The color-coded guide to microcomputers

ARTHUR GODMAN

BARNES & NOBLE BOOKS
A DIVISION OF HARPER & ROW, PUBLISHERS
New York, Cambridge, Philadelphia, San Francisco
London, Mexico City, São Paulo, Sydney

Library of Congress Cataloging in Publication Data

Godman, Arthur.
The color-coded guide to microcomputers.

(Everyday handbook; 590)
1. Microcomputers – Programming. I. Title.
QA76.6.G6 1983 001.64'2 83-47884
ISBN 0-06-463590-2 (pbk.)

This book was designed and produced by
BLA Publishing Limited, The Studio,
Newchapel Road, Lingfield, Surrey, England.

Artwork by Hayward and Martin Limited
Phototypeset in Britain by Composing Operations Limited
and Southern Positives and Negatives (SPAN)
Colour origination by Chris Willcock Reproductions
Printed in Italy by Arti Grafiche V. Bona

Contents

On using this book		*page* 5
Chapter 1:	**Computer technology**	7
Chapter 2:	**Using a microcomputer**	21
Chapter 3:	**Flowcharts and algorithms**	42
Chapter 4:	**Binary notation and computer codes**	52
Chapter 5:	**Arithmetic and operators**	62
Chapter 6:	**Strings**	76
Chapter 7:	**Arrays and logic**	94
Chapter 8:	**Central processing units**	119
Chapter 9:	**Machine code and machine code programs**	141
Chapter 10:	**Computer languages**	161
Chapter 11:	**Input, output and storage**	185
Chapter 12:	**Using BASIC as a language**	223
Appendix:	**The vocabulary of BASIC**	249
Index		253

Acknowledgements

The author would like to thank K. Walkinshaw and F. Stanger for their helpful comments and suggestions and Sylvia Brittenden for her meticulous typing of the manuscript.

The Publishers would also like to thank Elgin Press Limited and Rosie Vane-Wright for their assistance in the production of this book.

On using this book

How much do you know about computers and how much do you wish to find out? This book describes how to use a microcomputer or personal computer, at a simple level and at a more advanced level. It also gives a simple description of the way in which a microcomputer works, the principles of the use of the machine code and the methods of translation from BASIC to machine instructions. The choice is yours for starting at any one of these levels:

(i) You wish to understand programming in BASIC and to be able to write simple programs:

read Chapters 1, 2, 3, and 6

(ii) You wish to try and write more difficult programs in BASIC and to unravel complicated programs you see in magazines and periodicals:

read Chapters 7 and 12 as well as 1, 2, 3, and 6

(iii) You would like to understand how a microcomputer works without too great a detailed description:

read Chapters 4, 5, and 8

(iv) You want to have a simple explanation of how a microcomputer works, especially with regard to the use of peripheral devices:

read Chapters 9, 10, 11 as well as 4, 5, and 8

Remember that it is important to use a microcomputer yourself and to try all the programs on your own computer. Trying to follow the text without a computer is rather like trying to learn to play the piano without having a piano to practice on; it is possible, but very difficult.

It is also important to remember that different makes of microcomputers use different forms of commands and instructions, and, in addition, use these words in different ways. Trying out simple programs will make you understand the way in which your own computer obeys BASIC, and how it differs from the method of operation described in this book.

Binary logic

All microcomputers use logic to solve problems, therefore to get inside the working of a computer you have to look at the business of logical thinking. A problem generally presents a list of questions and. if the answers can be a simple YES or NO, then a computer can solve the problem.

The basis of computer logic is to use a code with 1 standing for YES or 0 for NO. This binary system is used by all electronic digital circuits where the presence of a voltage means a 1 and the absence means a 0.

Chapter 4 goes on to show how these two numbers only, are used to represent other letters and characters in the computer.

The color code

The color-coded guide shows the different sections of a computer such as the central processing unit, the control unit, input and output devices, memory and decisions taken through programs. It also indicates the use of binary notation, decimal notation and hexadecimal notation.

The following color codes have been used in this book to help you identify the different sections and functions of a computer.

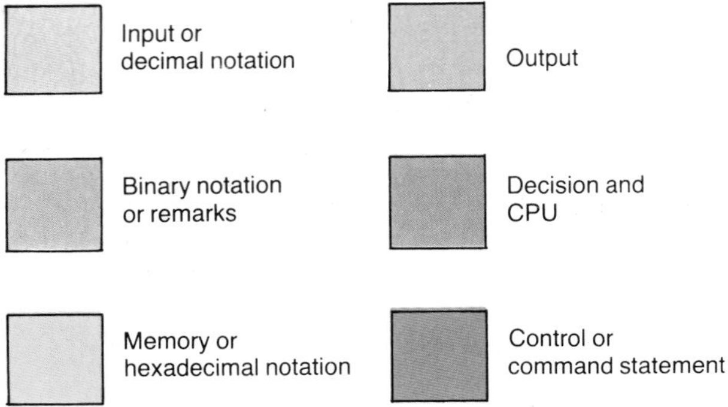

CHAPTER 1

Computer technology

There are many electronic devices or machines which can be called computers and so, in discussing computers, it is best to begin with a quick overall look at such devices. Starting with the largest, there are the big computers used by government departments or by banks, such as the computer which operates a cash-point (Automatic Teller Machine). These machines are called **mainframe computers**. Then there are the **minicomputers** used by medium-sized business firms, and the **microcomputers** (personal computers) used by small firms, or by individuals. The difference between these three types of devices is mainly one of size. **Word processors**, also a type of computer, can be of the same size as either minicomputers or microcomputers. **Electronic games** machines vary from the size of a minicomputer or microcomputer down to the size of a calculator. Some **calculators** can be held in the hand, some are programmable and more suitable for repetitive calculations than computers. Electronic watches, thermometers, thickness gauges, all have the same electronic technology as the computers, word processors and calculators, that is a solid state electronic system, usually in a silicon chip.

The different aspects of computers

Computers deal with data; they store it, they process it, and finally they print it. All information is concerned with two things, numbers and characters. The information is converted to data and some devices function better with numbers, others with characters. Here, then, are the ways in which information is treated.

Calculations: activities which are concerned with numbers and mathematical processes operating on numbers. A calculator, either a hand-held model or a larger model, is most suitable for everyday application. If the calculations are lengthy and numerous, then a computer is better; some computers are specifically designed to carry out especially lengthy and complex calculations; these are sometimes called **number crunchers**.

Word processing: information which is concerned solely with words. A word processor can store written text, rearrange the text for printing, check whether any words have been misspelt, and reproduce text in different styles of print. A computer can carry out similar tasks, but it is much more limited in what it can actually do, unless provided with additional facilities.

Information retrieval: information which can comprise both words and numbers. No processes are usually carried out and the information is displayed, when requested, on television screens, or printed out on pages. Such services are now available from telecommunications departments and television companies. They are concerned with the storage, updating, and retrieval of information useful to the general public.

Analysis of tabular information: information which combines both words and numbers arranged in a particular way. Simple arithmetical processes are going to be carried out on the information in the tables. This type of analysis can be performed by punched-card machines and, for some processes, is probably easier and cheaper. However, this is a process to which computers are well suited.

General purpose computers

A computer can carry out any type of process with words or numbers. It will not be as quick, or as efficient, as any device which is specifically aimed at a particular task. Thus a calculator is a computer specially designed to operate on numbers; a word processor is a computer specifically designed to operate with words. Some computers are designed to operate on lists and tables, while others are designed to operate best on numbers. A general purpose computer will perform all such tasks, but will be slower or less efficient than the computer or device designed for the specific purpose.

Simple organization of a computer

In a typical computer system there is an input device, by which information is fed into the computer; and an output device whereby the processed information, or the result, is made available to the operator. A central processing unit controls the working of the computer. It consists of an arithmetic and logic unit, which carries out mathematical operations and simple logical decisions, and a control unit

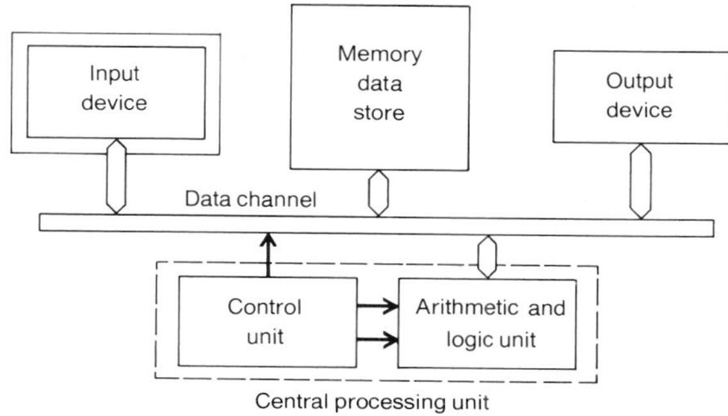

Simple organization of a computer

Keyboard input

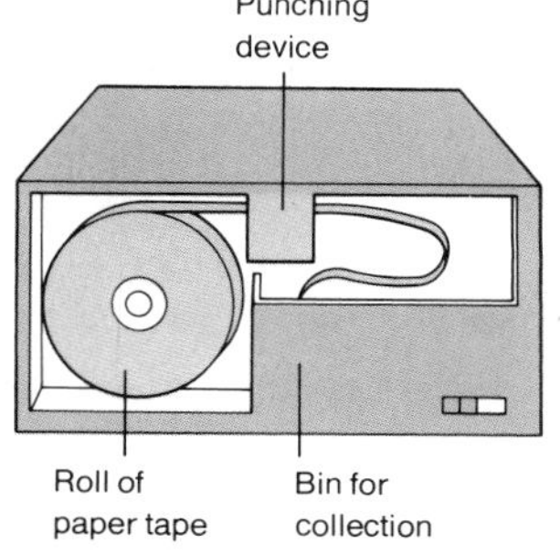

Punched paper tape input

which controls the execution of a program for the process. A memory store holds the data until required. The input, output and memory devices are connected to the central processing unit by a communications channel which allows any one device to be indirectly connected to any other device.

Input devices

These devices will be described in greater detail later. The usual input for a microcomputer, and many other computers, is a **keyboard**, which is very similar to a typewriter keyboard. It is commonly called a QWERTY keyboard, as these are the first six letters from left to right in the top row of letters. The information is typed in, using the keys. A cathode-ray tube, as in a television set, forms a screen, on which the typed information is displayed. Errors are rubbed out, that is erased, by a key on the keyboard. Typing over a piece of text has the same effect. The input goes straight into memory.

Another form of input is **punched paper tape**. The diagram shows punched paper tape being produced. Holes are punched in the paper and these holes represent coded information. An input machine reads the holes and the information is passed to memory. Punched paper tape is used, with programs operating on large quantities of data, mainly in minicomputers and larger computers.

Punched cards were used in offices where there were very large quantities of data to be processed but have been mainly replaced by computer systems. A card has eighty columns on it and each column can record either a number or a letter. A manual punch produces the cards, and the punched cards are fed by means of hoppers into the sensing machine which senses electrically the holes in the cards, and records the code represented by the holes. Punched card equipment can be used to process the cards, as well as computers, and some machines are almost as quick as computers for some specific tasks.

Other input devices include **optical character reading (OCR)**, a special method of printing numbers so that they can be recognized by an optical scanner. These are most frequently used on cheques, and the diagram shows a typical set of numbers used by banks in the sorting and

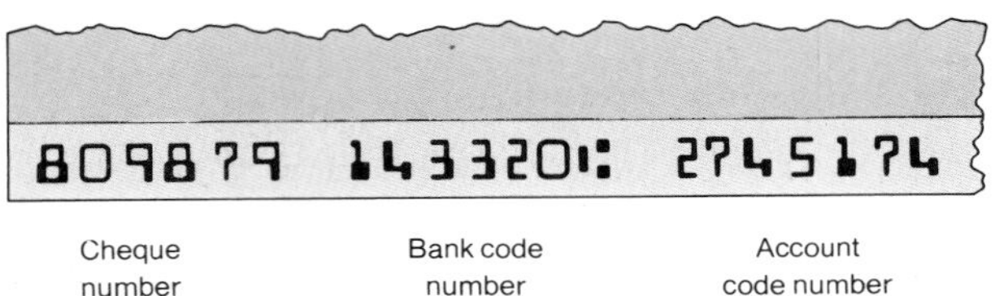

Optical character reading

recording of cheques. **Voice recognition devices** are the subject of experiment at present. Finally, backing storage devices can be used as input sources, but they will be discussed under memory devices.

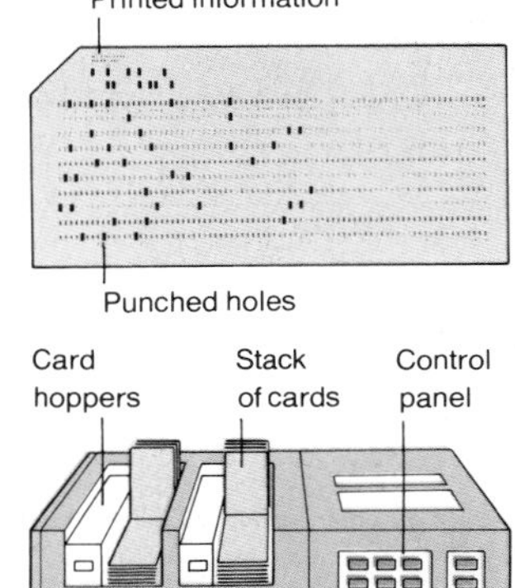

Punched card input

Output devices

The common output device for a microcomputer is a **visual display unit** (VDU). This can be a CRT (cathode-ray tube) monitor or a television set, the difference between the two being in the quality of the picture. The definition of the picture depends on the size of the smallest dot to be displayed, and on the response time of the amplifier. The definition of a picture is a measure of the smallest detail that can be seen in a picture or image on the screen. A TV set has difficulty in displaying sixty-four characters per line with clarity. If eighty characters per line have to be displayed then a CRT monitor has to be used. The VDU enables the keyboard input to be checked as well as displaying output on a microcomputer. The output on a VDU is *volatile*, that it, not permanent.

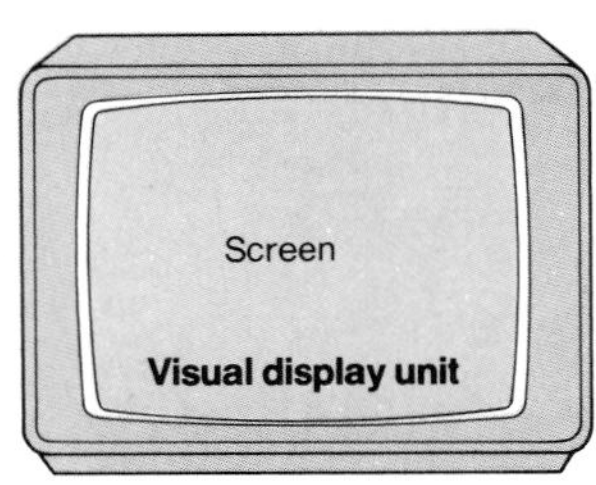

Visual display unit

A **line printer** is used only with minicomputers or mainframe computers. It produces a print-out on a continuous sheet of paper, usually with 120 characters per line and at a rate of 30-500 lines a minute. The letters, figures and punctuation marks are contained around the rim of a

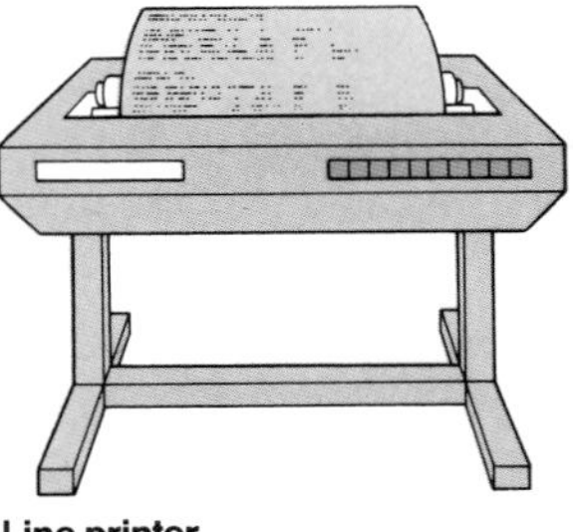

Line printer

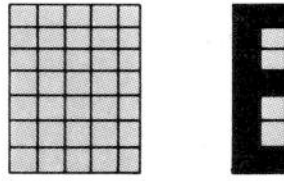

Matrix printing

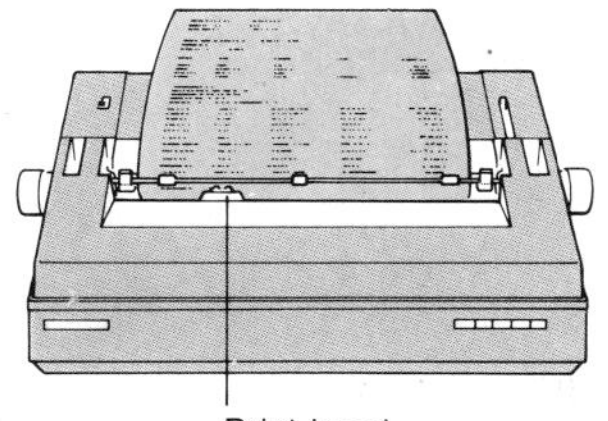

Matrix printer

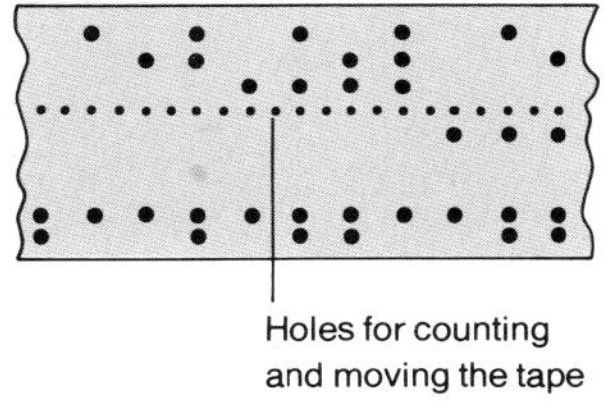

Punched paper tape

rotated wheel, and there are as many wheels as there are characters in the line. The output instruction momentarily halts the rotating wheels at the correct set of characters for a line, and an impression of the letters is then stamped on the paper.

A **matrix printer** uses a dot-matrix to print letters and figures. Each dot is made by a moving needle, and the needles are moved up to form a letter or figure as shown in the diagram. The needles are contained in a print-head which moves along a bar, generating a line of print, character by character. Printing instructions move the print-head and activate the needles in the matrix. The matrix can vary from 7 × 5 dots to 16 × 8 dots; the greater the number of dots, the better is the formation of each character. Matrix printing is a much cheaper method than line printing, and the fewer the dots in the matrix, the cheaper the printer.

Punched paper tape can be an output, using the machine illustrated before on page 9. **Punched cards** can also be an output. Both of these outputs can be physically transferred to another machine and become an input of that machine.

A **graph plotter** is an output device on some computers. It is an electromechanical device moving along an arm which itself moves to cover the extent of a sheet of paper. A pen, or pointer, on the moving arm draws diagrams on the paper. The diagrams can be graphs, maps, engineering design sheets, etc. Plotting can be carried out in several colours; cheaper models draw in black only.

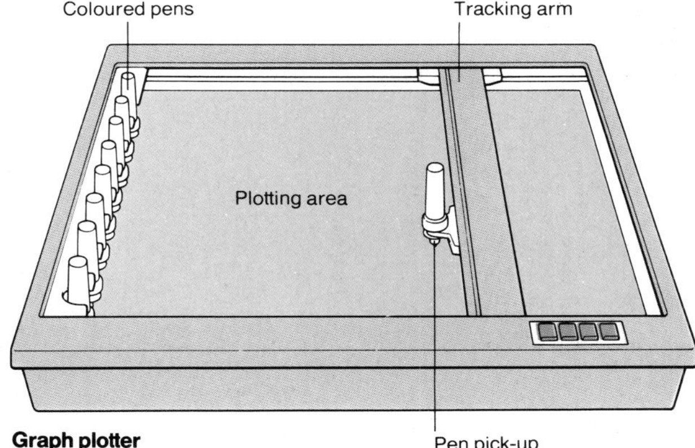

Graph plotter

Output devices include those capable of producing sounds. Voice simulation devices have been produced, but most of such devices are still at the experimental stage. However, musical notes can be produced to cover a wide variety of qualities; in this area computers approach electronic organs. Some toy computers combine the production of music with the ability to store a tune and provide an accompaniment, together with an ordinary arithematical calculator. Sound out-put is not, as yet, an important part of computer output.

All backing storage devices can be used as an output, as well as an input.

Memories and storage devices

A computer always contains two memories incorporated in its system. They are ROM and RAM.

The ROM (read-only memory) provides the computer with a list of instructions for its operation. It is a fast, non-volatile memory, that is information can be obtained from it rapidly, and the coded instructions do not disappear when the computer is switched off. The coded instructions are 'burnt in' during manufacture. The speed of obtaining an instruction from ROM is between 0.2 and 0.8 micro-seconds. No action in the computer can remove, or overwrite, that is replace, the coded instructions in ROM.

The RAM (random-access memory) is so called because it provides instant access to any item of information stored in it by means of horizontal and vertical coordinates. The coordinates provide an unique address for each storage location, and so any address can be selected at random. Information is 'read out' or 'written in', using the address of a location. Older type memories, and those used in some mainframe computers, use ferrite rings in RAM. In microcomputers, all RAM are solid state devices, usually on a silicon chip. RAM is a volatile memory, that is when the computer is switched off all data recorded in RAM is completely erased; in addition, data can be continually entered and removed. The speed of obtaining data from RAM is the same as for ROM.

More permanent storage of data is provided by **floppy disks**. These are thin, circular, ılexible plastic disks, coated each side with a magnetic material, similar to the material on magnetic tape in a cassette. There are two sizes of disk, the standard 5.25-inch and an 8-inch. A disk has circular tracks, the 5.25-inch disk having thirty-four tracks. A read/write head on an arm can read the tracks.

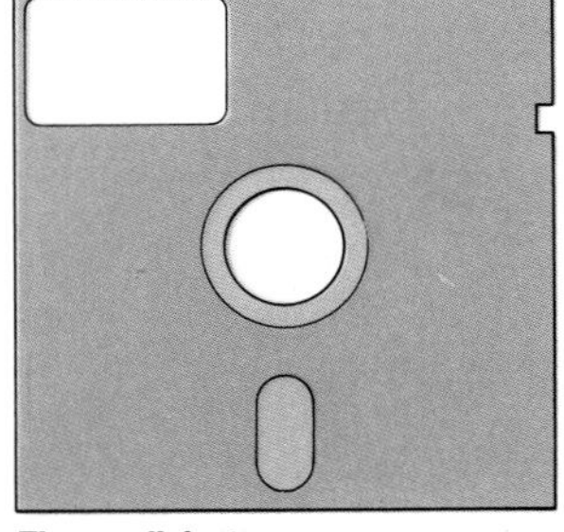

Floppy disk storage

Magnetic disk

Disk memory

Read/write heads

Multiple disks

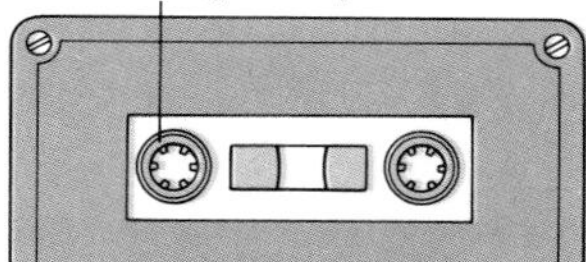

Tape cassette

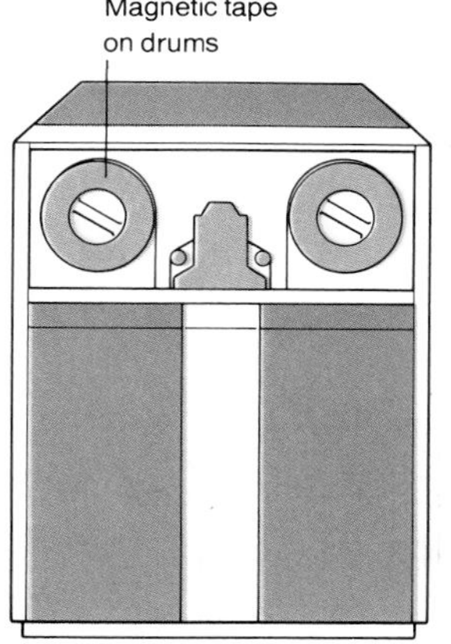

Magnetic tape unit

There is more than one read/write head, usually one for each sector of the disk. A floppy disk can hold up to 300,000 characters with a very fast access time due to the sector read/write heads. The memory is non-volatile, but the memory storage can occasionally suffer from corruption of some of the magnetized spots resulting in incorrect characters. Corruption is the appearance of errors on saved programs. Floppy disks are also known as **diskettes**.

Hard disks are rigid circular disks similar to gramophone records, and are coated with the same magnetic material as on diskettes. A read/write head on an arm can read the tracks on the disk. The speed of rotation is ten times faster than that of a floppy disk and an average access time for a random location on the disk is fifty milliseconds. A hard disk can store up to ten million items of information and data can be transferred at a rate of 800,000 items per second. (An item is taken as a byte, see p. 56). Hard disks, operated by disk drives, are used with some minicomputers, and with all mainframe computers. Floppy disks are used with a few minicomputers and with all microcomputers.

Tape cassettes are used as memory storage for microcomputers. Access time is very slow, so cassettes are generally used to store programs. Storage on tape is the same in principle as storage on disks, both methods using the same type of magnetic material coated on plastic.

Magnetic tape on spools is used with big mainframe computers. It is then used only with data required in a serial fashion, for example lists of customers, lists of stock, or tax data which needs updating from time to time in a serial order. Magnetic tape has generally been replaced nowadays by magnetic disks.

Memory devices can be divided into two types, **primary memories** and **peripheral memories**. A primary memory is one that is an integral part of a computer; ROM and RAM are primary memories, they cannot be separated from the computer. Disks, diskettes, cassettes, magnetic tape are peripheral memories; they can be detached from one computer, reconnected to another computer, or generally be made independent of a computer. Notice that peripheral memories are non-volatile, while primary memories may be volatile. Memories can also be **serial** or **random-access**. In random-access, any locations in memory will have an address that can be reached by an address command, that is instant access to any location in memory. A serial memory can be read only in sequence,

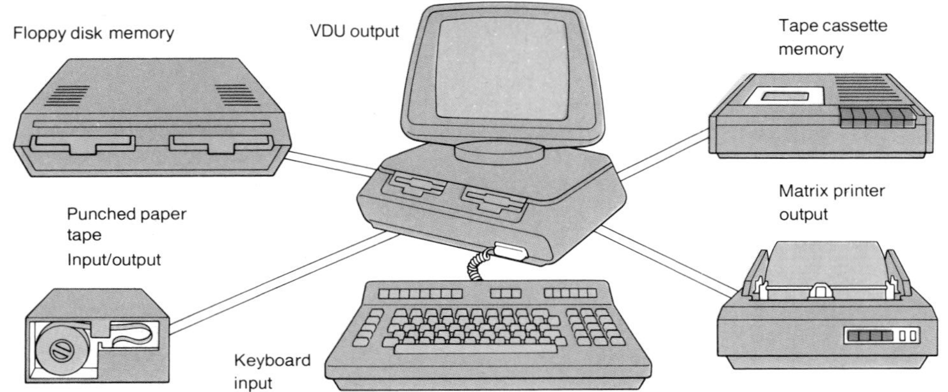

A computer system

starting from a specified location; a tape illustrates this type of memory, as reading commences at a particular point, and then continues sequentially along the tape. Tape cassettes and tape decks provide serial memories; they are read serially and loaded serially. Disks provide an intermediate type of memory. Random-access memory is very fast, and serial memory is slow for access. Disks and diskettes provide a medium-speed memory. Most computers use a **memory hierarchy**, consisting of a very high-speed silicon chip (integrated circuit or IC) memory, a medium-speed disk memory, and a large, slow-speed tape memory.

Other devices used with computers

A **light pen** is the same size as an ordinary pen. It contains a light-sensitive photoelectric cell in the tip. When pointed at a CRT display screen, it detects the displayed information. Using the pen an operator can draw, modify, or change the display on the screen. The computer can then calculate information drawn on the screen. A light pen is a very useful device for testing any type of problem which can be represented graphically.

A **joystick** control is a small stick, or lever, that is mounted on a base and can be moved in any direction, right and left, backwards and forwards. The movement of the joystick is converted to electrical pulses which are interpreted by the processor into the movement of a cursor, or other mark, on a CRT screen. Joysticks are mainly used in computer games, although there are other applications connected with graphic information on a screen.

Joystick control

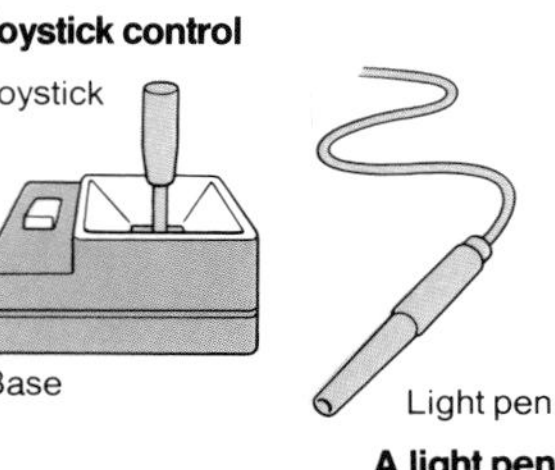

A light pen

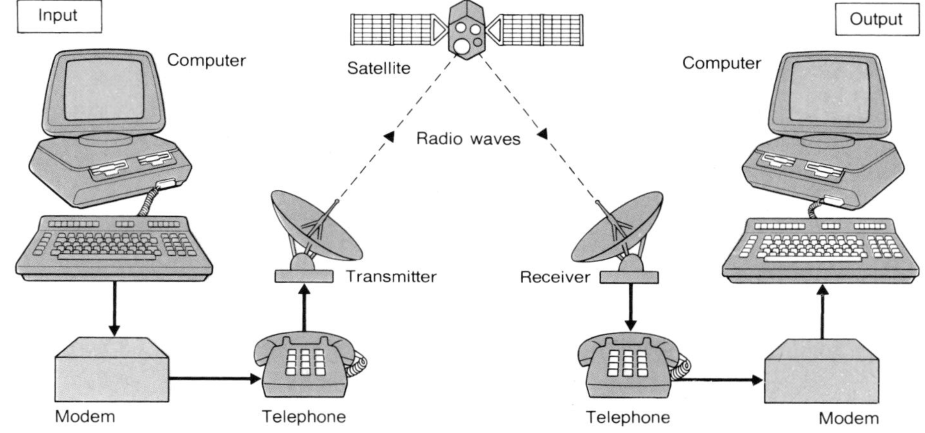

Use of a modem

A **modem** is a device that enables a computer to put out information over a telephone, and to receive information from a telephone for use by a computer. Modem stands for MODulation/DEModulation and refers to the action of modulating the computer output to suitable signals for transmission by telecommunications, and then demodulating them back to a computer input. The modem is an **interface** between the computer and the telephone. Once on the telephone communication system, radio telephony can be used and the computer can be linked to a computer anywhere else in the world, providing the two computers share a common computer code. Computers allow data exchange by using programs employing the same language and the same machine instructions.

The central processing unit

The central processing unit (CPU) controls the working of the computer. In a microcomputer it is called a microprocessing unit (MPU), and includes some form of memory. A CPU contains various **registers**. A register is a device capable of retaining items of numerical data. All data in a computer is processed through registers so all data must be coded into numbers before it is usable in a computer. A set of figures may represent data other than a number.

A computer deals with three types of information: **data, control, status**. **Data** can be alphabetical, numerical, or both. **Control** is information passed between different parts of the computer to produce a process. **Status** indicates the present condition of the microprocessor, that is sending or receiving data or control. Data are stored in memories, and these memories have addresses, so, in the flow of information, the CPU first controls the communication channel between RAM and itself, then selects the address, and when the correct channel is opened, the data are then transferred by the third channel of communication. At the same time, the status of the CPU, that is in control, addressing, or transferring data, is recorded in a status register.

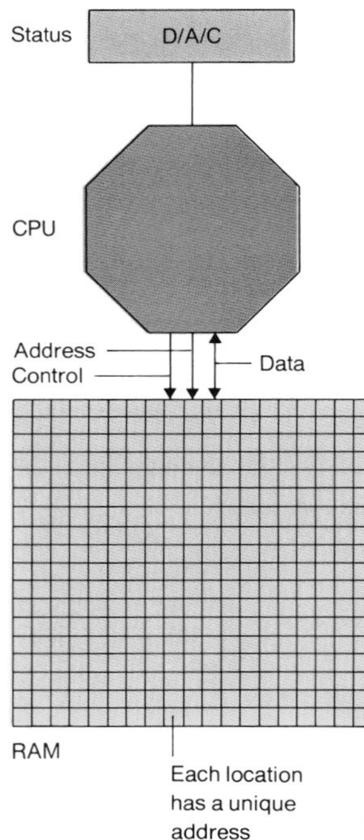

Information flow in a computer

Control circuit

This is a circuit which controls the execution of instructions in a regular sequence, interrupts instructions and restores instructions. It handles the decoding of microprogram instructions and generates internal signals for requested operations. It has stored information available in registers to deal with the sequencing of instructions.

A source program is stored in memory using a high-level language which is understandable from everyday speech. The instructions in this language are not understood by the computer and have to be broken down into smaller instructions called **micro-instructions**. A micro-instruction is a short, small, single command, for example add, shift, delete, which is understood by the machine. This requires an **interpreter**, a program which takes the instruction from the source program and translates it into a set of micro-instructions. The interpreter is usually part of ROM.

Arithmetic and logic unit (ALU)

The ALU usually consists of three or six registers, working in conjunction with a set of registers called **accumulators**. Under instruction from the control circuit, the ALU carries out the ordinary arithmetical operations, including exponentiation. The ALU also contains logic gates which deal with the mathematical signs for inequality and truth values. It has associated with it a condition code register (CCR) which deals with a limited number of processes such as borrow, overflow, or carry, which occur during arithmetical processes in the registers.

Information registers

The **accumulator** (ACC) is a holding register for arithmetical, logical or input/output operations. Data can be transferred from memory to ACC and vice versa. Any arithmetic or logical process operating on two numbers, or

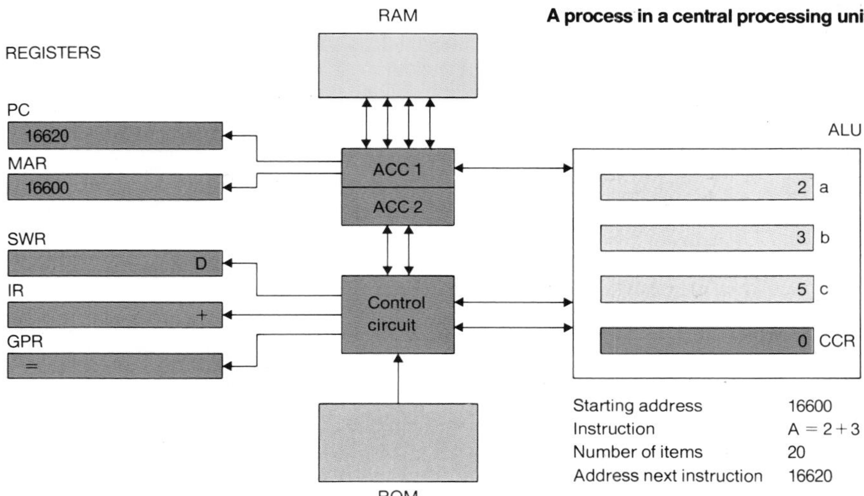

A process in a central processing unit

items, will have one in ACC, while the other is processed in the ALU, putting the final result in the ACC. An ACC can be cleared, complemented, tested, incremented, or rotated under program control. The ACC can also act as an input/output register, as in most computers all information passes through the ACC to the CPU. A CPU usually has two accumulators. The **memory address register** (MAR) holds the address of the location in RAM which is the starting address of the current instruction. This address can be altered by program instruction. The **program counter** (PC) contains the address of the start of the next instruction. It is automatically incremented after each fetch cycle where information is fetched from RAM. The **status word register** (SWR) shows the current status of the control circuit. The **instruction register** (IR) holds the code for the current instruction. The **general purpose register** (GPR) is used for simple arithmetical operations in computing and modifying addresses in a program.

A process in the CPU

An arithmetic operation, A=2+3, is illustrated. This instruction is located in RAM with a starting address of 16600. The instruction takes up twenty items of information, so the next instruction will start at location 16620. The control circuit shifts control to RAM, following instructions from ROM. The address is supplied by the register. When the process starts the registers MAR and PC show the relevant addresses for the current and the next instruction. The language instruction is broken down to micro-instructions. For example, **a** ADD 2 means putting the number 2 into register **a** (*see diagram*) from the accumulator, which itself has obtained the number from RAM. Although the diagram shows the information in numbers and symbols, in the registers all the information is in **binary code** used by digital computers.

Digital and analogue computers

An **analogue** measurement shows a **continuous** relationship between two quantities. Using an ordinary watch, the two hands show a continuous relation between time and the reading given by their movement. It is possible to guess what fraction of a minute is shown by the position of the large hand. A **digital** measurement shows a **discontinuous** relationship between two quantities. A digital watch shows a discontinuous relationship between time and the reading shown by the figures. The figures change every second, or every minute; they have no way of indicating fractions of a second. An ordinary watch with a seconds hand can show fractions of a second. The smallest digital change is called an **interval**, and all measurements are in multiples of this interval, making the measurement discontinuous.

Analogue measurement

Digital measurement

Analogue and digital computers make and use measurements in their separate ways. An **analogue computer** creates an electrical analogy of a mathematical problem; it usually measures varying voltages and makes them represent the mathematical variables in the problem. For example a varying temperature can be represented by a varying voltage and hence represented by a varying line on a CRT screen. The variation can represent *any value* between the defined limits of the temperature. With a **digital computer**, readings, results, or any measurements, are available only in steps, depending on the interval of measurement, that is the measurement is discontinuous. With very small intervals, the discontinuous

Analogue representation

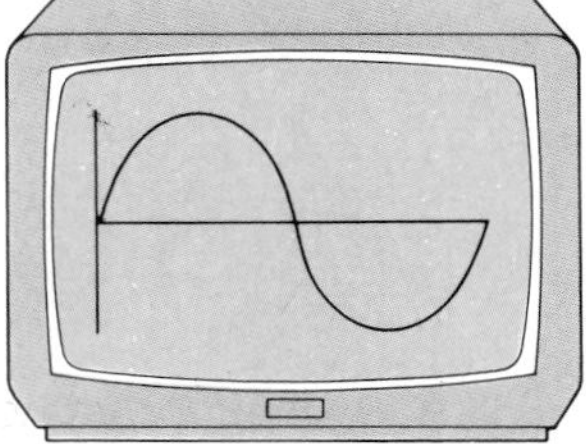

Digital representation

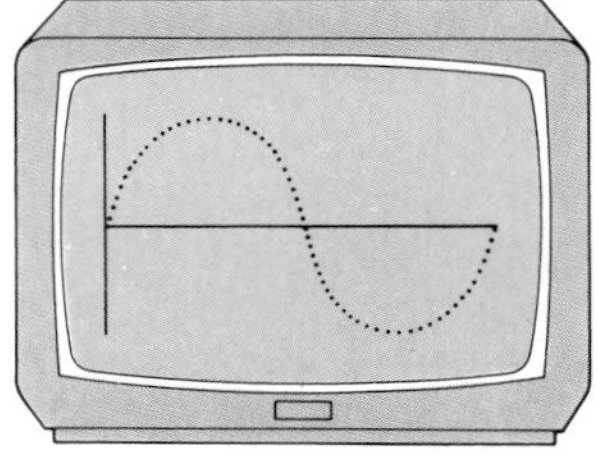

Analogue and digital representation

nature of the digital measurement offers little difference from a continuous, or analogue, measurement.

Analogue and digital measurements are interconvertible. A **digital-to-analogue converter** (DAC) is a computing device that converts digital quantities into analogue quantities, for example digital voltage reading changed to a scale reading. An **analogue-to-digital converter** (ADC) produces a digital reading from a scale reading.

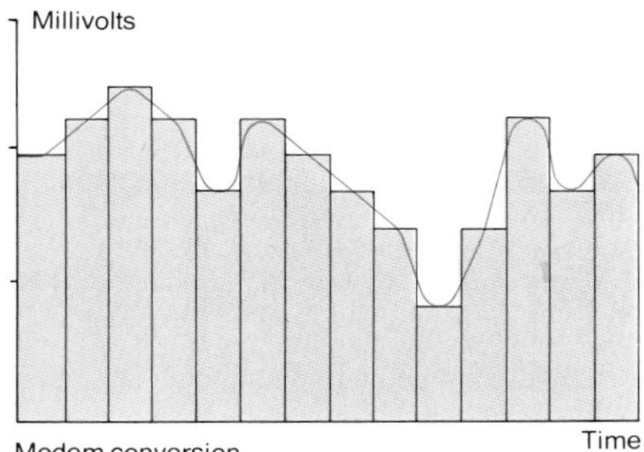

Modem conversion

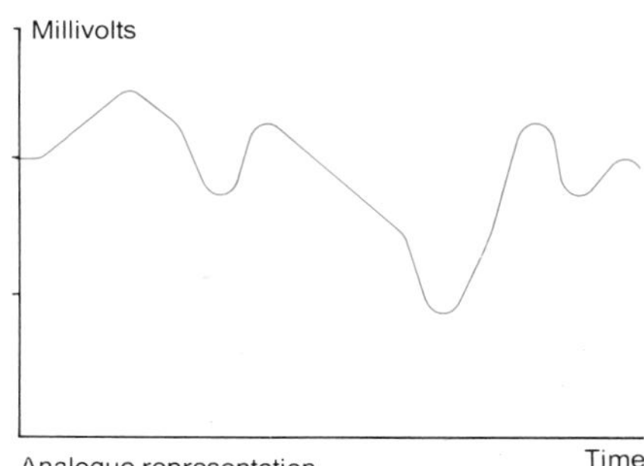

Analogue representation

Digital to analogue conversion

Modems are examples of DAC and ADCs. Telephones impose a continuous wave form on a transmitted direct current, hence they use analogue signals. The majority of computers use digital signals, so a modem is used to convert the digital signal to an analogue signal and then back again. The relationship between the two sets of signals is shown in the diagram. Each letter of a message is given a number code. The number code is then repres-

MESSAGE	C	O	D	I	N	G		A		W	O	R	D	·
DIGITAL REPRESENTATION	67	79	68	73	78	71	32	65	32	87	79	82	68	46

ented by a voltage. The digital representation is then made into an analogue representation, which is a continuous curve. This analogue signal is sent by telephone wire. In the reverse process, the continuous signal is split into time intervals, and the magnitude of each interval determined and produced as a specific reading. This number code is then converted back to letters. It can be seen that any distortion in the analogue curve, due to electrical disturbances, would affect the number code and produce an incorrect letter. The digital number code is described in more detail on page 57.

Summary

Three sizes of computer: mainframe computers, minicomputers, microcomputers (personal computers).

Capabilities of computers: calculations, word analysis, information lists, analysis of tabular information and data.

Simple **organization of a computer**: input devices; output devices; central processing unit; memory store.

Input devices: keyboard, punched paper tape, punched cards, optical character reading (OCR).

Output devices: visual display unit (VDU); line printer, matrix printer, punched paper tape, punched cards.

Memories: read-only memory (ROM), non-volatile; random-access memory (RAM), volatile; floppy disks/diskettes; hard disks; tape cassettes, magnetic tape.

Primary devices are an integral part of a computer; **peripheral devices** are separable from, and connected to, a computer.

Memories are **serial** (read in consecutive order) or **random-access** (any location available); they form a **hierarchy** based on speed of access.

A **light pen** can alter, delete, draw lines, on a VDU screen.

A **joystick** control can move a cursor over a VDU screen.

A **modem** connects a computer with a telephone.

Central processing unit (CPU) contains registers, control circuit, arithmetic and logic unit.

A **register** retains numerical data for subsequent use.

Status indicates the current condition of a device.

Control circuit handles instructions and generates signals for requested operations.

An **interpreter** is a program which takes instructions from a source language and translates them into micro-instructions; it is part of ROM.

Arithmetic and logic unit (ALU) contains three or six registers and an **accumulator** (ACC), together with a **condition code register** (CCR) for overflow, borrow, carry, etc.

Registers include: memory address register (MAR); program counter (PC); status word register (SWR); instruction register (IR); general purpose register (GPR).

Analogue describes continuous relationship between two quantities.

Digital describes a discontinuous relationship between two quantities, i.e. the readings, results, or measurements are available only in steps of an interval.

Digital-to-analogue converter (DAC) converts digital quantities to analogue quantities.

Analogue-to-digital converter (ADC) converts analogue to digital quantities.

CHAPTER 2

Using a microcomputer

It is very difficult to understand how a microcomputer works unless a person actually uses one. This is called 'hands-on' experience, and very often a few minutes of 'hands-on' a computer is worth an hour or so of reading about the subject. In addition, everyone should have the manual explaining how a particular microcomputer is operated, because the computer language used by each machine may differ.

BASIC language

BASIC stands for *'Beginner's All-purpose Symbolic Instruction Code'*. It is a computer language that is easily learned, and is used by almost all microcomputers. The language consists of a set of **reserved words** which have meaning for the computer and cause it to function. The first difficulty is that all computers do not spell the words in the same way, so it is necessary to consult the manual supplied by the manufacturer of the computer to see which variety of spelling is used. The second difficulty is that some computers use different words for the same instruction. In this book, either the standard ANSI spelling, or, if there is no standard, then the most common spelling, will be used for common BASIC words.

Words in BASIC

The words used in BASIC are either commands or statements; some words can be used as both statements and commands. **Commands** are words which cause the microcomputer to carry out a process. Two useful ones are: PRINT, GOTO. The command PRINT is the standard word, variations are: PRI and P. GOTO is the most common version of the word, variations are: GOT, G, and GO TO. RUN is the most common system command, variations are: RU and R. These spellings illustrate some of the differences between languages; always check the manual to verify the command used in your microcomputer. **Statements** used in **programs** are described below.

Printing on a microcomputer

The command, PRINT, produces a result on the VDU (or CRT screen) as follows. Use the keyboard to type PRINT, then key in a number, say 36. Now press the key marked for ENTER or RETURN, or any such key indicating a new line of typing on the keyboard. The figures, 36, appear on the screen. Next type: 36 – 16, and press the return key. The answer, 20, appears on the screen, in place of the figures 36. If letters are typed, as in: PRINT ABCD, followed by pressing the return key, nothing appears on the screen. To produce letters, they have to be enclosed in inverted commas ("), sometimes called quotes. For example, type: PRINT "ABCD" and then press the return key, and ABCD appears on the screen. The computer manual should be checked to ensure the correct commands and procedures are used to get the results shown in the diagram.

PRINT

TYPE
(*a*) 36
(*b*) 36-16
(*c*) "ABCD"

Printing on a visual display unit

Printing on a matrix printer

The common command is LPRINT to produce letters or numbers printed on paper by a printer connected to the microcomputer. However, it is best to check your manual to see the exact command needed to produce a copy printed on paper. The written statement typed on the keyboard is checked on the VDU, and when the return key is pressed, the statement is printed by the printer. The statement for printing has the same composition whether shown on a VDU by the command PRINT, or printed on paper by the command LPRINT.

TYPE IN STATEMENT
AND
PRESS RETURN KEY

Keyboard

LPRINT "BOTH LETTERS AND
NUMBERS SUCH AS 12, CAN
BE PRINTED"

VDU

BOTH LETTERS AND
NUMBERS, SUCH AS 12,
CAN BE PRINTED

Printed paper output

The microcomputer as a calculator

A microcomputer can be used as a simple calculator, although it is a waste of its capabilities. The four rules of arithmetic are represented on the keyboard as follows:

addition	+	multiplication	*
subtraction	–	division	/

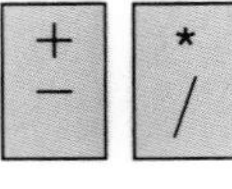

So 51×6 becomes 51*6 n the microcomputer, and 37÷4 becomes 37/4. Check from the manual whether your computer accepts decimal fractions; most do, but some popular machines do not accept decimals. If the machine accepts decimals, then the decimal fraction is separated from the whole number by a full stop (full point), e.g. 23.625 or 14.15. The next symbol is ↑, which indicates 'to the power of', e.g. 14 ↑ 3 represents 14^3, that is 14 to the power of 3. Some machines use ** (a double asterisk) instead of ↑.

The typed statement for a calculation is: PRINT 126*32/21 and the result is shown when the return key is pressed. If the statement is enclosed within inverted commas, then the actual statement and not the result is printed. So, using the arithmetical statement with PRINT:

TYPE IN STATEMENT

Syntax of printing

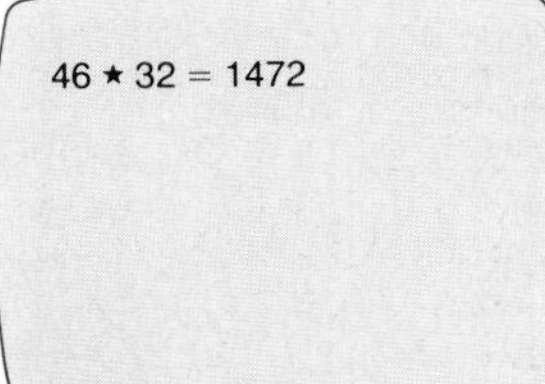

PRINT "46*32 ="; 46*32 produces the result 46*32 = 1472

Syntax in BASIC

In the statement just printed, a semicolon (;) separates the sets of figures; if it is omitted the text is not printed. The omission of the semicolon is a **syntax error**. A statement consists of words, numbers, and punctuation marks presented in an order dependent upon certain rules. These rules resemble the rules governing the order in which words are used in a spoken language, that is syntax. So the rules governing statements in BASIC are its **syntax**. The statement just printed consisted of two separate statements, and these must be separated by a semicolon. The syntax also governs the way statements are printed on a VDU, or on paper.

Any text, whether in letters or figures, enclosed in inverted commas (quotes), is shown on a VDU, or on paper, exactly as typed in.

Letters cannot be used in a statement without being enclosed in inverted commas.

Programs

A program is a series of statements arranged in a correct sequence for directing a digital computer to carry out a required process. The term, program, is applied to the actual list of statements, to the planning and encoding of statements in the process to be performed, and also the printing of the result.

Each statement must start with a number followed by a word* from BASIC; the first set of statement words is given below. Each statement forms a line in a program and each line must have a number. The sequence of numbers forms the sequence of the program.

INPUT

Action in the microcomputer stops and it waits for **data**, either figures or letters to be entered by the keyboard. While doing this the computer is in **input mode**, shown in various ways on different machines. A question mark is common, or a change in the **cursor** indicates the input mode.

LET

Gives (i.e. **assigns**) a value to a **variable**. A variable is usually given a letter, or several letters, to name it, and then it can have a numerical value which can change according to some known rules. For example, B can represent the price of a kilo of beef; T can represent the temperature at midday; EGGS can represent the price of one dozen eggs. Some computers do not use LET; in others it is optional; while some require its use. When the use is optional it is preferable to use it, because it helps to make a program clear.

STOP

The action of the microcomputer is stopped; it can be made to continue by the command CONT (continue). CONT is not used in programs. Some computers stop at the point in the program using STOP, while others go to the END of the program. Variations of STOP are STO., ST., S. Check the use of this statement in your manual.

GOTO

This statement causes the computer to 'jump' to another part of a program instead of continuing in sequence. GOTO is often used with other reserved words in statements. It can also be used in some machines to start the machine running a program; this is done by using GOTO *x*, where *x* is the number of a line in a program. Variations in spelling have been described; check your manual for the use of this statement.

*LET can be optional or omitted

RUN

This command instructs the microcomputer to execute a program held in RAM (see p. 12). Most computers permit the use of RUN *x*, where *x* is the number of a line in a program, and the program is executed, starting with that statement. Some computers allow RUN to be used as a statement, with a reference to a program held on disk or tape, for example RUN "FILE X". Variations in spelling have been described; check your manual for the use of RUN, for example type RUN then press the ENTER or RETURN key.

PRINT

This word has been used as a command. It can also be used as a statement. It instructs the microcomputer to display the result from a program on a VDU screen. The more precise use of it as a statement will be discussed later.

Variables in a program

A variable is a value, factor, quantity or condition that can be measured and can take any of a given set of values, e.g. a temperature, atmospheric pressure, cost of meat, composition of a material. Such a variable can be assigned, that is given, a letter, or even several letters, to identify it, and the letter, or letters, will assume the values given, or calculated, for it. For example let L = length of a room; B = breadth of a room; A = floor area of a room. The variables, L and B, can assume a variety of values. For any one particular room, A = B × L. These variables can be put into a simple program to calculate the floor area of any room; for example:

10	INPUT	L	Lines 10 and 20 assign values to L and B
20	INPUT	B	
30	LET	A = L*B	Line 30 calculates the area and
40	PRINT	A	line 40 prints the answer.

The program is typed on the keyboard, pressing the ENTER or RETURN key to indicate the end of each line of the program. RUN is then typed and entered, and the microcomputer goes into input mode. The value of L is typed, followed by the RETURN key, then the value of B is typed, followed by the RETURN key. The computer then displays the answer.

If such a calculation has to be performed many times, it would be useful to save the program and to describe it. Description is by means of a REM statement. REM stands for 'reminder' or 'remarks'; the microcomputer ignores it when working through a program. The lines are numbered, using whole numbers, in multiples of 10. This is to allow extra lines to be put in if it is necessary to amend the program. Suppose the cost of covering the floor is required. If L and B are measured in metres, then A will be in square metres. If the cost per square metre is S, then the cost of covering the floor is A × S. This will need an extra input, S, and a further calculation, which we will call COST = A × S. The revised program now looks like this:

Program 2.1

5	REM	A PROGRAM FOR THE COST OF COVERING A FLOOR
10	INPUT	L
20	INPUT	B
25	INPUT	S
30	LET	A = L*B
35	LET	COST = A*S
40	PRINT	A
50	PRINT	COST
60	GOTO	10

Lines 25, 35, 50, 60 have been added to the original program. Note that the variable, COST, has more than one letter. No units have been specified for cost in the program. A specimen calculation is shown in the diagram.

Input

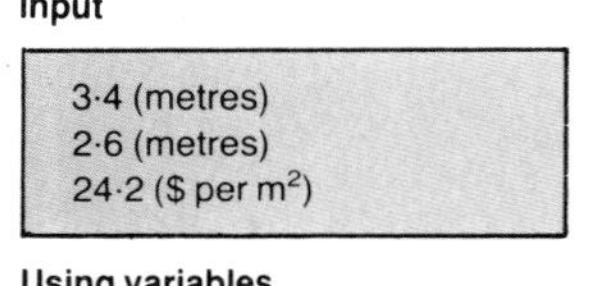

result

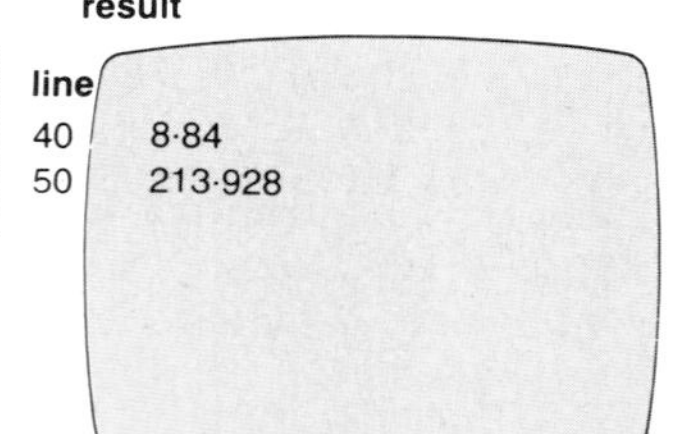

Using variables

The variables, L, B, S, A, could also be given more letters for their description. The number of letters that can be used depends upon the microcomputer. Some use only one letter, some two letters, and some up to six letters. Your manual will tell you how many letters can be used to define a variable. Using the word COST is suitable for all computers, since the first letter is C, not used previously in the program, and if the machine uses one letter only, it takes the first letter as defining the variable. Words such as COST can be used in a program, as used above, to make the program easier to understand, even if the machine is restricted to using one letter only for a variable.

In line 60, the statement, GOTO, sends the program back to line 10, ready to execute a second calculation when data are typed in. The computer will repeat the program cycle endlessly unless told to stop. When in input mode, the command STOP can be typed followed by pressing the RETURN key, or a STOP or BREAK key can be pressed, and the program halts. The statement in line 60 is a 'jump' command, as the program jumps from line 60 to line 10 instead of going to line 70. As line 70 is non-existent, the computer would stop at line 60 if the statement were not GOTO.

Erasing an error in a program

A microcomputer has a **cursor** on its screen; the design and use of the cursor varies from machine to machine, so it is necessary to consult your manual to find how your machine shows, and uses, a cursor. The cursor in all machines indicates the current position on the current line being typed. Normally it moves along, in sequence, from one position to the next, on a line. Four keys, in most machines, control the movement of the cursor; they can raise or lower it, move it right or left. The cursor can thus be moved to any part of a program. A key marked RUBOUT/ERASE/DELETE can be used to remove an unwanted figure or letter; if needed, a correct figure or letter can then be entered in its place.

Errors can be erased by overtyping; if a line of BASIC has errors, then the whole line is retyped, and on pressing the RETURN key, the new line replaces the old line.

Displaying information and results

This section considers the ways in which a microcomputer can be used to present information, including results, either on a screen, or printed on paper. The command used will be PRINT, for displaying on a VDU, but this command can equally be replaced by LPRINT, or its equivalent, to have the information displayed in print on paper.

The use of semicolons

;

On a line, a semicolon is needed to separate two pieces of data, when using a PRINT statement. (There are other ways of separating two pieces of data however.) For example: 30 PRINT "COST OF COVERING"; C where C is a variable number. In program 2.1, lines 40 and 50 were printed one below the other because line 40 did not have a semicolon. The effect of a semicolon is seen in the following program:

Program 2.2

5	REM	PROGRAM TO SHOW USE OF SEMICOLONS
10	PRINT	"JOE,22";
20	PRINT	"BILL,24";
30	PRINT	"sp sp SAM,23"
40	PRINT	"ROB,18"

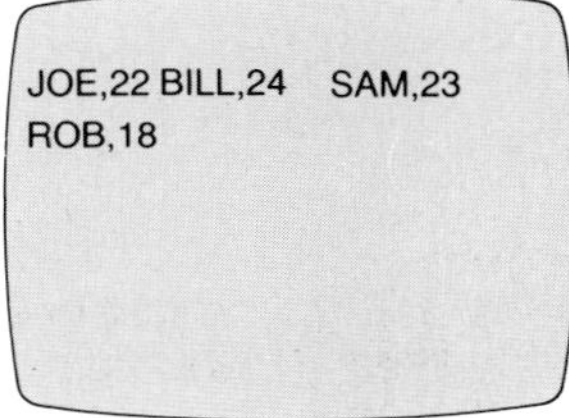

Use of semi-colons in printing

Notes

(1) 'sp' represents space, obtained by pressing the space key.

(2) Line 30 contains two spaces inside the inverted commas.

The result of the program is shown in the diagram; type RUN to start.

Notice that: (*a*) line 20 follows line 10 without a break; (*b*) line 30 has two breaks between it and line 20, the breaks provided by the two spaces; (*c*) line 40 is on the second line of print because there was no semicolon at the end of line 30; (*d*) lines 10, 20, 30 appear on one line of print because of the semicolons at the end of lines 10 and 20.

Semicolons and spaces can be used to print statements concerning variables, giving information about a program, or stating the reason for an input, or request, and make the format, or layout, similar to a printed text. For example, program 2.1 could be revised and extended to give more information, as follows:

Program 2.3

5	REM	THE COST OF FLOORING
10	PRINT	"WHAT IS THE LENGTH OF THE ROOM?"
15	INPUT	L
20	PRINT	"AND THE BREADTH?"
25	INPUT	B
30	LET	A = L*B
32	PRINT	"STATE COST PER SQ.METRE, IN DOLLARS"
34	INPUT	S
35	LET	COST = A*S
40	PRINT	"AREA OF ROOM = sp sp";A;"SQ.METRES"
50	PRINT	"COST OF FLOORING = sp sp $"; COST
60	GOTO	10

WHAT IS THE LENGTH OF THE ROOM?
AND THE BREADTH?
STATE COST PER SQ. METRE, IN DOLLARS
AREA OF ROOM = 8·84 SQ. METRES
COST OF FLOORING = $213·928
WHAT IS THE LENGTH OF THE ROOM?

Printing descriptive information

The diagram of the screen shows the result of executing this program.

The use of commas

,

A comma is used with PRINT to divide the screen into zones, each containing a maximum of 16, 15, 12, or 10 letters, figures or symbols. For a screen with a display of 64 letters, and 16 letters in a zone, this gives four zones, that is each line of print can be divided into four parts. For smaller screens with 32 characters, only two zones of 16 letters are formed.

Program 2.4

```
5  REM   THE USE OF COMMAS IN PRINTING
10 PRINT "JOE", "22"
20 PRINT "BILL", "24"
30 PRINT "NO MORE",
40 PRINT "NAMES"
```

Notes
(1) No comma after line 10
(2) Commas after lines 20 and 30
(3) Type RUN to get result

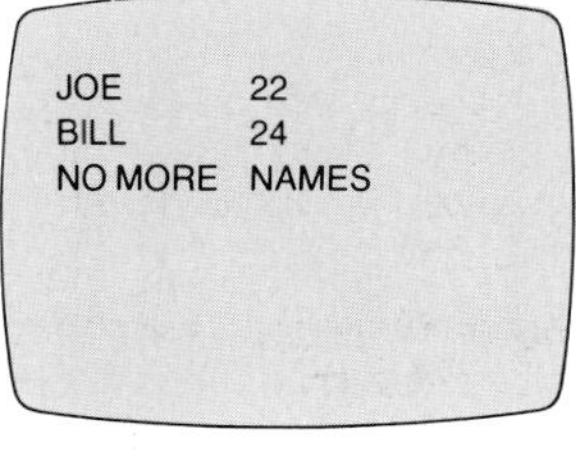

Use of commas in printing

The diagram shows the result on a 32-character screen with zones of 16 letters. With a 64-character screen, the first two lines become one line. A comma allows simple tabulation to be performed by dividing the screen into zones for printing.

The use of TAB

TAB

This statement, used with PRINT, allows a letter, figure or symbol, to be printed at any position along a line. The syntax of BASIC demands:

(a) TAB shall be followed by a number
(b) The number shall be followed by a semicolon, e.g. TAB (16);
(c) The semicolon shall be followed by the character to be printed, e.g. TAB(16); "SQ."

The number after TAB indicates the number of places to the left of the character to be printed, e.g. TAB (16); "S" means that S is printed at the seventeenth position along the line of print.

TAB allows information to be printed, or presented, in tabular form. Care must be taken, though, that sufficient space is left in a column for all the information to be inserted. This will be shown in the next program.

Program 2.5

5	REM	THE USE OF TAB
10	PRINT	"SMITH"; TAB (16); "JOE"; TAB (26); "22"
20	PRINT	"JONES"; TAB (16); "BILL"; TAB (26); "24"
30	PRINT	"12345678901234567890 12345678901234"

```
SMITH          JOE       22
JONES          BILL      24
12345678901234567890123456789012
34
```

Use of TAB in printing

In the tabulated data, the first column contains the family name, the second column contains the first name, and the third column contains the age of a person. If a person has a family name longer than sixteen letters, then it will overflow the space allowed for it. When designing a table, sufficient space must always be allowed for the maximum word length.

Variables with letters

Program 2.5 takes a long time to type for each individual entry; to reduce the time needed for typing, variables can be used. For program 2.5 there will be three variables needed: family name, personal name and age. The names will use letters, and a variable using letters has to be described by a letter followed by a dollar ($) sign. A general program can now be written:

$

Program 2.6

5	REM	FURTHER USE OF VARIABLES
10	INPUT	F$
20	INPUT	P$
25	REM	F$ IS FAMILY NAME; P$ IS PERSONAL NAME
30	INPUT	AGE
40	PRINT	F$; TAB (16); P$; TAB (26); AGE
50	GOTO	10

Input

SMITH	JONES	BROWN
JOE	BILL	SAM
22	24	18

```
SMITH   JOE    22
JONES   BILL   24
BROWN   SAM    18
```

Compiling tabular information

When the program is executed by the command RUN, the first demand for an input requires the family name, the second requires the first name and the third requires the age. The program will continue to run, because of line 50, until the command STOP is given.

Variables used with commands or statements

The statement for TAB can have a variable instead of a number. When the variable is assigned a value, then PRINT is executed at that tabulated position. The following program illustrates several points connected with this use of TAB:

Program 2.7

5	REM	VARYING TABULATION
10	INPUT	X
15	INPUT	F$
18	REM	F$ IS FAMILY NAME; X IS USED FOR TAB
20	INPUT	Y1
25	INPUT	P$
30	INPUT	Y2
35	INPUT	Q$
38	REM	P$ AND Q$ ARE PERSONAL NAMES; Y1 AND Y2 ARE THEIR TAB POSITIONS
40	INPUT	Z
45	INPUT	AGE
48	REM	AGE IS GIVEN IN YEARS; Z IS USED FOR TAB
50	PRINT	TAB (X); F$; TAB (Y1); P$; TAB (Y2); Q$; TAB (Z); AGE
60	GOTO	10

Input

1	1	3
SMITH	JONES	BROWN
12	12	12
JOE	BILL	SAM
20	20	20
sp	ALFRED	–
28	28	28
22	24	18

Result

```
SMITH      JOE                   22
JONES      BILL    ALFRED        24
   BROWN   SAM     –             18
```

An input and the displayed result are shown in the diagram. Points to notice about the program are:

(1) By altering X, a name is indented in the table; this can be useful to pick out certain items in the table; in this case the indentation shows the surname of a person aged less than 20.

(2) The variables Y1 and Y2 are both used to represent different numbers. Some computers may not have this facility; check with your manual.

(3) Every position in the table must be filled; if the person does not have a second personal name, then a space or a dash (–) is entered; notice that the computer will accept a space to print, and enters nothing on the VDU.

Limits of a screen

A screen is split into columns and rows. Most microcomputers have 48-64 columns in a screen, allowing for 48-64 characters to be printed. The smallest screen display is 32 columns and the largest 128. The number of rows that can be printed varies with the computer; generally it is between 22 and 32 rows, giving that number of printed lines. Check the display limits of your screen from your manual.

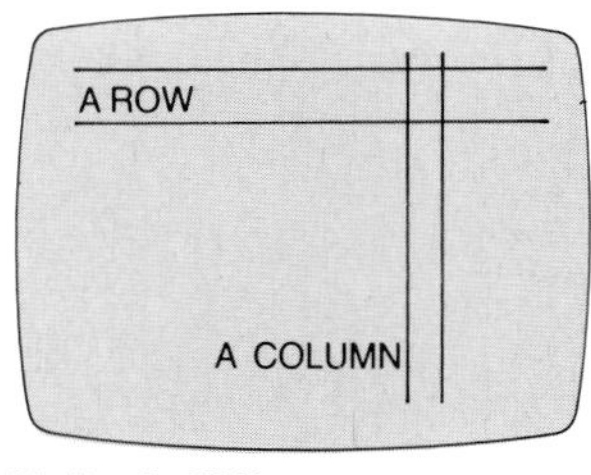

Limits of a VDU screen

Arithmetical calculations

A microcomputer is useful when an arithmetical calculation has to be made many times. Suitable examples are often found in engineering; here is such an example.

When gases pass through a duct they meet a resistance due to the duct work, for example cool air passing in ducts in air-conditioning plants for large buildings. The loss in pressure of the gas is calculated in centimetres of a water gauge. The formula is:

$$wg = \frac{LV^2 (A + B)}{CABT}$$

Where: wg = loss in pressure in cm of water
L = length of duct (in metres)
V = velocity of gas (in metres per sec.)
A = breadth of duct (in metres)
B = width (depth) of duct (in metres)
T = absolute temperature
C = a constant

The value of C is given by: new metal ducts 70; old metal ducts 57; smooth concrete ducts 51; rough concrete ducts 44. The absolute temperature is found from T + 273 where T is the temperature in degrees celsius. The formula thus becomes:

$$wg = \frac{LV^2 (A + B)}{CAB (T + 273)}$$ where T is measured in degrees celsius

This formula has now to be expressed in BASIC, and it becomes wg = (L*(V ↑ 2)*(A + B))/(C*A*B*(T + 273)).

Notes on the BASIC version

(1) Two variables multiplied together must have an asterisk (*) between them.

( )

(2) Brackets, also called parentheses, i.e. ( ), enclose separate calculations, e.g. V ↑ 2 is V^2; it is enclosed in brackets otherwise L*V ↑ 2 becomes $(LV)^2$.

(3) The whole of the numerator, i.e. $LV^2(A + B)$, must be enclosed in brackets in order to be divided by the whole of the denominator, i.e. CAB(T + 273).

Program 2.8

```
5   REM    CALCULATION OF PRESSURE LOSS IN DUCTS
10  INPUT  A
20  INPUT  B
30  INPUT  C
40  INPUT  L
50  INPUT  V
60  INPUT  T
70  LET    WG=(L*(V↑2)*(A+B))/(C*A*B*(T+273))
80  PRINT  "TEMP = sp";T;"DEG.C.",WG;"CM"
90  GOTO   10
```

Result

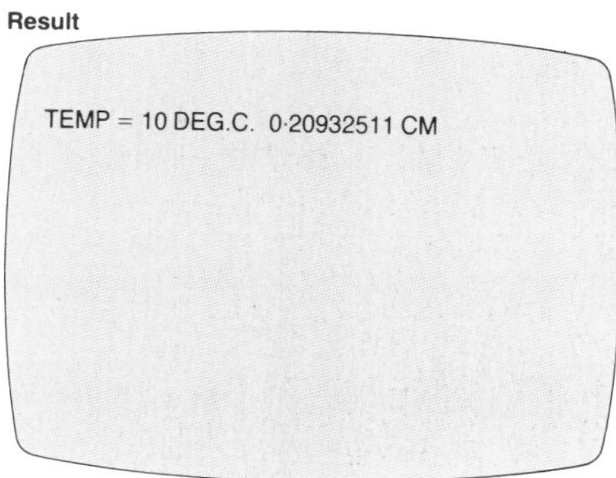

Pressure loss in ducts

A typical result is shown in the diagram.

Exponentiation by computer

The calculation in program 2.8 could be done without great difficulty on a pocket calculator. The advantage of a microcomputer is best seen in exponentiation, that is, raising a number to a given power. A common problem using exponentiation is the calculation of monthly or annual payments to repay a loan at a given percentage interest rate. The formula to calculate this is:

$$A = P(R \div 100)^{-1}/(1 - (1 + R/100)^{-N})$$

where P is the sum owed, R is the interest rate, N is the number of years over which repayment is spread, and A is the sum repaid annually. If the loan is repaid monthly, then the calculation is:

$$M = P(R \div 1200)/(1 - (1 + R/1200)^{-12N})$$

Both these calculations would be difficult using the normal pocket calculator. The program in BASIC for the calculation of monthly repayments is given on page 34.

Program 2.9

5	REM	CALCULATIONS ON LOAN REPAYMENTS
10	INPUT	P
20	INPUT	R
30	INPUT	N
40	LET	I = R/100
50	LET	J = I/12
60	LET	A = (P*I)/(1 − ((1 + I) **(−N)))
70	LET	M = (P*J)/(1 − ((1 + J) **(−12*N)))
80	PRINT	"MONTHLY sp $";M
90	PRINT	*ANNUALLY sp $";A
100	PRINT	"12 TIMES M sp = sp $"; 12*M
110	GOTO	10

Input

P = 100,000
R = 8%
N = 10 YEARS

Result

MONTHLY $1213·2759
ANNUALLY $14902·949
12 TIMES M = $14559·311

Calculations on loan repayment

Notes on program

(1) The alternative symbol, **, has been used in place of, ↑, to show exponentiation; in this case a negative exponent.
(2) The sum owed is given the identifier P.
(3) The percentage rate of interest is given the identifier R.
(4) The number of years is given the identifier N.
(5) P, R, N are the three variables for the input; the additional variables I, J, A, M are calculated.

The diagram shows the result of a calculation.

Constants

A constant is a value that does not change. Most computers store one constant in their BASIC list, it is the value of π. The BASIC statement is the word PI. The area of a circle is given by $A = \pi R^2$, where A is the area and R is the radius. The written program is:

PI

Program 2.10

5	REM	TO FIND THE AREA OF A CIRCLE
10	INPUT	R
20	LET	A = PI*(R ↑ 2)
30	PRINT	R, A
40	GOTO	10

Program bugs

A bug is an error in a program which causes its failure to be executed correctly. Great care must be exercised when typing a program, as the slightest error in syntax can cause a bug. With the calculations illustrated in the last few programs the most frequent bug that appears is in the use of brackets (parentheses). It is as well to check any statement with brackets by counting the left-hand brackets; (, and the right-hand brackets:), and ensuring they are equal in number. The omission of the multiplication symbol, *, is another frequent syntax error. A common program fault is putting a variable in a statement before it has been assigned a direct value, or is the subject of an INPUT, or is defined from a previously known variable. If a bug appears through incorrect use of a variable, the program will halt at the line containing the unassigned variable. A variable is assigned in three ways as described above. Getting rid of bugs in a program is called 'debugging'.

Tabulation and headings

One use of tabulation is to find an average performance of some aspect of work. For example, a firm uses lorries to transport goods. It would like to know what use is being made of its vehicles. This could be ascertained from (*a*) the number of kilometres per litre of petrol used by each of the vehicles; and (*b*) the average distance driven by a vehicle in a set period. Each vehicle could be compared with the average performance of all vehicles to check on its use and its actual performance.

Use of conditions in programs

IF

The number of vehicles in use may vary, so the input of data may have an indefinite number of entries. A method of stopping the program in order to find totals of data is required. This is met by the conditional statement IF . . . THEN. This sets a condition to show the end of a program. The next requirement is a counter to count the number of items; this is achieved by adding one to a variable which acts as the counter.

The data, then, consists of a number of lorries, identified by registration numbers, providing at the end of one week, the distance, in kilometres, they have travelled, and the quantity of petrol, in litres, that they have used. The information required is: (*a*) the performance in kilometres per litre of each vehicle and (*b*) the average performance for all the vehicles; (*c*) the average distance travelled by a vehicle in the week.

Program 2.11

```
5   REM    TABULATION AND AVERAGE PERFORMANCE
10  LET    N = 0
20  LET    L = 0
30  LET    H = 0
35  PRINT  "REG.NO.";TAB (14);"KM.";TAB (19);"LTS";
           TAB (25);"KM/L"
40  INPUT  R$
45  IF     R$ = "XXX" THEN GOTO 140
50  INPUT  M
60  INPUT  G
70  LET    P = M/G
80  LET    L = L + M
90  LET    H = H + G
100 LET    N = N + 1
120 PRINT  R$;TAB (14);M;TAB (19);G;
           TAB (23);P
130 GOTO   40
140 PRINT
145 PRINT  TAB (16);"KM/VH";TAB (23);"KM/L"
150 PRINT  "AVERAGE";TAB (16);L/(N−1);TAB (23);L/H
160 STOP
```

Input

R$	M	G
AH 213	762	89
K 116	38	9
BD 417	421	74
XXX	(0.00001)	(0.00001)

Result

REG.NO.	KM.	LTS.	KM/L
AH 213	762	89	8·5617978
K 116	38	9	4·2222222
BD 417	421	74	5·6891892
	KM/VH	KM/L	
AVERAGE	407	7·0988	

Tabulation, headings and averages

Notes on the program

(1) Line 45 has the conditional statement IF . . . THEN. If the *condition is correct*, the program jumps to line 140; this is a conditional jump. If the *condition is not met*, the program continues in sequence to line 120. The condition has been specified as R$ = XXX, but any suitable condition could be made.

(2) Lines 20, 50, 80 show the method of totalling individual items. The total, L, is set at 0 to begin with; each addition of M is then made in line 80, using the individual input from line 50. The total for L is held in line 80, ready for a further calculation when all entries have been made, and used in line 150 for the total distance.

(3) Similarly the variable, H, is used to total the number of litres of petrol used and the total is held in line 90.

(4) The variable, N, acts as a counter. It is set to 0 in line 10, then in line 100, it has 1 added, i.e. it counts the number of times an input is made for lines 40 to 60.

(5) The program has a **loop**, starting at line 40 and ending at line 130. Each loop has an input of the details of an individual vehicle. The loop is executed as long as there are vehicles to be listed. The condition in line 110 ends the loop. Line 130 is an unconditional jump.
(6) The data for each vehicle are: (*a*) R$ for the registration number; (*b*) L for the distance travelled in kilometres; (*c*) G for the number of litres of petrol used. The figures are for one week.
(7) When all the data have been entered, the INPUT is XXX for R$. This causes the program to jump to line 140, which just has the statement, PRINT. The result is a blank line of printing, separating the individual details from the results for all the vehicles.
(8) At TAB (16) is printed "KM/VH", i.e. the average distance travelled. At TAB (23) is printed "L/H", i.e. the total distance divided by the total quantity of petrol, giving the average performance of all vehicles.
(9) The program is stopped by the statement STOP. This allows the program to be repeated by the command RUN or GOTO.

An input and its result is shown in the diagram. The following point should be noticed:
(1) The results for performance, i.e. KM/L and average distance, KM/VH, are given to too great an accuracy. This is because a microcomputer always gives results to eight significant figures. To curtail this accuracy, different computers have different methods; these will be discussed in later chapters.

Maintaining a commercial file

A simple example of a file will now be demonstrated using BASIC. The example maintains a stock account of books, and includes sales and price changes. The information needed is:
(*a*) The ISBN reference number of the book. (It is easier to define an object from a number than from a name.)
(*b*) The amount of stock bought, i.e. the number of books, labelled A.
(*c*) The selling price of the books, labelled COST.
(*d*) The number of books sold in a particular period, labelled SOLD.
(*e*) The period defined as a month with a three-letter label for the month and the stock, labelled STOCK, defined as the balance at the end of each month.

The procedure will be:

(*a*) A balance of stock, B, defined as: B = previous B + stock – SOLD.

(*b*) A calculation of money credit from SOLD × COST.

(*c*) A total of books sold to date.

(*d*) A total of credit to date.

(*e*) Totals to be calculated in June and December.

The program from these considerations is as follows:

Program 2.12

```
5   REM    BOOK STOCK DATA FILE
10  LET    T = 0
15  LET    Q = 0
20  LET    B = 0
25  REM    T AND Q ARE TOTALS FOR SALES AND CREDIT; B IS
           BALANCE OF STOCK
30  PRINT  “ISBN NO.”;TAB (11);“STOCK”;TAB (18);“COST”;
           TAB (23);“SOLD”;TAB (28);“MON”
35  PRINT  21
40  INPUT  A$
50  INPUT  A
55  REM    A$ IS ISBN NO.; A IS STOCK BOUGHT
60  INPUT  C
70  INPUT  S
75  REM    C IS COST, S IS NUMBER SOLD
80  LET    B = B + A – S
85  LET    T = T + S
90  INPUT  M$
95  REM    B IS BALANCE UNSOLD; T IS TOTAL SALES;
           M$ IS MONTH
100 PRINT  A$;TAB (11);B;TAB (17);“$”; TAB (18);C;TAB (23);S;
           TAB (28);M$
105 LET    R = S*C
110 LET    Q = Q + R
120 IF     M$ = “JUN” THEN GOTO 150
130 IF     M$ = “DEC” THEN GOTO 150
140 GOTO   40
150 PRINT
160 PRINT  “ISBN NO.”;TAB (10); “SALES”;TAB (20); “CREDIT”
170 PRINT  A$;TAB (10);T;TAB (19);“$”; TAB (20);Q;TAB (28);M$
180 STOP
```

Notes on the program

(1) Line 35 PRINT makes a one-line space between the printed headings and the data.

(2) Line 80 calculates the balance of stock at the end of the month.
(3) In line 100, TAB (17) prints a dollar sign in front of the cost, and in line 170, TAB (19) does the same. Both of these signs could be altered to show any other form of currency, e.g. £, ¥, F, M, etc.
(4) Lines 105 and 110 calculate the sum received for each month and the running total of SALES.
(5) Lines 120 and 130 give the conditions, i.e. the relevant months of June and December, for printing the totals. In a full program, the December figures will include the June figure.
(6) Line 140 gives an unconditional jump to form the loop for the input of data between the months of January to June and July to December.
(7) If line 140 is changed to GOTO 35, then each line of data will be separated by a one-line space in the table.
(8) Line 150 gives a one-line space between the table of data and the summary result. This space could be increased by adding 152 PRINT 154 PRINT 156 PRINT giving a four-line space.
(9) Lines 25, 55, 95 contain REM statements for the information of anyone reading the program to make understanding of the program easier.

The diagram on page 40 shows the result of a small but typical input below.

Book stock data file

Input

ISBN NO.	A	C	S	M$
09074.32	20000	8·5	2350	JAN
09074.32	0	8·5	4200	MAR
09074.32	5000	9·5	4890	NOV
09074.32	0	9·5	3642	DEC
RUN				
04750.35	10000	10·0	310	JAN
04750.35	4019	10·0	5671	APR
04750.35	2802	10·5	1217	JUN

Notes on the result

(1) The program, as designed, has to have data supplied for one book at a time. More advanced programming, described later, is needed to overcome this difficulty.
(2) When the data for one book have been completed, the command RUN removes all the printed results from the VDU; data for the second book can then be entered.

Result

ISBN NO.	STOCK	COST	SOLD	MON.
09074.32	17650	$8·50	2350	JAN
09074.32	13450	$8·50	4200	MAR
09074.32	13560	$9·50	4890	NOV
09074.32	9918	$9·50	3642	DEC

ISBN NO.	SALES	CREDIT	MON.
09074.32	15082	$136729	DEC

ISBN NO.	STOCK	COST	SOLD	MON.
04750.35	9690	$10·0	310	JAN
04750.35	4019	$10·0	5671	APR
04750.35	2802	$10·5	1217	JUN

ISBN NO.	SALES	CREDIT	MON.
04750.35	7198	$72588·5	JUN

Tabular information

The last two programs show some of the simple methods of tabulating data and extracting summary information concerning totals and averages. Using methods such as these, reasonably complex programs can be developed to deal with tabulated information. Further BASIC reserved words are needed, however, to compile programs to make full use of tabulation. This will be the subject of the text chapters on programming.

Summary

BASIC is a computer language using **reserved words** which have meaning for the computer.

PRINT is a command word to produce a result on a visual display unit (VDU).

Printing on a line or matrix printer has a command LPRINT, or similar word.

Calculation on a computer uses the signs +, −, *, /, ↑ (or**) for the arithmetical signs of addition, subtraction, multiplication, division, exponentiation.

Syntax in BASIC is the set of rules for forming a statement.

A **program** is a series of statements written in sequence.

INPUT stops action in a microcomputer and puts the machine in input mode.

LET assigns a value to a variable; this word is not necessary in many computers.

STOP stops the action in a microcomputer.

GOTO causes an unconditional jump in a program either backwards or forwards.

RUN is the normal command for a microcomputer to execute a program.

A **variable** is a value, factor, quantity, condition that can be measured.

REM makes a reminder statement; the microcomputer ignores it, but it is useful for the reader to understand the program.

A **variable** can be identified by a letter, or by a word, if the variable is a number.

GOTO can be used to make a program jump back to the beginning so that the program forms a loop and runs continuously

Typing errors can be erased by a key, or by over-printing.

A **semicolon** (;) causes printed data to follow on the same line of print.

A comma (,) causes a print statement to be divided into zones containing a maximum of 16 characters.

TAB is a statement which fixes a position along a line of print.

Variables with letters have to be defined by a letter followed by a dollar sign ($).

Variables can be used with commands or statements.

Arithmetical conditions are most useful in repetitive operations.

Brackets (parentheses) group variables together in a calculation to ensure that the intended order of calculation is maintained.

Exponentiation is the raising of a number to a given power, e.g. 25^5 is an example of exponentiation.

A **constant** is a value that does not change, e.g. PI is a constant.

A **bug** is an error in a program causing errors in a result or making the program inoperable.

Tabulation is the setting out of information in columns with suitable headings for description.

Conditions in programs are made by IF . . . THEN statements.

Totals can be accumulated in programs.

Averages can be calculated from totals and counters in a program.

A **counter** in a loop has an increment of 1 for each time the loop is executed.

IF . . . THEN statements make a condition; if the condition is met, the program jumps to another line; if the condition is not met, the program continues in sequence.

CHAPTER 3

Flowcharts and algorithms

A flowchart is a method of writing down a sequence of operations to be followed by a computer, any other machine, or even a person, in solving a particular problem. To do this, a set of conventional symbols are used and these are shown in the diagram. To illustrate their use, a

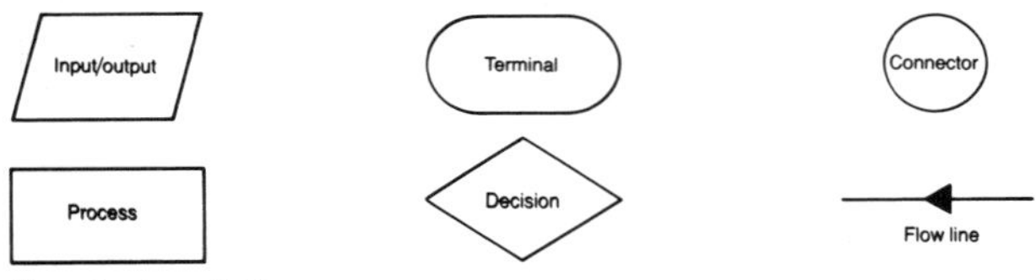

Flowchart symbols

simple problem is presented as a flowchart; it is the problem of boarding the correct bus to go to a required destination. First, an **outline** of the problem is needed. Here is the outline: (1) get to bus stop; (2) board correct bus; (3) dismount at correct stop. This is now put into a flowchart. The flowchart must always have a START and an END, both using the appropriate symbols. The information needed is: (*a*) which is the correct bus for the destination? (*b*) recognition of the destination. The two decisions to be taken are: (*a*) is the bus going to the destination? (*b*) has the bus arrived at the destination? The remaining boxes show the necessary actions to use the information and to take the decisions. This is obviously a very simple problem and the purpose is to show the use of flowchart symbols.

Flowcharts for mathematical processes

A mathematical process can always be broken down to a number of sequential steps, that is a number of steps, one after the other, with a reason for the order. The steps are shown by a flowchart, and the flowchart can be used to test the accuracy of presentation of the problem.

An arithmetical example

The calculation of an electricity bill with a fixed rate of 45 cents a unit and a standing charge of a fixed amount provides a simple example. The **input** of information is the

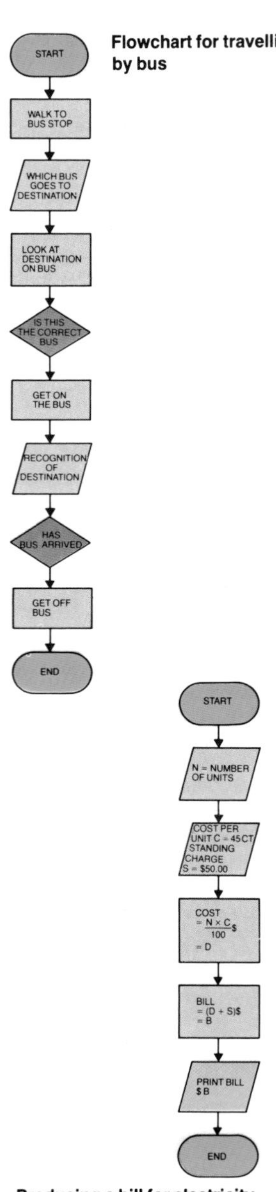

Flowchart for travelling by bus

Producing a bill for electricity

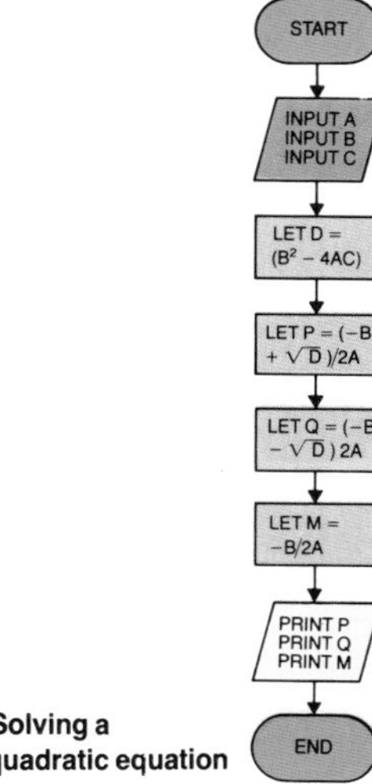

Solving a quadratic equation

number of units of electricity used, the cost per unit and the standing charge. If N units are used, at a cost of C cents per unit, then the cost, D, for electric current is given by D = (N × C)/100. (Divide by 100 to convert to dollars and cents). If S is the standing charge, then the total bill for electricity, B, is given by B = D + S. The calculation can be written as: B = (N × C)/100 + S, where only N will vary, providing charges remain the same. This expression is an **algorithm** to give the value of B.

A mathematical example

The solution of a quadratic equation is frequently required and also the maximum or minimum value of a quadratic expression. Let the equation be $Ax^2 + Bx + C = 0$. Then the solutions to the equation are

$$(a)\ \frac{-B + \sqrt{B^2 - 4AC}}{2A} \qquad (b)\ \frac{-B - \sqrt{B^2 - 4AC}}{2A}$$

and the maximum or minimum value is given by $x = \frac{-B}{2A}$. This can be set out in a flowchart. The input is the values respectively of A, B and C. The first calculation finds D from D = (B^2 – 4AC). The value of D may be negative, in which case the program stops there. A decision box would be useful to say if D is negative, then the solutions are imaginary. Otherwise the calculation proceeds to find the value of each of the two solutions, P and Q, and the maximum or minimum value, M. These are then printed and the sequence ends.

A repeated operation

An iterative process is one that is carried out time and time again. An example is a multiplication table where a number (in sequence) is multiplied by the same number several times, for example the twelve times table where the numbers 1 to 12 are each multiplied by 12. The outline of the task then is:

(1) To present a number from 1 to any other number, in sequence.

(2) To multiply the first number by a chosen number, say 16.

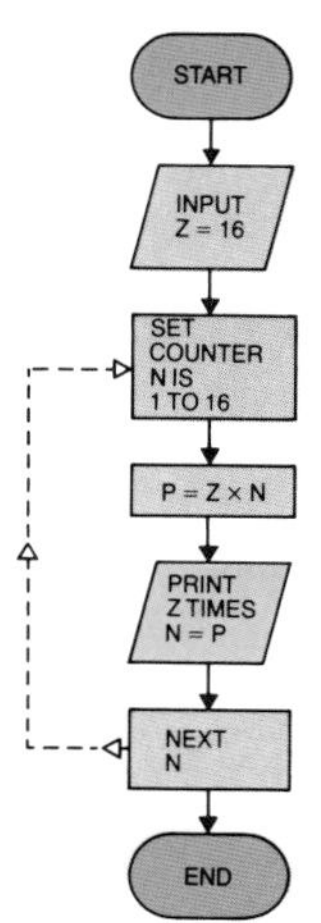

A loop for the sixteen times table

To produce the sixteen times table we have 1 × 16; 2 × 16; and so on up to 16 × 16. If we put Z = 16 (any letter will do, Z happens to be chosen) and then let N have successive values from 1 to 16 (any letter can be chosen), the result of

P = Z × N produces the sixteen times table. The table can be printed as: Z times N = P, with numbers substituted for the letters, e.g. 16 times 3 = 48. The numbers are produced by the computer following the program of the flowchart and could be printed.

Loops

One process, multiplying 16 by a number, is repeated several times. A **loop** can be used to perform this task; at the start of the loop is the number of times the process has to be carried out, in this case 16 times. The instruction, then, is to set up a counter, which will go from 1 to 16, it being assumed in steps of 1. The process is then followed. At the end, the flow has to be directed back into the loop; this is done by the instruction process of 'next N' (*see diagram*). When N has reached 16, there is no next N, so the flow carries on to END. This is an example of a simple loop without conditions; the loop has to be executed a specified number of times.

A loop with conditions

A loop may have to be executed an unknown number of times until a particular condition is met. An example of this is the flowchart for the conversion of a number in any radix less than 10 to a number in decimal notation. A radix, or base, is the number given to a place value for a digit, for example if the radix is ten, i.e. decimal notation, then the number 10 represents ten; but if the radix is eight, then the number 10 represents eight; if the radix is two, then the number 10 represents two. Let a number be 354 and the radix be 6, then to find the equivalent number in decimal notation we have:

$$\text{number equals } 3 \times 6^2 + 5 \times 6^1 + 4 \times 6^0$$

now $6^0 = 1$ and $6^1 = 6$, so the number equals

$$3 \times 36 + 5 \times 6 + 4 \times 1 = 108 + 30 + 4 = 142$$

So 354 (radix 6) ≡ 142 (radix 10).

As calculations are invariably carried out in decimal notation, the flowchart opposite is used to convert a number in any radix (less than 10) to a number in decimal notation. The outline of the problem is:

(1) Number the digits 0 to N beginning with the right-hand digit.

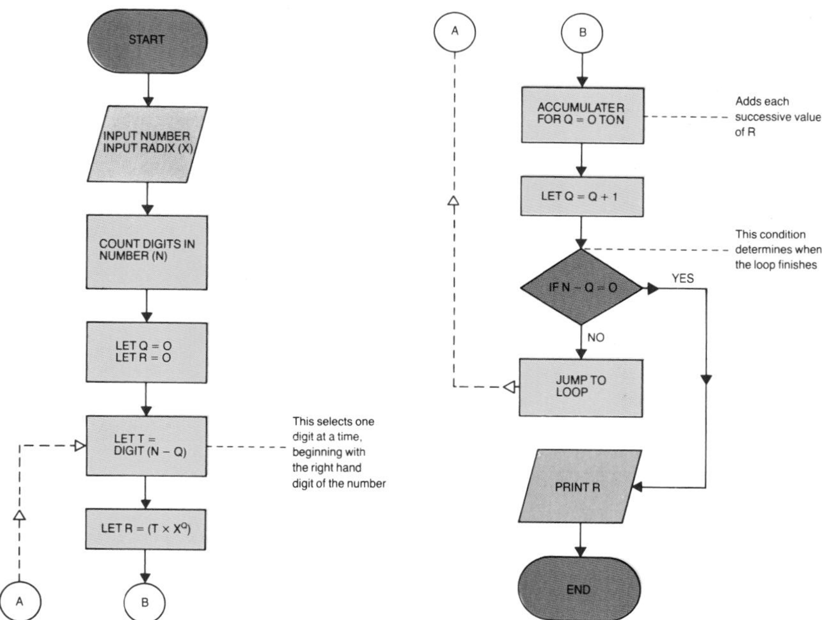

Conditional loop for conversion of notation in radix (< 10) to decimal notation

(2) If X is the radix, multiply each digit by X^Q, where Q is the numbered digit.
(3) Add the values obtained from each digit.

Example: The number is 783, the radix is X, thus the decimal equivalent is $(7 \times X^2) + (8 \times X^1) + (3 \times X^0)$.

A loop is required in the flowchart as one process is repeated. Each digit (T) is multiplied by X^Q, giving a decimal value, R. The letter Q is then given an increment of 1 ($Q = Q + 1$). The condition is then tested for $N = Q$, that is have all the digits in the original number been used in the calculation? If not, the loop is repeated; if so, the result is printed.

In this method of controlling a loop, a counter, Q, is set at zero, and then incremented by 1 for each individual process, until a condition is fulfilled to stop the process looping. Using this method the number of loops is not preset. The flowchart also illustrates a conditional jump, that is if N is not equal to Q, then jump back to the start of the loop.

Flowcharts: business and technical

Tabulation is of frequent use in business records. A table is to be constructed showing:

Name of salesman Commission payable Number of sales

The information required is (*a*) average commission per salesman (*b*) average number of sales per salesman and (*c*) average commission per sale. The first two items require the number of salesmen to be known. When the data for each salesman is recorded, a counter must be set up to count the number of salesmen. This is done by using a counter, T, which has an increment of 1 added for each item of data entered. A condition for a loop is needed; this is supplied by assigning a symbol, in this case '??', which shows the end of the data. The totals for commission and number of sales have also been recorded, so the averages can be calculated and printed.

In this type of loop, the number of events is counted by an increment of 1 for each time the loop is used. The number of loops needed is controlled by the entry of a predetermined symbol.

Multiple conditions

A desired result is dependent on 3 or 4, or more, conditions simultaneously. A suitable example is landing an aeroplane on an airstrip. On landing, the height and location have to be correct; in addition, the landing speed has an upper limit, and so has the angle of approach. All four conditions must be realised simultaneously for the aeroplane to land safely, otherwise it will crash. When flying and while landing, the speed of the aeroplane must exceed its stalling speed; this makes a fifth condition.

The problem will now be attempted in a simple fashion, without detail of attraction due to gravity, consumption of fuel, or excessive speed and angle of descent. The **variables** necessary for the calculation are: V = speed of aeroplane (in knots); H = height of aeroplane (in metres); D = distance from airstrip; A = angle of descent/approach. Other information needed is: VS = stalling speed (minimum); VL = landing speed (maximum); AL = angle of approach (maximum).

The relation between H, D and A is shown in the diagram. From the triangle H/D = tan A, hence A can be calculated from H and D, or, alternatively, if an angle of descent is given, then H can be calculated from A and D.

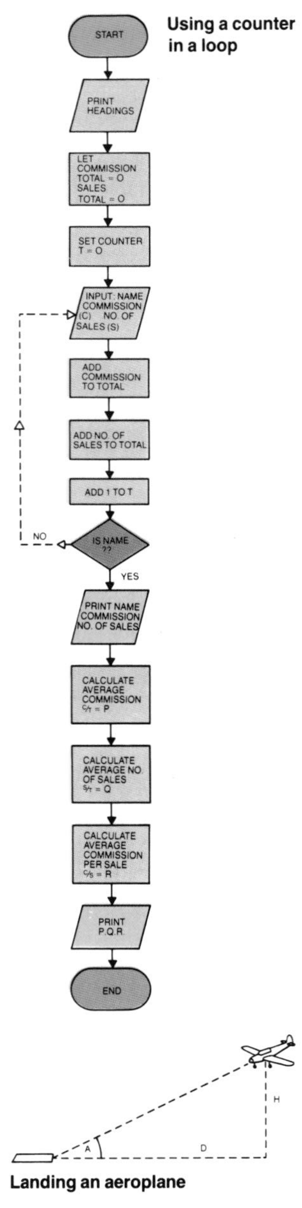

Using a counter in a loop

Landing an aeroplane

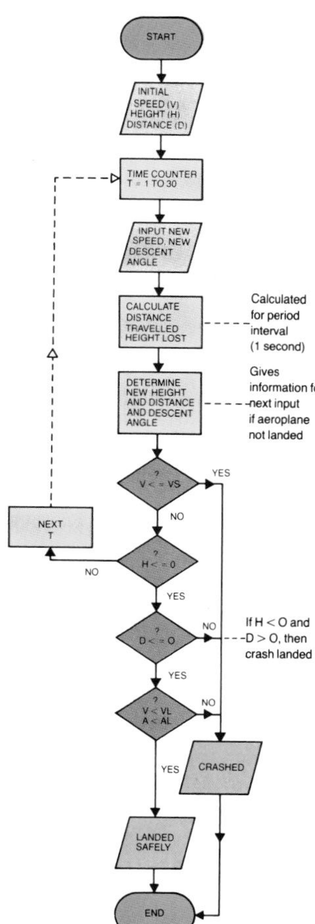

Multiple conditions; landing an aeroplane

The conditions can be calculated for a specified time interval, say 1 second, an unrealistic time interval for a modern jet aeroplane, but suitable for a simple calculation for aeroplanes with lower flying speeds.

The initial conditions will give the values of V, H and D, and assume A is zero for the plane, but calculate a value of A from H and D. The priority of the conditions must be decided first of all. Is the aeroplane at zero height? Is it at the airstrip? These come first. Then the landing conditions: (*a*) speed correct? (*b*) approach angle correct? These are conditions that must be realised simultaneously so (*a*) and (*b*) form one condition in a decision box in the flowchart.

The flowchart does not give an algorithm for the calculation of distance travelled and height lost. This calculation can be simple for an elementary, approximate exercise, or it can be complex for a more accurate calculation. The decision box on stalling speed would be slightly better immediately after the input box on new speed and angle of descent. The flowchart has not allowed for overflying the airstrip, that is $D < 0$, but $H > 0$ when the aeroplane is above the airstrip but not on it.

Nesting loops

One loop can be inside another loop, this is called **nesting** loops. Nested loops are useful in searching through tabulated information. For example, an insurance company keeps records of different policies for individual clients; for this example a maximum of six different policies for a client has been made permissable. The code letter at the head of the policy number describes the type of policy. The policy number can incorporate the date of birth of the insured. The tabulated information would look like this:

Smith A.	Policy 1	Policy 2	Policy 3		
Jones D.	Policy 1	Policy 2			
White B.	Policy 1	Policy 2	Policy 3	Policy 4	Policy 5

Set out briefly, the full file of information would be:

	Smith A.	P.1	P.2	P.3			
M items	M names						
	Lee B.A	P.1	P.2	P.3	P.4	P.5	P.6

N = 6 items (maximum)

The search is for the number of insured persons born between the years 1935 and 1939 with an annuity policy. Two nested loops are needed. The N-loop searches through the policy details of one individual, hence N will run from 1 to 6. The maximum number of documents has been fixed at 6, so the loop must have the same count each time it is carried out. The J-loop runs through the list of insured; the limit M must be included with the other information in the data file. The search is carried out by:

J = 1	N = 1 TO 6
J = 2	N = 1 TO 6
⋮	
J = M	N = 1 TO 6

Notice that the N-loop must be completely inside the J-loop. This is true for all nested loops; an inner loop must be completely enclosed by an outer loop. Each loop will end when terminated by the FOR . . . TO statement, that is when N = 6, in this case, the N-loop is terminated by the statement, the next J number is taken, and N goes back to 1 again. Some computers have the loop terminated by NEXT.

Any number of loops can be nested, but care must be taken to make sure every inner loop is completely enclosed by an outer loop. For a nest of:

FOR R = 1 TO 4	where R is the innermost loop
FOR Q = 1 TO 3	where Q is the middle loop
FOR P = 1 TO 2	where P is the outermost loop

then the order of presentation of data is:

P = 1	Q = 1	R = 1, 2, 3, 4
	Q = 2	R = 1, 2, 3, 4
	Q = 3	R = 1, 2, 3, 4
P = 2	Q = 1	R = 1, 2, 3, 4
	Q = 2	R = 1, 2, 3, 4
	Q = 3	R = 1, 2, 3, 4

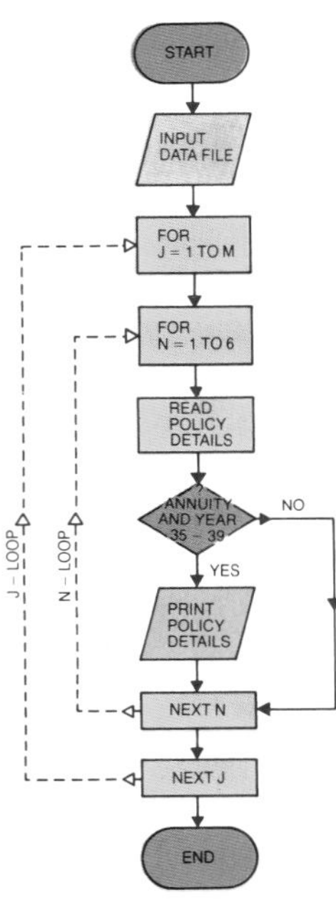

Nested loops for searching tabulated information

The increment in a loop

The step in a loop need not go up by 1 for each event; most computers will allow any other integer. Most computers will allow negative steps or even decimal increments. Such steps are useful in making tables for trigonometrical constants. For example, let Y = SIN A, where A is expressed in degrees. To get all values of Y, A must

The use of 'step' in a loop; successive loops

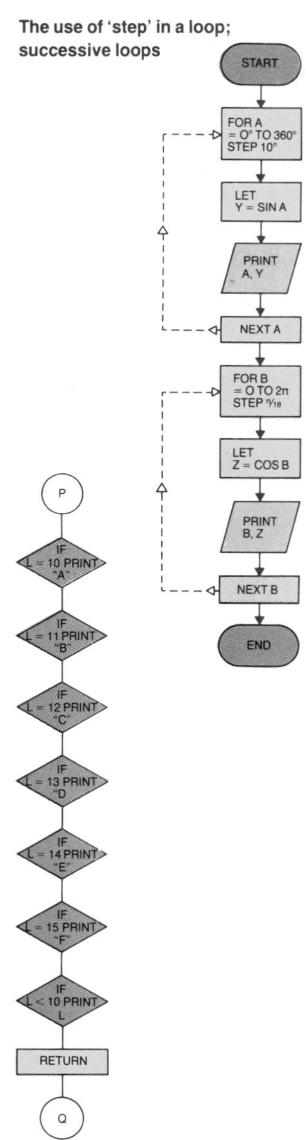

Subroutine for hexadecimal conversion

change from 0° to 360°. A suitable increment for this is 10°, so the statement is: FOR A = 0° TO 360° STEP 10°. A list of values of Y will now be produced for values of A in increments of 10°. Now many computers will not accept degrees for calculation of trigonometrical ratios, as they accept only radians. For conversion 360° = 2π radians, so increments of 10° will become increments of $\pi/18$ radians, an increment definitely not an integer. Using the expression Z = cos B, values of Z can be found using the statement FOR B = 0 TO 2*π STEP $\pi/18$

The values of A and B now correspond. In the flowchart, both loops have been used, one after the other. This is a successive use of loops, in this particular example, not to be confused with the nesting of loops. The flowchart is not applicable to most computers, as degrees would need to be converted to radians. Negative steps can be used, providing counting runs in decreasing numbers, for example: FOR X = 10 TO 1 STEP –1. Such a count often is useful in arranging printing statements.

The use of subroutines

A subroutine is called by a main routine. There are two uses of subroutines. Firstly, a part of a process is repeated several times; this part can be removed from the process and put in a subroutine. This is the general use of a subroutine in most programming. However, in advanced programming, several subroutines can be written and then joined together in a linking program to make a full program. This use allows different parts of a program to be tested before the whole program is run.

The first use of a subroutine can be demonstrated by the following flowchart. A number in decimal notation is to be changed to a number in hexadecimal notation (see p. 54). Here we have the problem of converting 10 to A, 11 to B, 12 to C, 13 to D, 14 to E and 15 to F; this problem will obviously appear several times in a process, so a subroutine can be made for it. The subroutine is shown in the diagram. The value of L is tested, then printed when the correct one is found. At the end of the subroutine is the statement RETURN. This returns the flow of data to the point *immediately* after it left the main routine.

The conversion of decimal to hexadecimal is carried out by dividing the decimal number successively by 16 and putting the remainder for each division into the hexadecimal number (see p. 54). Some high-level languages allow the use of a remainder, but some do not, so the flowchart has an algorithm to produce a remainder. The function INT produces an integer by *truncation*, that is it gives an integer less than or equal to the number. The flowchart produces successive figures, but does not show how to print them. A conditional loop produces conversion figures until the calculation is completed and no further figures are left to divide. Each digit, as it is produced, is printed by the subroutine.

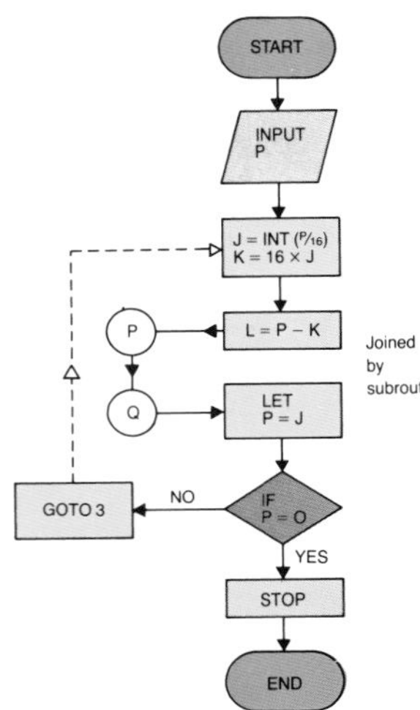

Flowchart for conversion of decimal to hexadecimal

General practice for flowcharts

For a long flowchart, it is convenient to construct it from several subroutines, joining the subroutines in a main flowchart. This allows each part of the flowchart to be tested on a computer. An example of this is provided by a list of names and ages which has to be arranged (*a*) alphabetically (*b*) by age. Assume that the original list is in random order and is given with name first and age second for each entry.

The first subroutine tests whether a list is either alphabetically or numerically correct. This is done by testing item I against item J, where J = I + 1. If the order is correct then item I < item J.

The second subroutine, Q, exchanges two incorrectly placed items. This three-part statement is a standard piece of program (or flowchart) for a computer. Note that subroutine Q is a subroutine itself of subroutine R. Subroutines can be embedded in other subroutines, in this way.

The third subroutine, P, prints the final list when it is arranged correctly in either alphabetical, or numerical order for age.

The three subroutines are now gathered together in a main flowchart. Beginning with an input in random order, an alphabetical list is produced by the first arrangement. This list is now labelled list M – alphabetical order. The original list, L, now has the data rearranged so that age comes before name. In arranging age, the number of years is put before the number of months. If age has been recorded by date of birth, then year of birth is put before month. A second process is now carried out, using the same subroutines, and a list by age is produced. This list is labelled N – by age. A final print of lists M and N gives the data in two lists, as required. This flowchart is restricted to ten items in a list. By replacing 10 in the various loops by the letter Y, and giving Y a value, the flowchart can be made available for any number of items.

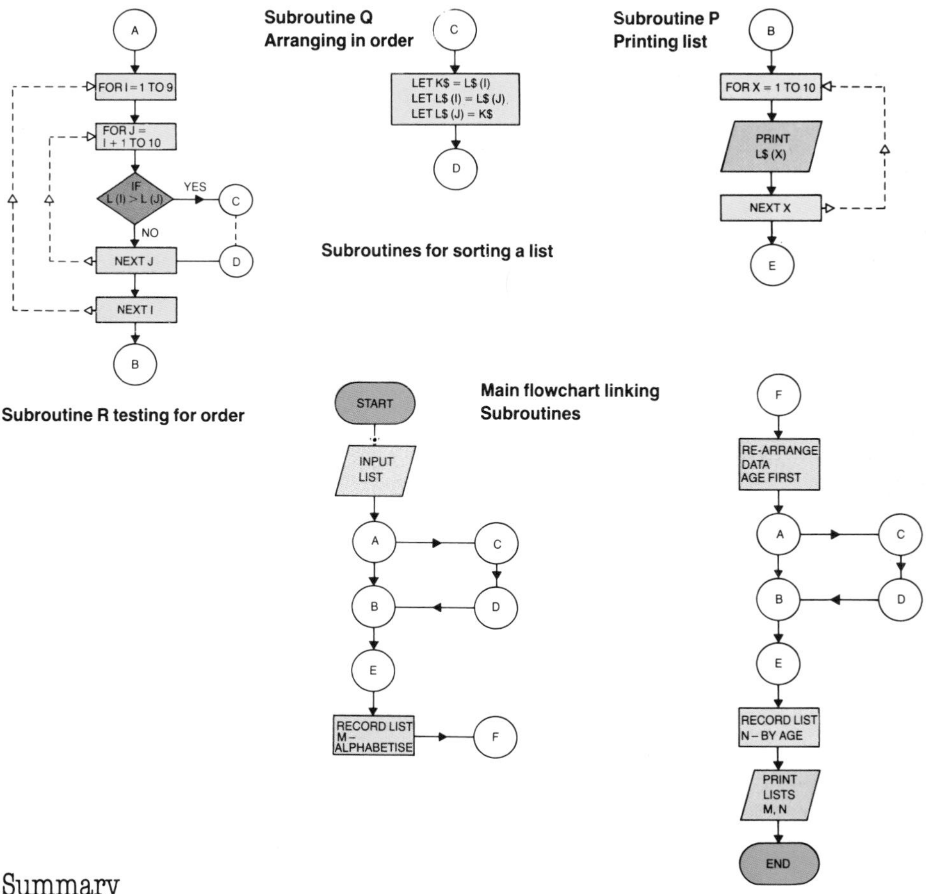

Subroutine R testing for order

Subroutines for sorting a list

Main flowchart linking Subroutines

Summary

A flow chart is used to break down a process into a succession of simple steps; steps are either terminators; input/outputs; decisions; processes.

An **algorithm** is an expression, with variables, for solving a problem.

An *iterative* process is carried out by **looping**.

Loops are controlled by statements: FOR . . . NEXT.

Conditional loops are controlled by statements: IF . . . THEN and increments.

Multiple conditions can be used in loops; it is important to get conditions in correct order.

Nesting loops: every inner loop must be completely enclosed by an outer loop.

Steps in loops: increments can be other than 1. Negative numbers can also be used.

A **subroutine** is a part of a flowchart that is used in different parts of the process. A main flowchart can also be composed of a collection of subroutines.

Binary notation and computer codes

Binary notation

Binary notation is a method of counting using two figures, 0 and 1. A **notation** is a method of recording information, in this case numerical information. The **base**, or **radix**, is 2, that is the place value of each digit in a number represents a multiple of 2. A comparison of numbers in binary and decimal notation (i.e. the common method of counting) is:

BINARY NUMBER	1	10	11	100	101	110	111	1000	1001	1010
DECIMAL NUMBER	1	2	3	4	5	6	7	8	9	10

Conversion of binary to decimal notation

The conversion is:

Binary number	1	0	1	1	0	0	0	1	1
Digit value (in decimal)	2^8	2^7	2^6	2^5	2^4	2^3	2^2	2^1	2^0
Decimal value	256	128	64	32	16	8	4	2	1

101100011 (binary) $= 1+2+32+64+256 = 355$ (decimal)

Binary numbers and equivalent decimal numbers

Binary number	1	1	0	0	1	1	0
Decimal value	64	32	16	8	4	2	0

1100110 (binary) $= 2+4+32+64$
$= 102$ (decimal)

Conversion of decimal to binary notation

This is done by dividing repeatedly by 2, and the remainder at each stage is the binary digit. The numbers above, that is 355 and 102, can be converted back from decimal to binary notation as follows:

		(remainder)
2	355	
2	177	1
2	88	1
2	44	0
2	22	0
2	11	0
2	5	1
2	2	1
	1	0

355 (decimal) ≡ 101100011 (binary)

		(remainder)
2	102	
2	51	0
2	25	1
2	12	1
2	6	0
2	3	0
	1	1

102 (decimal) ≡ 1100110 (binary)

Exercise

(1) Show that 179 (dec) ≡ 10110011 (binary)
(2) Show that 11001000 (binary) ≡ 200 (decimal)
(3) (*a*) Find the decimal values of 1101011 and 1000100 (*b*) Convert 281 (decimal) and 256 (decimal) to binary

Octal notation

Octal notation uses a **base**, or radix, of 8; the figures used are 0, 1, 2, 3, 4, 5, 6 and 7. A comparison of numbers in octal and decimal notation is:

1	2	3	4	5	6	7	8	9	10	11	12	DECIMAL NUMBER
1	2	3	4	5	6	7	10	11	12	13	14	OCTAL NUMBER

Conversion of octal to decimal notation

The conversion is:

5	4	1	Octal number
8^2	8^1	8^0	Digit value (in decimal)
64	8	1	Decimal value

541 (octal) = (5 × 64) + (4 × 8) + (1 × 1) = 353 (decimal)

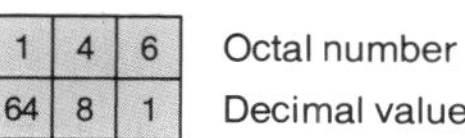

1	4	6	Octal number
64	8	1	Decimal value

146 (octal) = (1 × 64) + (4 × 8) + (6 × 1) = 102 (decimal)

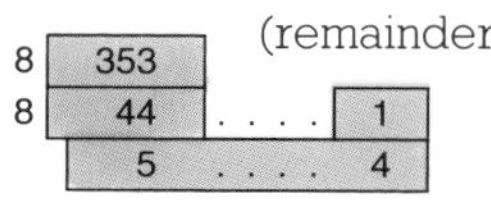

353 (dec) ≡ (octal)

Conversion of decimal to octal

The decimal number is divided repeatedly by 8 and the remainder at each stage is the octal digit. The numbers, 353 and 102, above can be converted back from decimal to octal as shown here.

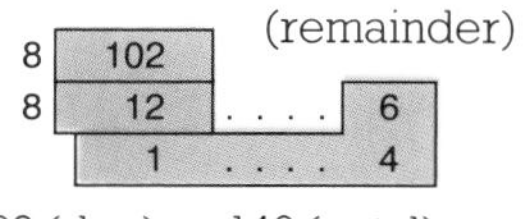

102 (dec) ≡ 146 (octal)

Conversion between octal and binary

Conversion between octal and binary is easy because $2^3 = 8$, so the binary number 1000 is equivalent to the octal number 10. In the figure the octal number 146 is compared with the binary number 1100110. When the binary number is split into groups of three digits, one group in each of the locations *a*, *b*, and *c*, each group, counted in binary, is equal to the digit value of the octal number. In location *a*, 1 ≡ 1; in *b*, 100 ≡ 4; in *c*, 110 ≡ 6, so 541 (octal) is equivalent to 101100001 (binary). Converting decimal to octal is easier than converting decimal to binary, so to convert a decimal number to binary, first convert to octal, then write down the binary number, for example 367 (octal) ≡ 11,110,111 (binary). (The commas show the equivalent groups.)

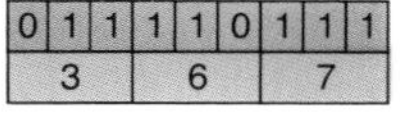

BINARY	0	1	1	1	1	0	1	1	1
OCTAL	3			6			7		

Hexadecimal notation

This notation is also used in computer work. The **base** is 16, so figures are required for the decimal numbers 10, 11, 12, 13, 14, 15. These are:

HEXADECIMAL	1	2	3	4	5	6	7	8	9	A	B	C	D	E	F	10
DECIMAL	1	2	3	4	5	6	7	8	9	10	11	12	13	14	15	16

Conversion of hexadecimal to decimal notation

The conversion is:

2	E	A	Hexadecimal number
16^2	16^1	16^0	Digit value (in decimal)
256	16	1	Decimal value

2EA (hex) = $(2 \times 256) + (14 \times 16) + (10 \times 1) = 512 + 224 + 10$
= 746 (decimal)

Hexadecimal number and equivalent decimal number

Conversion of decimal to hexadecimal notation

The decimal number is divided repeatedly by 16 and the remainder at each stage is the hexadecimal digit. The number above can be converted back from decimal to hexadecimal.

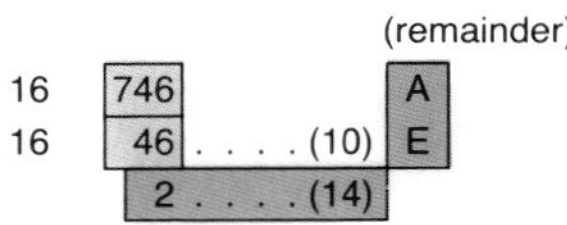

746 (decimal) ≡ 2EA (hexadecimal)

An easier method of conversion is through an octal number.

Conversion between hexadecimal and binary

Conversion between hexadecimal and binary is easy because $2^4 = 16$, so the binary number 10000 is equivalent to the hexadecimal number 10. In the figure, the hexadecimal number 2EA is compared with the binary number 1011101010. When the binary number is split into groups of four digits, one group in each of the locations *a*, *b* and *c*, each group, counted in binary, is equal to the digit value of the hexadecimal number, for example in location *c*, 1010 ≡ decimal) ≡

Location	a	b	c
Binary number	10	1110	1010
Hexadecimal number	2	(14) = E	(10) = A

2EA (hex) ≡ 1011101010 (binary)

Conversion between binary and hexadecimal numbers

The relation of octal, binary and hexadecimal notations

An octal number can be readily converted to a binary number by replacing the octal digits by groups of *three* binary digits. If the binary digits are then placed in groups of four digits, the hexadecimal number can be written down. In the figure, 1352 (octal) ≡ 101101010 (binary) ≡

746 (decimal)

Octal	1	3	5	2
Binary	1 0	1110		1010
Hexa-decimal	2	(14) = E	(10) = A	

Relation between binary, octal and hexadecimal notation

2EA (hexadecimal). Since conversion of decimal to octal is the easiest arithmetical calculation, so conversion of decimal to hexadecimal can be through decimal to octal to binary to hexadecimal. This can be used instead of the method of dividing any decimal number repeatedly by 16. Hexadecimal codes are a useful shorthand way of writing down any binary number.

Exercise

(1) Change the decimal numbers 168, 1709 to octal and then to binary notation.
(2) Change the octal numbers 264, 312, 512 to decimal and binary notation.
(3) Change the decimal numbers 618 and 377 to hexadecimal numbers.

Information flow

Binary notation is very useful for the flow of information through a computer, or other electronic device. The numbers 1 and 0 are represented by an ON and OFF characteristic.

Voltage characteristics

A high and a low voltage are used. A high voltage represents 1 and a low voltage represents 0. A timer sends a series of voltage pulses through the computer at a fixed frequency. The frequency is between 3 MHz and 48 MHz, depending on the individual computer. 48 MHz $= 48 \times 10^6$ pulses per second, that is 1 pulse lasts for approximately 20 nanoseconds, i.e. 20×10^{-9} seconds. The pulse is then recorded as a high or low voltage, to give the binary code.

Coding binary by voltage

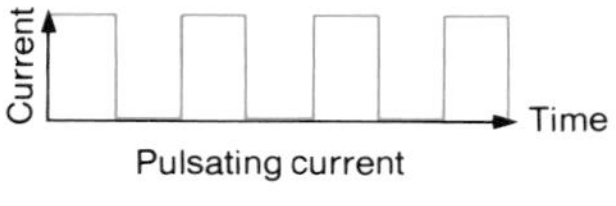

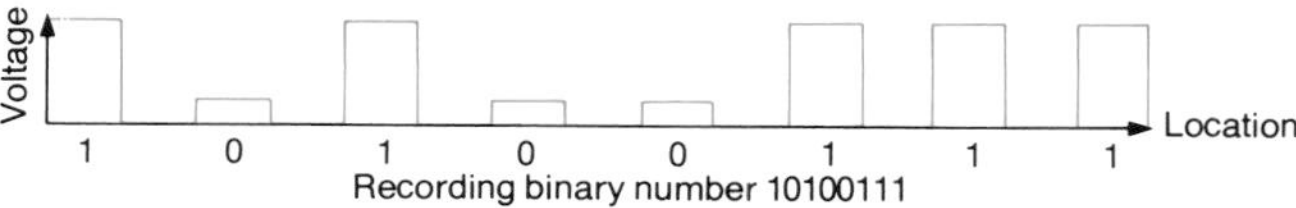

Magnetic characteristics

A magnetic recording surface is put on disks or on tape. The disk, or tape, passes under a read or write head, as on a cassette recorder. A **track** on the disk, or tape, passes under the read/write head and spots, at a fixed distance apart, can either be magnetised or left unmagnetised. The result is shown in the figure, and a recorded binary number indicated. A magnetised spot represents 1 and an unmagnetised spot represents 0.

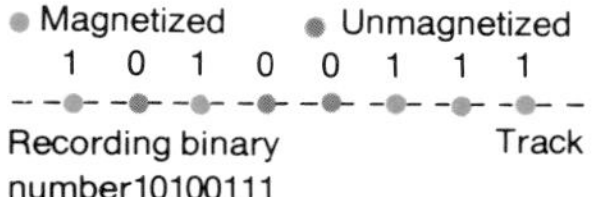

Coding binary by magnetized spots on track

Mechanical characteristics

Paper tape is used and holes can be punched in it. A hole represents 1 and no hole represents 0. The paper tape in the illustration is divided into groups of holes, with each group representing an octal number.

Paper tape

247 156 316

Recording octal numbers

● Hole ○ No hole

Coding octal by holes on paper tape

A bit

Each representation of binary code, whether by voltage, magnetisation, a hole in paper, or a figure 1 or 0, is called a **bit**. Bit is a shortened form of **BInary digiT**. The binary number 10100111 has eight bits. These bits are used to encode information as well as to represent numbers. A computer carries out all its processes using information coded in bits.

Binary-coded decimal (BCD)

A decimal number can be coded using a group of four bits. The diagram shows the method of coding on magnetic tape, using four tracks. Binary-coded decimal was used in earlier computers, but was subsequently replaced by octal coding. Some recent computers are now using

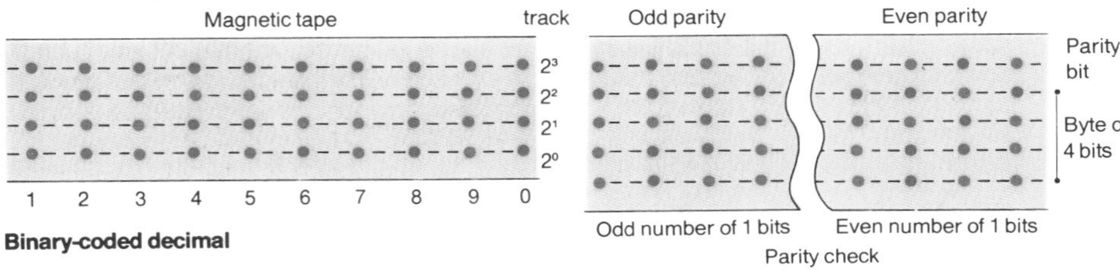

Binary-coded decimal

Parity check

binary-coded decimal for quicker arithmetical calculations. In binary-coded decimal, not all the possible combinations are used. The numbers 0-9 are shown in the diagram, but the tracks could also be used to show 10, 11, 12, 13, 14 and 15. (How would you do this?)

● Magnetized (= 1)
● Unmagnetized (= 0)

A byte

A group of bits, considered as a unit, is called a **byte.** Most microcomputers use a byte of eight bits. A few, more advanced, microcomputers use a 16-bit byte and a 32-bit byte is also used. Two or more bytes make a **word**, in which the bytes have different uses, but most microcomputers use a byte as the standard unit.

Testing bytes by parity

When bytes are transferred in a microcomputer, it is possible for a fault to cause the loss of a bit. To test whether a byte has been transferred accurately, a bit is added to a byte to form a **parity** check; this bit is called a **parity bit**. The parity bit is not part of the information coded in the byte, the computer uses it solely for checking purposes.

Parity

There are two types of parity, called **odd parity** and **even parity**. A computer uses either one or the other for checking purposes. In odd parity, the sum of 'one' bits, including the parity bit, is odd. In even parity, the sum of the 'one' bits, including the parity bit, is even. For example, in an 8-bit byte, if the binary number is 10110110, then in odd parity the parity bit is 0; in even parity the parity bit is 1. In the diagram, various bytes, each consisting of four bits, is shown with its parity bit for checking.

Computer code

Information is stored in a byte. The information can be a letter, a figure, a punctuation sign, a mathematical symbol, or an instruction to the computer. For each of these types of information, a computer has a code. The codes are not standard for all computers, thus making it impossible, generally, for one computer to work with another. A standard set of codes exists called the ASCII standard (ASCII is short for American Standard Code for Information Interchange). A list of some of these codes is given in the tables below.

Sample of ASCII number codes (decimal numbers)

ASCII character	Decimal code	ASCII character	Decimal code	ASCII character	Decimal code	ASCII character	Decimal code
space	32	1	49	<	60	G	71
(	40	2	50	=	61	H	72
)	41	3	51	>	62	I	73
*	42	4	52	?	63	J	74
+	43	5	53	A	65	K	75
,	44	6	54	B	66	L	76
—	45	7	55	C	67	M	77
.	46	8	56	D	68	N	78
/	47	9	57	E	69	O	79
0	48	;	59	F	70	P	80

ASCII character	Decimal code	Hexadecimal code	Binary code	
Q	81	51	0101	0001
R	82	52	0101	0010
S	83	53	0101	0011
T	84	54	0101	0100
U	85	55	0101	0101
V	86	56	0101	0110
W	87	57	0101	0111
X	88	58	0101	1000
Y	89	59	0101	1001
Z	90	5A	0101	1010
			Byte of 8 bits	

Some ASCII characters with decimal, hexadecimal and binary codes

Many computers now use the ASCII codes for characters, but have their own codes for instructions.

Characters and operators

Strictly speaking, characters are those symbols used in printing, that is, all the letters of the alphabet, all the figures, and the punctuation marks (i.e. ; , . : " ? '). Operators are those symbols used in mathematics (i.e. < > = + − * / ↑) where the symbols have the following meanings:

COMPUTER OPERATOR	MATHEMATICAL SYMBOL	MEANING
+	+	addition
−	−	subtraction
*	×	multiplication
/	÷	division
>	>	greater than
<	<	less than
=	=	equals
↑	index	4 ↑ 3 is 4^3
**	index (alternative)	4**3 is 4^3
<>	≠	not equal to
>=	⩾	greater than or equal to
<=	⩽	less than or equal to

Characters and operators are sometimes all included in the set of characters. **Numeric characters** are figures alone; **alpha characters** are letters alone; **alphanumeric characters** are letters and figures. All microcomputers use alphanumeric characters.

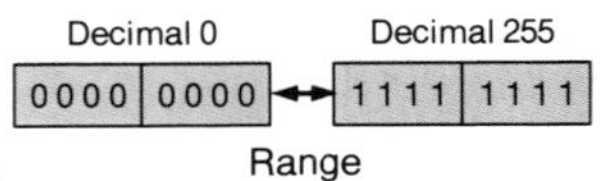

Range of computer code in 8-bit binary

Character code

The character code for a computer must be held in a byte. For an 8-bit byte, the range is 0–255 (see diagram) as 255 is

Instruction/ character	Computer decimal code	Instruction/ character	Computer decimal code
PRINT	01	STOP	14
LET	02	line end	15
TAB	05	;	18
"	10	number	23
CLEAR	12	INPUT	27

Dummy code for instruction purposes only

the largest binary number that can be held in the byte. The code of 256 separate numbers must have a single number for each character, operator and instruction used by the computer. Although the ASCII code is widely used by many computers for alphanumeric characters, and most operators, there is not much standardisation on instructions or on the codes used for them. This applies particularly to the computer's method of dealing with *peripheral* devices. In order to understand the functions of a computer code, here is a list of fictitious codes for computer instructions. The actual instructions are fairly standard for most computers. Note that two of the instructions, (line end, number) are printed differently. These are not instructions from a keyboard or other input device, but instructions that the computer adds for its own information. These fictitious, or dummy, instructions will be used to show how a computer acts on a program.

Transmission of bytes

Information can be sent out or received in two ways, called serial and parallel. In **serial transmission**, a byte is transferred from one location, at the start, to another location, at the end, by sending one bit at a time along a single wire. Extra bits are added to the byte to show where the byte starts and where it ends. In **parallel transmission**, separate wires are used for each bit in the location, so the whole byte is transferred in one action. Parallel transmission is obviously much quicker than serial transmission, but the wire connections needed for parallel transmission are greater in number and more complicated than the connections for serial transmission. Serial transmission is thus cheaper and slower than parallel transmission.

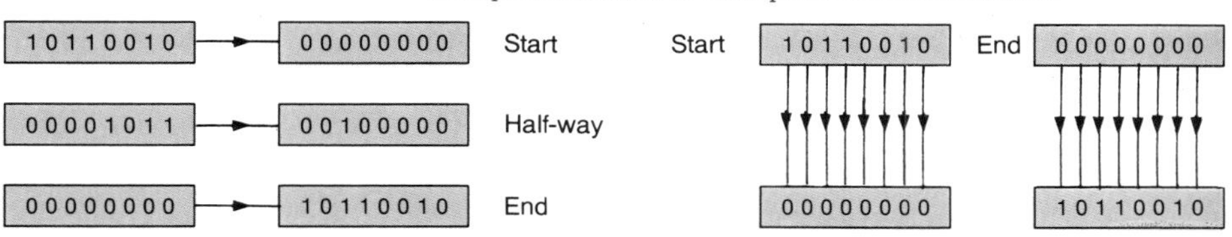

Serial transmission of a byte of binary with 8 bits

Parallel transmission of a byte of binary with 8 bits

Registers

A register is a special location used temporarily for the storage of a byte before it is sent on for the next process. The use of registers varies from one computer to another, but almost all arithmetical units use registers for calculations.

Storing a program

Using a keyboard, or other input device, a program is written and appears on a VDU for visual checking by the operator. This program is then stored in the computer memory, using the computer code.

Compiler

Part of the central processing unit is called a compiler. It puts the program into memory and also interprets the instruction. An **interpreter** converts the instruction, character, or operator into computer code. The computer code is stored in binary in a byte. An 8-bit byte is the most common one. In addition to translating the instructions from the input, the compiler arranges the information in memory. An example will show how this is done. Note that different computers will store the coded information in different ways, so this is only an illustration. It will show, however, certain principles that all computers have to follow. A simple program is shown here. Differences for computers appear immediatelty, as many computers do not need the instruction LET, and there are variations of STOP.

```
10  LET    A = 12
20  LET    B = 5*A
30  PRINT  A; TAB 8; B, 6*B
40  STOP
```

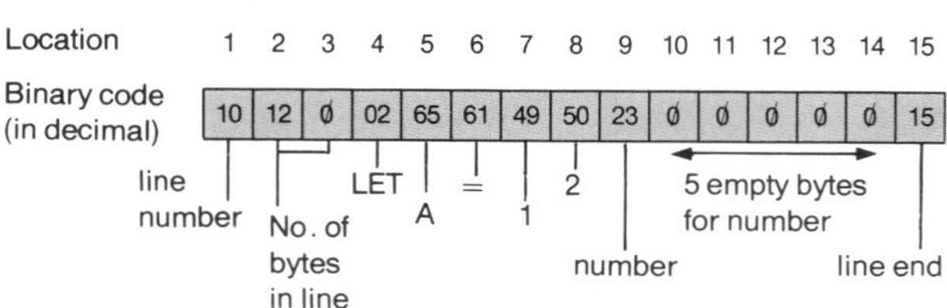

Storing a coded program in memory

The diagram shows the storage memory of the first line of the program. The compiler puts information into memory to show the line number, the number of bytes in the line (it has to count them first), and then the character code for each character and operator. It adds, in location 9, an instruction, labelled 'number' to show that the number, 12, must be converted to another form before it can be used by the arithmetical unit. The last byte shows the end of the line. The information coded in locations 2, 3, 9 and 15 is thus additional to the written program and is supplied by the compiler. The information in location 9 sets aside five empty bytes for translation of the number. Although the codes are shown in *decimal*, this is only for ease of reading, the codes are stored in each location in *binary*. Remember that there is a maximum of 255 codes plus a code for an empty location, when using 8-bit bytes.

Program in memory

The next program shows the storage of letters as well as numbers. Once again, different computers will have different instructions for printing alpha characters, and using LET.

10	PRINT	"A NEW PROGRAM"
20	INPUT	A
30	LET	B = 15*A/100
40	PRINT	A, B
50	STOP	

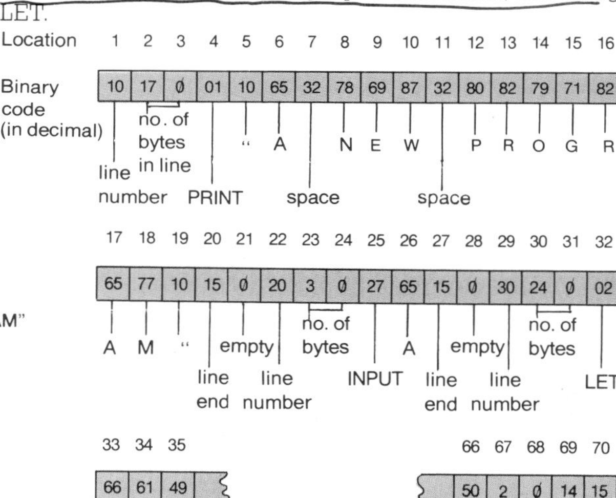

Storing a coded program

The diagram shows the start and the end of the program when stored in memory. Complete the program and show that the last locations are numbered correctly.

Summary

Notation. A number can be written using different **bases**. The base in everyday use is 10, forming decimal notation. A computer stores all its information in binary notation. Octal notation uses a base of 8 and hexadecimal notation uses a base of 16. Hexadecimal notation is used to show the contents of an 8-bit byte. If every bit is 1, then the decimal value is 255 and the hexadecimal value is FF. Hexadecimal is much more convenient to write than binary, so it is used to indicate a binary number.

Bits. A bit is a binary digit, and it can have only one of two values: 1 or 0. Bits can be recorded by: high/low voltage; magnetised/unmagnetised spot; hole/no hole in paper tape. A set of bits is a **byte**. A byte in a particular computer always contains the same number of bits. Most computers use an 8-bit byte.

Computer code. A numerical code, of value between 0 and 255, is used to describe any letter, figure, punctuation mark, mathematical operator, or instruction.

Program store. A program is stored in computer code in the computer's memory. All information is thus stored in binary bytes.

CHAPTER 5

Arithmetic and operators

Numbers

Numbers in arithmetical calculations can be divided into integer numbers and real numbers. A real number has a decimal fraction as part of the number; an integer has no decimal fraction. Examples are:

Integers:	4; 604; 1 328 967; 21; 100; 2 000 000
Real numbers:	4·23; 604·5; 1 328 967·217; 21·5; 100.62985

Some computers will accept only integers for calculations, but most computers will accept real numbers.

Integer arithmetic

Arithmetical operations on integers are carried out in some computers by using binary-coded decimal numbers (*see Chapter 4*). The computer stores the binary-coded decimal number in a 2-byte register in its arithmetic unit. The number, recorded in memory in the computer code, is translated and fed into the register, as shown in the diagram. The 8-bit registers contain the number, 361, in

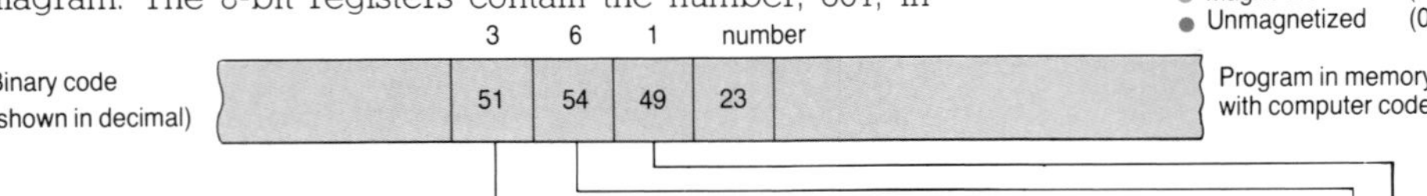

binary-coded decimal; the parity bits are not included in the diagram, so that the binary-coded decimal number can be recognised more easily. The largest number that can be held in an 8-bit register is $10^8 - 1$, that is 99,999,999. Integer arithmetic is a part of fixed-point arithmetic.

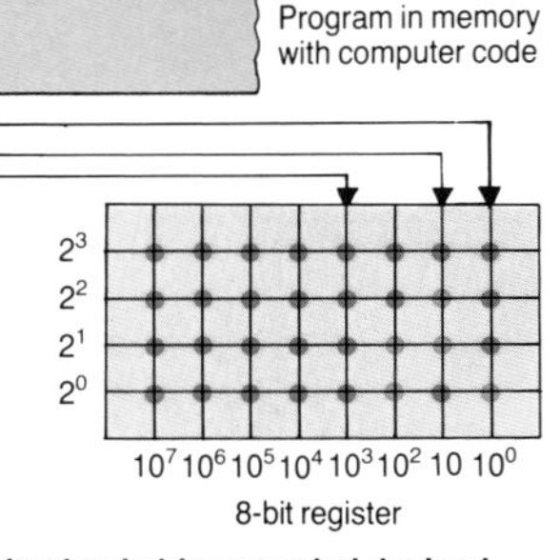

Number in binary coded decimal (no parity bits shown)

Parity bits

When the number is fed into the arithmetic register from memory, **parity bits** are added, where necessary, to make either odd- or even-parity. In the figure, parity bits are added to each column to make an odd-parity check. An extra **parity column** is added to the register so that the odd-parity of each row can be checked by parity bits. The parity bit, or lack of it, in the position for the parity row and

Odd-parity check

parity column, checks the bits for both rows and columns, and thus checks the adding of the parity bits. Check that odd-parity is maintained for all rows and columns in the diagram. Whenever a register is used, a parity check is made on its contents.

Addition in binary-coded decimal

The bits are added in an arithmetic register, that is 2 bits on the 2^2 row become 1 bit on the 2^3 row. A total of 10 on one column becomes 1 bit on the next column.

Subtraction using complements

Subtraction in computers is carried out by forming the **complement** of a number and then adding the complement instead of subtracting the number. A **complement** is obtained by subtracting each digit of a number from one less than the base, or radix, of the notation (*see Chapter 4*). In decimal notation, the base is 10, so each digit is subtracted from 9. The **true complement** is then given by adding 1. For example, the complements of 354 and 1938 are:

```
 999                                    9999
-354                                   -1938
 645 + 1 = 646 (true complement)        8061 + 1 = 8062 (true complement)
```

Here is a comparison of ordinary subtraction, and subtraction using a complement:

```
  796 minuend          796
 -354 subtrahend      +646 complement
  442 difference      1442
```

In the arithmetic register, a true complement of 354 in an 8-bit register is:

```
99999999
00000354
99999645 + 1 = 99999646
```

so when the addition of the complement takes place, we have:

```
      | 00000796 |
      | 99999646 |
1<--- | 00000442 |
```

The 1 is suppressed outside the register, leaving the correct value of the difference in the register.

Binary complement

A binary complement is obtained by subtracting each digit of a number from 1, and then adding 1 to get the true complement. For example:

```
  11111111
- 01100101
  10011010 + 1 = 10011011 (true complement)
```

Observe the complement, it can be obtained by reversing each digit of the binary number, that is changing 0 to 1 and 1 to 0. For example:

Binary number	10011101	01110100
Complement	01100010	10001011
True complement	01100011	10001100

A comparison of ordinary subtraction, and subtraction using a complement is:

```
  10110110 minuend                  10110110  minuend
- 01100101 subtrahend           +   10011011  true complement
  01010001 difference     (1) ←     01010001  difference
```

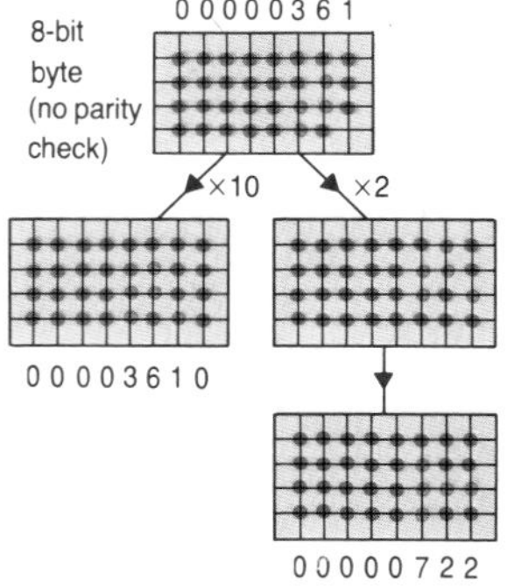

Multiplication in binary coded decimal

Multiplication with BCD

In an arithmetic register, a bit can be moved up, or to the left. Moving a bit to the left is equivalent to multiplying by 10, as shown in the diagram. Moving a bit up by one row is equivalent to multiplying by 2. This allows multiplication of a number to be carried out very quickly. The following multiplication shows the action in the arithmetic unit:

```
  361 multiplicand
× 154 multiplier
55594 product
```

There are four registers, A, B, C, D, in the arithmetic unit, shown in the diagram. The multiplicand is put in register A, and the multiplier in register B. The central processing unit (CPU) puts the multiplicand number in register C by using clear add, that is removing any previous number before adding the number 361. This number is then multiplied by 4, that is by 2 and then by 2 again. This result is transferred to register D. The original multiplicand is then clear added to register C. This time it is multiplied by 10, then by 5. The result is added to register D. Finally, 361 is

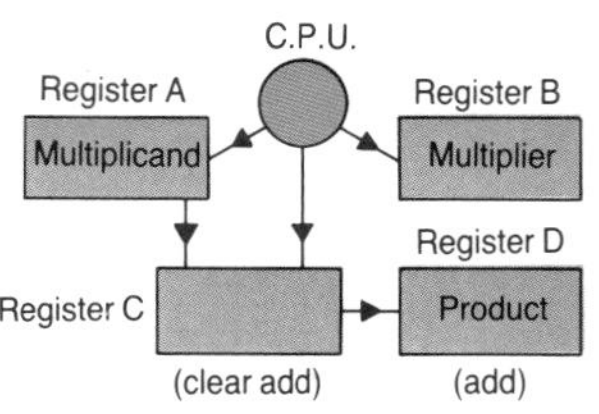

Simple multiplication in binary coded decimal

clear added to register C and the number multiplied by 100, that is by 10, then by 10 again. The result is added to register D giving the final product.

In all these operations the arithmetic unit carries out only four operations, that is multiplication by 10, 2, or 1, and addition.

Division with BCD

Division is carried out by successive subtraction, counting the number of subtractions made before a negative number is obtained. For example:

3749	÷	238	=	15	+(179)
dividend		divisor		quotient	remainder

The divisor is multiplied by 10; the result is subtracted from 3749. 3749 − 2380 = 1369. 2380 cannot be subtracted from 1369, as a negative number is formed, so the quotient has 10 in its register. 238 is now repeatedly subtracted from 1369. After five subtractions, a remainder of 179 is left. So the result is a quotient of 15; the remainder can be displayed or can be suppressed in integer arithmetic.

Real numbers

Very large or very small real numbers are best written in **standard index form** (also called scientific notation), which is based on powers of 10. For example:

number	537·62	67400	0·00000652	14.000361
standard index form	$5{\cdot}3762 \times 10^2$	$6{\cdot}74 \times 10^4$	$6{\cdot}52 \times 10^{-4}$	1.4000361×10

The convenience of standard form is seen when numbers such as the number of molecules in 1 mole of substance ($6{\cdot}03 \times 10^{23}$) or the mass of an electron (9×10^{-31}kg) are used in calculations.

Standard index form can be used with any notation. For decimal notation, a number is expressed as $a \times 10^x$ where a is any number from 1 to 9 together with any decimal fraction. This is expressed mathematically as $1 \leqslant a < 10$. The index of 10 is x. A computer displays standard index form, using the letter, E. For example, $6{\cdot}03 \times 10^{23}$ is displayed on the VDU as 6·03E23, while 9×10^{-31} is displayed as 9E−31. The part a of the standard form number is called the **mantissa**, and the index x is called the **exponent**; in the display of 6·03E23, 6·03 is the mantissa, and 23 is the exponent.

Multiplication/division with standard form numbers

If $6{\cdot}03 \times 10^{23}$ and 9×10^{-31} are multiplied together, then the two **mantissae** are multiplied and the two exponents are added. So the product is $54{\cdot}27 \times 10^{23-31} = 54.27 \times 10^{-8} = 5{\cdot}427 \times 10^{-7}$. The product could appear on a VDU as 5.427E9 or as 5427000000. If $6{\cdot}03 \times 10^{23}$ is divided by 3000 (3×10^{3}), the mantissa 6·03 is divided by the mantissa 3, and the exponent 3 is subtracted from the exponent 23. So $(6{\cdot}03 \times 10^{23}) \div (3 \times 10^{3}) = 2{\cdot}01 \times 10^{23-3} = 2{\cdot}01 \times 10^{20}$.

Standard form in binary

Standard form in binary notation will express a number as $a \times 2^{x}$. The mantissa, *a*, will be equal to 1 or more, but not equal to 2, that is $1 \leqslant a < 2$ and the exponent will be the index of 2. The fractional part of the mantissa will have digit values of ½, ¼, ⅛, 1⁄16, etc., that is 2^{-1}, 2^{-2}, 2^{-3}, 2^{-4}, etc. These values are shown in the diagram, where the binary number 1·1011 is equivalent to the decimal number $1\frac{11}{16}$.

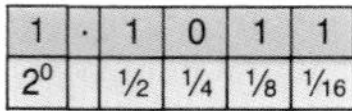

1.1011 (binary) = 1 + ½ + ⅛ + 1⁄16
= $1\frac{11}{16}$ (decimal)

Decimal number 3 = 2 × 1½ = 1·1 × 2 in binary standard form.

Decimal number 9 = 8 × 1⅛ = $1{\cdot}001 \times 2^{3}$ in binary standard form.

If these two numbers are multiplied together, using binary standard form, we have:

```
              1·001
            ×1·1     for the mantissae
            ------
             1001
            1001
            ------
product =   1·1011   and 2 × 2^3 = 2^4 (2^4 = 16) for the exponent
```

The product is $1{\cdot}1011 \times 2^{4}$. The mantissa is equal to $1\frac{11}{16}$ (*see diagram*), so the number, in decimal, is $16 \times 1\frac{11}{16} = 27$, which is equal to 3×9. There are other standard methods for dealing with numbers in computers.

Floating-point arithmetic

In this arithmetical form, standard form binary notation is used in a computer. The great advantage of standard form (i.e. scientific notation) is that the computer can deal with very large numbers using only five bytes of memory. A word of two bytes can store 65535 as its highest number

1 1 1 1 1 1 1 1	1 1 1 1 1 1 1 1	≡	65535

Largest binary number in 2 bytes

($65535 = 2^{16} - 1$) (*see diagram*). A word of five bytes can store $2^{40}-1$ as its highest number; this is $1{\cdot}1\times10^{12}$ approximately. Using standard form binary notation for five bytes, with one byte for the exponent and four bytes for the mantissa, the highest number that can be stored is approximately 1×10^{38}. In addition to storing the number, the stored number has the sign of the mantissa recorded, and the sign of the exponent. In the figure, the binary standard form of the number 1048575 is shown as stored in the computer memory. The left-hand bit of the exponent byte

(a) Number stored in memory in standard form binary

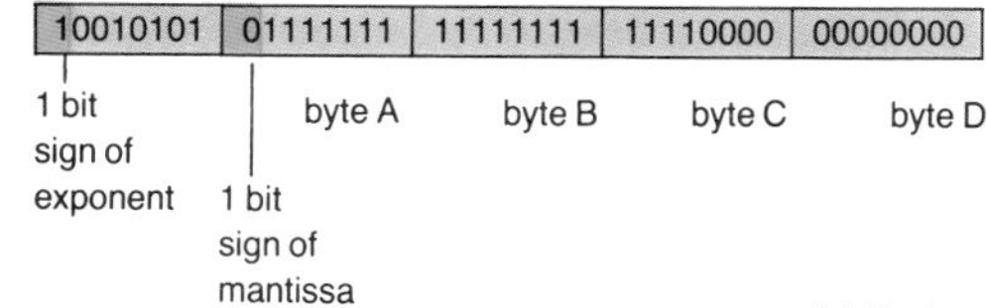

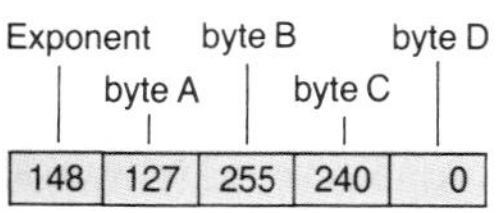

(b) Number represented on VDU in decimal notation

(c) Real number

$2^{19} \times 1\frac{8388592}{8388608} = 1048575$

indicates the sign of the exponent. The left-hand bit of byte A gives the sign of the mantissa.

If the contents of the memory are displayed on the VDU, then the binary numbers in the bytes are displayed as decimal integers. These decimal integers are shown in the diagram. Finally, the calculation from the binary number to a decimal integer is shown.

Scientific notation with binary numbers

The standard form binary notation for several decimal numbers is shown in the table. Remembering that $256 = 2^8$; $32 = 2^5$; $4 = 2^2$; $1 = 2^0$, the exponent can be obtained by

Exponent and mantissa in floating point arithmetic

Decimal number	Exponent	A	B	C	D
256	137	0	0	0	0
32	134	0	0	0	0
4	131	0	0	0	0
2	130	0	0	0	0
1	129	0	0	0	0
0	0	0	0	0	0
0.5	128	0	0	0	0
0.25	127	0	0	0	0
0.75	128	64	0	0	0
0.03125	124	0	0	0	0

Decimal number	Exponent	A	B	C	D
3	130	64	0	0	0
9	132	16	0	0	0
12	132	64	0	0	0
27	133	88	0	0	0
1.5	129	64	0	0	0
1.024	129	3	18	110	152
−0.12524414	126	128	64	0	0
−0.25	127	128	0	0	0
−0.75	128	192	0	0	0
2.892E+12	170	40	86	40	126

subtracting 129 from the value in the exponent byte. Test this for fractions. The exponent for decimal 0·5 is:

$$128 - 129 = -1, \text{ that is } 0{\cdot}5 = 2^{-1} \text{ and } 2^{-1} = \tfrac{1}{2},$$

so the exponent is correct.

The mantissa of the binary number

The mantissa of the standard form binary number is contained in four bytes, labelled A, B, C, D. The first byte, A, has only seven bits available for recording the number, as the first bit shows the sign of the mantissa. The mantissa

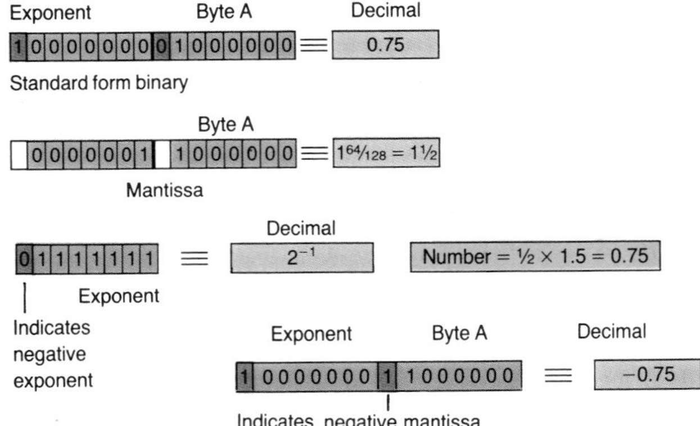

Exponent and mantissa in floating point arithmetic

must be a number between 1 and 2. Look at the standard form binary for the decimal number 0·75. The mantissa is 1½ or 1·5 and the exponent is 2^{-1}. The fraction part, that is ½, is stored in byte A, and the unit part is stored as the digit 1 in the exponent byte. The actual exponent is thus 1 less than the number stated in the exponent byte, that is 128 − 1 = 127; this makes the left-hand bit of the exponent byte equal to 0. When the left-hand bit of the exponent byte is 0, the exponent has a negative sign. Remember that a negative index gives a fractional power, for example $2^{-6} = 1/2^6$; $2^{-4} = 1/2^4$, etc. The exponent is found by subtracting the actual exponent from 128, that is 128 − 127 = 1. Since the exponent is negative it is 2^{-1}.

For negative numbers the mantissa is negative. This is recorded by a 1 in the left-hand bit of byte A. So any number in byte A which is 128 or more indicates a negative number. In the number −0·75, the mantissa has stored in it 128 + 64 = 192; the 128 indicates a negative number, the 64 indicates 0·75 as obtained previously.

Each byte of eight bits can store the number 255. Adding 1 to give 256 puts 1 in the next byte. With four bytes, labelled A, B, C, D, in byte D, the right-hand digit has a value of 1, in byte C a value of 256, in byte B a value of

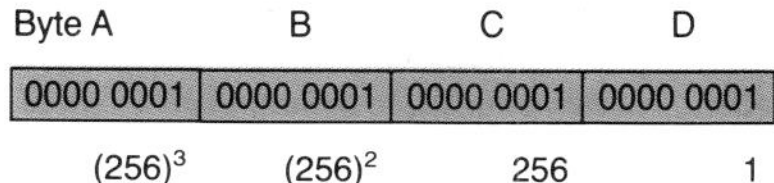

Relating binary values of bytes

$(256)^2$ and in byte A a value of $(256)^3$. When all four bytes are used in a mantissa, the value for the next digit outside the four bytes is $(256)^3 \times 128$; 128 because byte A has only seven digits available, the eighth digit, on the left, stores the sign of the mantissa.

Look at the value for 2·892E+12 given in the table on page 67. The exponent is $170 - 129 = 41$, hence it is 2^{41}. The mantissa is:

$$1 + \frac{126 + 40(256) + 86(256)^2 + 40(256)^3}{(256)^3\,(128)}$$

$$= 1 + \frac{341190780}{2147483700} = 1{\cdot}3151293$$

The exponent $= 2^{41} = 2199023300000$

$\therefore$ number is $2199023300000 \times 1{\cdot}3151293 = 2{\cdot}8919999\text{E}+12$

The number in byte D has little effect on the final answer; it is called the **least significant byte**.

Using numbers in a computer

A computer can use a number in four different ways; they are:

(1) In a word of two bytes, used for integers (i.e. whole numbers only), a binary number between 0 and 65535 can be stored or used.

(2) In computer character code using a byte for each decimal digit; the number stored in this way could be limitless, but the central processing unit could not handle it if it were too large.

(3) In binary standard index form, using five bytes. Any number between $+2^{126}$ and -2^{126} which is approximately $+10^{38}$ to -10^{38} can be stored and used.

(4) In binary-coded decimal. This can be used only in the central processing unit, and then for integers only.

Location	1201	02	03	04	05	06	07
Stored in memory	0000 0001	0010 1100	0001 0000	0000 0000	1111 0001	0010 0110	0001 0100
Interpretation	256	44	16	0	241	38	20
	Line no: 300		No: of bytes = 16		LET	A	=

Location	1208	09	10	11	12	13	14
Stored in memory	0001 1111	0001 1110	0001 1101	0001 1011	0010 0001	0010 0010	0111 1110
interpretation	31	30	29	27	33	34	126
	3	2	1	·	5	6	number

Location	1215	16	17	18	19	20
Stored in memory	1 0001001	0 0100000	1100 0111	1010 1110	0001 0100	0111 0110
interpretation						118
	Exponent 2^8	Byte A(32)	Byte B(199)	Byte C(174)	Byte D (20)	New line
	Positive exponent	Positive mantissa				

The use of numbers in a computer

The use of binary numbers for storing data is shown in the diagram. In locations 1201 and 1202 is stored the line number. This uses a 2-byte word, and the total of the bits is 300, that is the line number. Notice that location 1202 is the least significant byte. Locations 1203 and 1204 store the number of bytes in the line. Location 1203 is the least significant byte of the 2-byte word. The binary numbers in these locations are for the use of the central processor, and are used as reference numbers; the processor needs to refer to the line number, and it needs to know the number of bytes in the line.

Locations 1205 to 1213 inclusive store the character codes for the statements and characters in the line. The codes, mainly ASCII codes, operate the VDU through the interface system, and also any printing machines. Cathode-ray tubes in both monitors and TV sets use the same codes for ASCII characters as the computer. Location 1214 contains an instruction code which causes the central processor to change the decimal number in character code to standard form binary; this code is labelled 'number' in the character set.

Locations 1215 to 1219 inclusive are the five bytes for the standard form binary. These bytes are passed straight into the arithmetic unit for processing.

The last byte in location 1220 contains the character code for the signal showing the end of the line. This code is a number which activates the central processor.

Three methods of storing numbers are shown in the diagram, together with their main uses. Binary-coded decimal is used in the arithmetic registers only.

Arithmetic functions

These functions are available from the keyboard of a computer. There may be a little variation in use of the spelling according to the dialect of BASIC used by the computer, or the dialect of any other high level language.

The integer function

INT

This function in BASIC removes all digits after the decimal point in a positive number, so it *rounds down* to the lower whole number. For example:

INT(31·96) = 31; INT(297·164) = 297.

With negative numbers the function rounds down to the next *smaller whole number*, for example:

INT(−4·65) = −5   INT(−101·96) = −102

To round a decimal fraction to the nearest whole number, first add 0·5, for example:

INT(31·96 + 0·5) = 32   INT(297·164 + 0·5) = 297

If the number is negative, then first add 0·5, for example:

INT(−4·15) = −5 INT(−4·15 + 0·5) = −4 INT(−101·96 + 0·5) = −102

Most microcomputers give a numerical answer using eight digits. If such answers are to be used in further computation, then a lot of memory will be used up in storing such numbers. It is often useful to work with four digits only in a decimal fraction. This can be achieved in the following way. Let Y = 0·12345678. Now multiply this by 10,000, and we have Y = 1234·5678. Next take the integer value, rounded off to the nearest whole number, i.e. INT(1234·5678 + 0·5). This gives the value 1235. Now divide by 10,000 and we have 0·1235, that is the value of Y correct to four decimal places. This calculation would be entered as

LET Y = INT((0·12345678*10000) + 0·5)/10000

Alternative function symbols are I., instead of INT.

The absolute function

ABS

This function determines the modulus, or absolute value, of a number or of a numeric variable. The number can be an integer or a real number. The modulus, or absolute value, is the positive value of a number or numeric variable. For example:

ABS (−32·6) = 32·6   ABS (32·6) = 32·6   ABS (−101·96) = 101·96

Most microcomputers, and all other types of computer, will allow the absolute function to be used with mathematical expressions involving variables, for example

ABS(((X − Y)**2)/(−3*Z))

can be used. The computer evaluates the expression first, and then determines the absolute value. The entire expression must be enclosed in parenthesis following the ABS function.

Alternative spelling used on some computers allows A., instead of ABS.

The square root function

SQR

The function calculates the square root of any positive number within the arithmetical capacity of the computer. In the statement SQR(225), the number 225 is the *argument*, or operand, of the function SQR. For example:

SQR(225) = 15 SQR(256) = 16

The function can be used with mathematical expressions involving variables, for example:

Y = SQR(((A − B) + (B**3))/2·14159)

An alternative spelling is SQRT instead of SQR.

The constant π

PI

This is the constant relating the circumference of a circle to its radius; for a circle of radius R, the circumference is $2\pi R$. As a function, the computer spelling is PI, and many computers have this function as a keyboard entry. The numerical value is held in the central processor, and the constant is given a character code. The value of π is used in many calculations; usually it is one of two constants available on a keyboard. In addition to its use in calculating, it is also useful in giving a variable a value of 1 or 0. The following program shows how this is done.

```
10 LET   A = PI − PI
20 LET   B = PI/PI
30 LET   C = 1
40 PRINT A; B; C
```

Result

The program stored in RAM is shown below. The important thing to notice is the number of bytes needed to store lines 20 and 30. Line 20 is four bytes shorter than line 30. It is useful, therefore, in a program to use line 10 for a value of 0 and line 20 for a value of 1, as this saves space in memory.

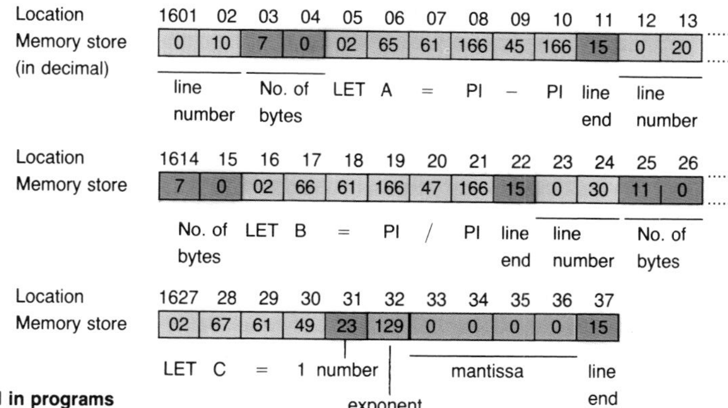

The use of PI in programs

The sign function

SGN

The sign function is often called the signum function to distinguish it from the trigonometrical function of sine. The result of the function is 1, 0, or −1, according to whether the argument is positive, zero, or negative. For example:

SGN(36·3) = +1; SGN(0) = 0; SGN(−36·74) = −1

The operators

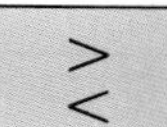

Besides the arithmetic operators of +, −, ×, ÷, which are indicated by +, −, *, /, in computer operators, there are other useful operators dealing with inequalities. The two simplest are > which means 'greater than' and < which means 'less than'. For example:

A > B: A is greater than B
C < D: C is less than D

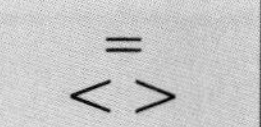

These rational operators are most frequently used in conditional statements.

The equals sign is used in statements of assignment, where a value is assigned to a variable. It is also used in conditional statements. The sign < > means 'is less than or is greater than', that is it is 'not equal to'. For example:

A < > 10 means A is not equal to 10.
X < > B means X does not equal B.

This operator is used in IF . . . THEN statements. The symbol shown is the official symbol; other symbols are: > < and ≠.

Use of the operators with strings

The central processor compares the character code, of each character in the string (*see* p. 76) in turn, moving from left to right in the string. The numbers of characters that can be compared varies with the type of computer. Some computers allow only the first character to be compared, others allow any word, or group of words.

For alpha characters, the earlier a letter is in the alphabet, the lower is its character code, for example A has code 65, Z has code 90 on the ASCII code (in decimal). An operator thus puts AB < BB. This allows words to be sorted into alphabetical order. For example:

BATH < BATS BATHE > BATH BATHS > BATH

The diagram shows each letter compared in turn. The three words would be sorted into BATH, BATHE, BATS according to the character code numbers.

Word input	B	A	T	H
Character code	66	65	84	72
	=	=	=	<
Character code	66	65	84	83
Word input	B	A	T	S

Word input	B	A	T	H	
Character code	66	65	84	72	32
	=	=	=		<
Character code	66	65	84	72	69
Word input	B	A	T	H	E

Comparison of alpha characters in strings

Use of operators in expressions

Operators can be used in expressions such as (A < 128). Using a program, as follows, the value of such expressions can be found.

```
10 INPUT A
20 LET   Y = (A < 128)
30 PRINT A, Y
40 GOTO  10
```

Values of A to be 127, 128, 129

The result is either 1 or 0 for each input. On examination of the result it can be seen that if the expression is true, then the result is 1*, and if the expression is false then the result is 0. For example if A is 127, then (127 < 128) is true and the result is 1; but if A is 129, then (129 < 128) is false and the result is 0. IF . . . THEN conditions use the true/false result to indicate how a program will continue.

Use of operators

Expression	Value of A		
	127	128	129
(A < 128)	1	0	0
(A > 128)	0	0	1
(A = 128)	0	1	0
(A <> 128)	1	0	1

Compound operators

One compound operator is > =, which means 'greater than or equal to'. The other is < =, which means 'less than or equal to'. These operators are used in IF . . . THEN statements, or with strings. They can also be used in expressions such as (A < = 128). Using (A > = 128) in the same program as before, the value of such expressions is found to be 1 or 0, as shown in the table. For example: (127 > = 128) is false, so the result is 0.

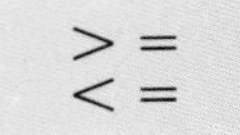

*In many microcomputers the result will be −1 for true, and not 1.

Expression	Value of A		
	127	128	129
(A < = 128)	1	1	0
(A > = 128)	0	1	1

Use of operators

Alternative symbols for operators

In some computers, the following letters are used in place of the standard operator symbols given above.

EQ means 'equal to', but is used only in an expression such as IF . . . THEN; it is not used in assigning a value to a variable.
NE is the equivalent of < >.
GT means 'greater than' and is the equivalent of >.
GE means 'greater than or equal to' and is the equivalent of > =.
LT means 'less than', and is the equivalent of <.
LE means 'less than or equal to', the equivalent of < =.

Summary

Numbers: either integers (whole numbers) or real numbers (with decimal fractions)

Parity bits: extra bits added to a number or any character, whether in memory or in a register or in any storage device, to check the number has been stored or transferred correctly.

Complements: The true complement of a number is found by subtracting each digit from 1 less than the radix, and then adding 1 to that result. Complements of numbers are added instead of subtracting the number.

Binary-coded decimal: used with integer arithmetic.

Standard index form (scientific notation): in decimal notation a number such as $3{\cdot}613 \times 10^4$; in binary notation, a number such as $1{\cdot}01101 \times 10^{1110}$; in general $a \times r^x$ where a is the **mantissa** and $1 \leqslant a < r$, r is the radix, or base, of the notation, and x is the index of the **exponent**. A number in standard form = mantissa × exponent.

Fixed-point arithmetic: includes arithmetic using integers alone.

Floating-point arithmetic: arithmetic using standard form numbers.

Numbers in memory: can be (1) a number for reference by the CPU; (2) a character code for alpha numeric characters and statements, commands and operators; (3) a number in standard binary form for calculation purposes.

Arithmetic functions: these operate on a number to produce a result; they include INT, ABS, SQR, SGN. The constant, π, is usually available on a keyboard.

Operators: there are six: >, <, =, < >, < =, > =. They operate on alpha characters as well as numbers.

Truth table: operators can be used in a simple expression to produce a result of true or false. True is given the value of 1 and false the value of 0.

CHAPTER 6

Strings

Description

A group of characters forms a string. The characters can be letters, figures, signs, spaces, functions, and even operators. A string of characters is written with quotes (inverted commas) at the beginning and end of the string. A string is designated by the dollar symbol ($). It is given a name beginning with a letter. So A$, C$, H$, Z$ are allowable names of strings. Different BASIC dialects have different rules for string names but all begin with a letter. A string named by a letter can be of any length, and can include any character in that length. Program 6.1 shows assigned string statements, and the result of a print command.

$

Program 6.1

```
 5  REM    A STRING PROGRAM
10  LET    A$ = "THIS PROGRAM DEMONSTRATES"
20  INPUT  B$
30  INPUT  C$
40  INPUT  D$
50  PRINT  A$
60  PRINT  B$; "sp"; C$, "sp"; D$
```

Input

B$	"THE"
C$	"USE OF"
D$	"STRINGS"

Result

```
50  THIS PROGRAM
    DEMONSTRATES
60  THE USE OF STRINGS
```

Notes

(1) A string is named by a letter (A to Z) followed by the $ symbol.

(2) The characters in a string are enclosed in quotes.

(3) Any statement marked by a letter and a dollar symbol indicates a string and must be enclosed in quotes.

The empty string

A string name with no characters between the quotes forms an empty string, for example A$ = " " forms an empty string. There must be no space between the quote symbols, otherwise it is not an empty string. A space counts as a character.

Numeric strings

A number in quotes forms a string and a PRINT command causes the number to be printed. An arithmetical or mathematical expression can also be put in quotes and forms a string, for example "4600*2" is a numeric string.

Use of VAL

VAL

The statement VAL produces the evaluation of a numeric expression. If the result is to be printed, then the instruction is PRINT VAL (A$), where A$ is the numeric expression. Program 6.2 shows the effect of PRINT instructions with strings.

Program 6.2

```
10 PRINT "4600"
20 PRINT "4600*2"
30 PRINT VAL "4600*2"
40 LET   A$ = "4600*2"
50 PRINT A$, VAL (A$)
60 PRINT LEN (A$)
70 LET   B$ = "123"
80 PRINT LEN (B$)
```

Result

10	4600
20	4600*2
30	9200
50	4600*2 9200
60	6
80	3

Use of Len

LEN

The statement LEN produces a count of the characters in a string. If A$="4600*2" there are six characters, five figures and one arithmetic sign. If the string consists of figures or letters only, then LEN produces a count of their number, that is the length of the string. If B$ = "123", then the length is 3. Program 6.2 shows the effect of LEN in a statement.

Changing numbers into strings

STR$

The instruction PRINT 234 produces 234 on the VDU. If STR$ is put in front of the number, the PRINT instruction produces the same result. However, the length of the number can now be measured by the statement LEN STR$ (234), the result (3) is shown in program 6.3. The statement

Program 6.3

			RESULT
10	PRINT	234	234
20	PRINT	STR$ (234)	234
30	PRINT	LEN STR$ (234)	3
40	LET	A = 2367	
50	LET	A$ = "23456"	
60	PRINT	LEN (A$)	5
70	PRINT	VAL (A$)	23456
80	PRINT	A$	23456
90	PRINT	LEN	NOT ACCEPTED

Notes

(1) Putting STR$ in front of a number changes it to a string.

(2) As a string, its length can be found.

LEN (234) cannot be carried out. If the number has been assigned to a variable, named A, then LEN A is also not acceptable, whereas LEN STR$ (A) is produced by a PRINT instruction. Program 6.3 shows the results.

VAL and LEN with variables

The two statements can be used with a variable to which a value has been assigned. A string A$ is created as a variable with the number 23456 assigned to it. The string and its value, in this case, are one and the same as the PRINT instructions shown in program 6.3.

Changing mathematical expressions into strings

Two methods of dealing with mathematical expressions are shown in program 6.4. The first assigns a variable, A, to the expression, and the second changes it into a string, C$. VAL can be applied to STR$ (A) as the statement, STR $, converts the number into a string. VAL cannot be used with alphabetical strings, as the evaluation cannot be expressed.

Program 6.4

```
5   REM   TYPES OF STRINGS AND OPERATORS
10  LET   X = 20
20  LET   A = 1024*X
30  PRINT STR$ (X), VAL STR$ (A)
40  PRINT "A", A
50  PRINT X, LEN STR$ (X)
60  PRINT
70  PRINT
80  LET   B$ = "BELIEF"
90  PRINT B$, LEN (B$)
100 LET   C$ = "1024*X"
110 PRINT C$, VAL (C$)
120 PRINT LEN (C$), VAL (STR$ LEN C$)
```

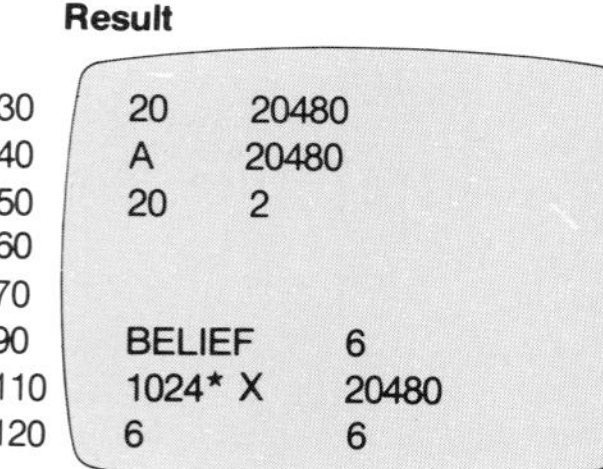

Notes

(1) VAL produces the answer to a numerical calculation if the expression is written as a string. VAL has no effect on an alphabetical string.
(2) LEN produces the length of a string, i.e. the number of characters.
(3) STR$ converts a number or an arithmetical expression into a string.

(4) VAL and LEN always precede STR$.
(5) VAL (LEN C$) is not accepted.

Using strings for calculations

In program 6.5, the value of arc cosine 0, where 0 is the value of the cosine, is calculated, giving an angle of $\pi/2$ ($\cos\frac{\pi}{2} = 0$). This angle is multiplied by 2, giving a value of π. The value of π is printed by line 20. A mathematical expression is put in a string, named B$, in line 30 of the program. The PRINT instruction in line 40 both lists and calculates the answer to the expression. The answer is given as a decimal, whereas a mechanical method of calculation would give a fraction. The value of the fraction is shown in line 50. A string can thus be used to print both the expression and the answer. The two calculations in the program are entirely separate; they are put in together for convenience.

Program 6.5

5	REM	CALCULATIONS USING STRINGS
10	LET	A$ = "ACS Ø*2"
20	PRINT	A$, "="; VAL (A$)
30	LET	B$ = "((5*2) + (12*−2) − 6)/SQR(25 + 144)"
40	PRINT	B$, "="; VAL (B$)
50	PRINT	"20/13"; "1 space"; "="; 20/13

Result

```
ACS Ø*2 = 3.1415927
((5*2) + (12* − 2) − 6)/
SQR(25 + 144)
= − 1.5384615
20/13 = 1.5384615
```

Notes

(1) Using the string notation, both the expression and the result can be readily printed.
(2) In line 20, the value of π is calculated.
(3) In line 10, ACS is arc cos.

Using strings for repetitive calculations

Program 6.6 shows the use of strings in a loop to give a repetitive calculation.

Program 6.6

5	REM	A USE FOR STRINGS
10	FOR	C = 1 TO 10
20	LET	D = 2**C
30	LET	D$ = "2 TO THE POWER OF"
40	PRINT	D$; TAB (19); C; TAB (21); "="; TAB (23); VAL STR$ (D)
50	NEXT	C

Result

```
2 TO THE POWER OF 1 = 2
2 TO THE POWER OF 2 = 4
2 TO THE POWER OF 3 = 8

2 TO THE POWER OF
10 = 1024
```

Notes

(1) A string is useful for printing a repetitive statement.
(2) Both D and D$ can be used to name a variable in the same program without confusion.

Joining strings

+

Strings can be joined, or combined, by using the plus symbol. The result of this statement is seen in program 6.7. The strings are joined without a break. If there are spaces in the separate strings, they are preserved; in other words, the number of characters, spaces included, in the combined string is equal to the number of characters in the separate strings. Strings cannot be subtracted, multiplied or divided. The only instruction allowed is A$ + B$ + C$ + . . ., etc.

Program 6.7

```
10 LET   A$ = "CONCATENATION"
20 LET   B$ = "MEANS"
30 LET   C$ = "CHAINING"
40 LET   D$ = "TOGETHER"
50 PRINT A$ + B$ + C$ + D$
60 PRINT A$; "sp"; B$; "sp"; C$; "sp"; D$
```

Result

```
50  CONCATENATIONMEANSCHAININGTOGETHER
60  CONCATENATION MEANS CHAINING
    TOGETHER
```

Notes

(1) Strings can be joined, or combined, together by the use of the plus (+) symbol.
(2) Strings cannot be subtracted, multiplied or divided.

Slicing strings

TO

A string can be divided into substrings by a notation called 'slicing'. A group of consecutive characters from a string is removed by slicing and forms a substring.

The notation for slicing is: string variable (first TO last). The string variable can be changed to a string expression. In the string "ABCDEFGH", the characters ABCD are a group of consecutive characters and can be sliced by the notation (1 TO 4). Different BASIC dialects have different instructions for slicing. One dialect uses:

LEFT$ (A$, N) which is the substring of the first N characters.
MID$ (A$, N1, N2) which is the substring of the characters N1 to N2.
RIGHT$ (A$, N) which is the substring of the characters from the Nth onwards.
TL$ (A$) which is the substring of all the characters, leaving out the first.

In the notation (1 TO 4) the initial number (1) can be left out, so the notation becomes (TO 4). Similarly, the last number can be left out, and the end of the string is assumed. Here are some comparisons of the difference in dialects acting on a string "LMNOPQRS".

A$ (1 TO 5)	A$ (TO 2)	A$ (3 TO)	A$ (3 TO 5)	A$ (2 TO)
LMNOP	LM	NOPQRS	NOP	MNOPQRS
LEFT$ (A$, 5)	LEFT$ (A$, 2)	RIGHT$ (A$, 6)	MID$ (A$, 3, 5)	TL$ (A$)

Program 6.8

```
5  REM   SLICING STRINGS
10 LET   A$ = "LMNOPQRSTV"
20 PRINT A$
22 PRINT "1234567890"
25 PRINT
30 PRINT A$ (TO 5)
32 LET   B$ = A$ (TO 5)
35 PRINT
40 PRINT A$ (6 TO)
42 LET   C$ = A$ (6 TO)
45 PRINT
50 PRINT "NEXT LINE IS A$ (8 TO 3)"
55 PRINT A$ (8 TO 3)
60 PRINT A$ (3 TO 8)
70 PRINT
80 PRINT "A$ =", B$ + C$
```

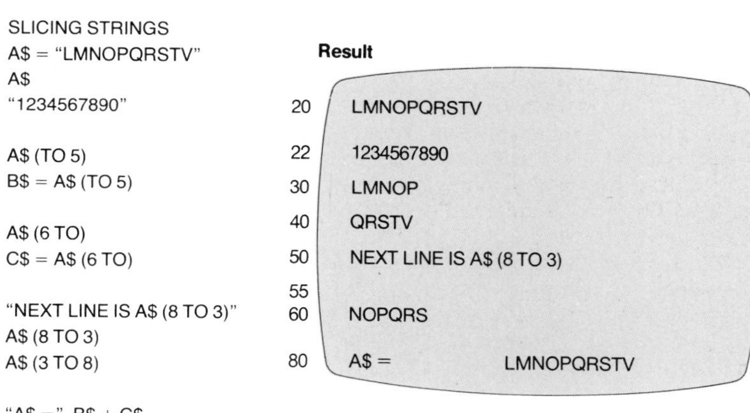

Notes

(1) Strings can be sliced by a command enclosed in brackets showing the first and last character in the slice.
(2) If no initial character is given, 1 is assumed.
(3) If no final character is given, the end character is assumed.
(4) Statement 55 cannot be executed, as the numbering of the characters for the slice is the wrong way round.

Exercises

(1) Which of the following cannot be used to name strings if only one letter can be used:
AA$; B$; C2$; 3$; D$; DB$; VAL$; TIM$?
(2) What is wrong with (*a*) STR$ LEN; (*b*) LEN (C); (*c*) G$ = 203*62; (*d*) L = "COST PRICE"; (*e*) A$/B$?
(3) Using the following data: 356,284; 3612; 43,768; 12,368,891; write a program to determine the length of each of the four numbers. Start with an input A.

(4) Write a program to correct the words WHEEL CHAIR to the word WHEEL-CHAIR, using only one variable and the slicing notation. (Remember one space counts as a character).
(5) Write a program, using a loop, to print out the 12-times table.
(6) Write a program to show both the expression $3X^2 - 2X - 6$, and its value when X = 6, in a printed statement.

A use for slicing

Program 6.9 detects the suffix –ED found in the past participle of regular verbs. It produces a printout of the original verb and of the suffix. Other suffixes, or prefixes, could be examined by a similar program, and a text could be examined to list the verbs, or other words, without such suffixes or prefixes. This is useful in compiling frequency counts of words. Notice that the program does not give correct answers for verbs such as 'ban, stun, trim, drop'.

The important feature of the program is lines 30 and 40. Whatever the length of the word, the last two letters are recognised and deleted from the word. The statement (TO (N–2)) shows this use in the slicing of a variable.

Program 6.9

```
 5 REM    PROGRAM TO DETECT SUFFIXES
10 INPUT  A$
20 LET    N = LEN (A$)
30 LET    B$ = A$ (TO (N – 2))
40 LET    C$ = A$ ((N – 1) TO)
50 PRINT  B$; TAB (10); C$; TAB (20); A$
60 GOTO   10
```

Input

```
BUMPED
TRIGGERED
FOSTERED
```

Result

```
BUMP     ED  BUMPED
TRIGGER  ED  TRIGGERED
FOSTER   ED  FOSTERED
```

Notes

(1) Line 30 removes the last two letters from the word, leaving the root word.
(2) Line 40 slices the last two letters.
(3) By joining, A$ = B$ + C$, whatever the length of A$.

The use of quotes

" "

Quotes are used to enclose a string of characters for a PRINT statement. All letters must be enclosed in quotes. If an alphabetic statement requires quotation marks, then image quotes (" ") are used, or in other dialects of BASIC, an apostrophe (') is used. Quotes cannot be nested, as loops are; the computer recognises only a pair of quotes and the characters between them. In some dialects of BASIC, an apostrophe is used instead of quotes to enclose a string, and then quotes are used as quotation marks in a string.

Replacement in strings

A segment of a string can be extracted and replaced. In program 6.10, each segment replaced by lines 50, 60, and 70 consists of one character only. The statement gives a new value to each segment, and this is put into the final expression for the string. The replacement also takes place if the initial string variable consists of strings that have been added, as shown in lines 120, 130 and 140 of program 6.10.

Different dialects of BASIC use the following statements for extracting a single character from a string.

B$ (2)	B$ (2 TO 2)	SEG$ (B$ 2, 1)	MID$ (B$ 2, 1)

Program 6.10

```
5   REM   REPLACEMENT IN STRINGS
10  LET   A$ = "PQ" + "RS"
20  LET   B$ = "PQ"" + ""RS"
30  PRINT A$; "< >"; B$
35  PRINT
40  LET   B$ = "PQ+RS"
50  LET   SEG$ (B$, 2, 1) = "sp"
60  LET   SEG$ (B$, 3, 1) = "sp"
70  LET   SEG$ (B$, 4, 1) = "X"
80  PRINT B$
90  PRINT LEN (B$)
100 PRINT
110 LET   C$ = "PR" + "QT"
120 LET   SEG$ (C$, 1, 1) = "R"
130 LET   SEG$ (C$, 2, 1) = "A"
140 LET   SEG$ (C$, 3, 1) = "P"
150 PRINT C$
```

Result

```
30    PQRS      PQ" + "RS

80    P     XS
90    5

150   RAPT
```

Notes

(1) The symbol, " ", image quotes are used to put quotation marks in strings; the ordinary quotes cannot be used as line 30 shows the difference.

(2) In line 90, the LEN instruction counts the spaces, i.e. the length of B$ remains the same in spite of deletions.

(3) In lines 120-140, the count for characters assumes the two strings in 110 are already joined.

Using brackets with strings

In program 6.11, lines 10 and 20 slice a string. Alternative statements would be the same as for replacement in strings. The extractions depend upon the position of brackets. In line 50, the extraction operates on the second string. In line 60, the extraction operates on the addition of the two strings, that is the addition is carried out first as the strings are enclosed in brackets. In line 70, the operations within the left hand bracket are performed first; this produces "HJNPQ". The final operation (1 TO 3) is then carried out.

Program 6.11

```
 5 REM    USING BRACKETS WITH STRINGS
10 PRINT  LEN "LMNPQR" (2 TO 5)
20 PRINT  LEN ("LMNPQR") (2 TO 5)
30 PRINT
40 PRINT  "LMN" + "PQR"
50 PRINT  "LMN" + "PQR" (1 TO 2)
60 PRINT  ("LMN" + "PQR") (1 TO 2)
70 PRINT  (("HJKLM")(1 TO 2) + ("NPQR") (1 TO 3)) (1 TO 3)
```

Result

```
 4
 4
LMNPQR
LMNPQ
LM
HJN
```

Notes

(1) Lines 10 and 20 produce the same result.
(2) Check the functions of the brackets in line 70.

Deletions in phrases

An IF statement is used to identify a word, that is a string of letters. The word is a substring beginning at the Nth letter

Program 6.12

```
 5 REM    DELETIONS IN PHRASES
10 INPUT  A$
20 PRINT  A$
25 PRINT
30 FOR    N = 1 TO LEN (A$)
40 IF     A$(N TO N + 4) = "MONTH" THEN GOTO 60
50 NEXT   N
60 LET    A$(N TO N + 4) = "....."
70 PRINT  A$
80 STOP
90 GOTO   10
```

Input A$

```
ITS A HOT MONTH
A MONTH AGO
WAIT ONE MONTH
```

Result

```
A MONTH AGO

A ..... AGO
```

Notes

(1) There are five characters in MONTH, so the slice is N TO N + 4
(2) LEN A$ can be used in a FOR . . . TO statement.
(3) Line 60 replaces MONTH by a line of dots.

of the string. As the word MONTH (in program 6.12) has five letters, these are the Nth to the (N + 4)th letters. (If N = 1, then N + 4 = 5, that is five letters in the word). A loop program (30-40-50) identifies the word, which is then deleted by using a row of periods (.); any other symbol could be substituted. The same word is deleted from different phrases; it could also be replaced by another word.

Replacements in phrases

Program 6.13 is similar to program 6.12. One phrase has one word successively replaced by different inputs. The replacement cannot be longer than the original word. When the program reaches STOP, the command CONT is used. This directs the computer to the next line, that is line 90, and the program starts again.

Program 6.13

```
5  REM    REPLACEMENTS IN PHRASES
10 LET    B$ = "WAIT ONE MONTH"
15 PRINT  B$
17 PRINT
20 INPUT  C$
30 FOR    N = 1 TO LEN (B$)
40 IF     B$ (N TO N + 4) = "MONTH" THEN GOTO 60
50 NEXT   N
60 LET    B$ (N TO N + 4) = C$
70 PRINT  B$
80 STOP
90 GOTO   10
```

Input C$

```
DAY
WEEK
MINUTE
```

Result

```
WAIT ONE MONTH
WAIT ONE DAY
WAIT ONE MONTH
WAIT ONE MINUT
```

Note

The replacement has the same number of characters as the original word. If the INPUT has more characters, then only the same number as the original are replaced.

Multiple replacements in strings

More than one replacement can be made in a string, but it needs a loop to examine the string for each replacement. In addition, a new variable must be assigned to the string after each replacement. In program 6.14, the two loops are lines 40, 50, 60 and lines 100, 110, 120. The initial string variable is D$, changed to E$ in line 80 after the first replacement. The statement must be written as E$ = D$, the reverse statement is not acceptable. Notice that E$ incorporates the replacements in D$ and G$. The use of four spaces in the original string allows G$ to have thirteen characters, utilised in line 130, although E$ is restricted to nine characters for recognition of YESTERDAY in line 110.

Program 6.14

```
5   REM    MULTIPLE REPLACEMENTS
10  LET    D$ = "THE POLICE CAME YESTERDAY six spaces"
20  PRINT  D$
30  PRINT
40  FOR    N = 1 TO LEN (D$)
50  IF     D$ (N TO N + 5) = "POLICE" THEN GOTO 70
60  NEXT   N
70  LET    D$ (N TO N + 5) = "ARMY"
80  LET    E$ = D$
90  INPUT  G$
100 FOR    N = 1 TO LEN (D$)
110 IF     E$ (N TO N + 8) = "YESTERDAY" THEN GOTO 130
120 NEXT   N
130 LET    E$ (N TO N + 14) = G$
140 PRINT  E$
150 STOP
160 GOTO   10
```

Input G$

```
LAST WEEK
FAST
LAST MONTH
TWO YEARS AGO
THREE YEARS AGO
```

Result

```
THE POLICE CAME
YESTERDAY

THE ARMY CAME
LAST WEEK
```

Notes

(1) Two loops needed for two changes
(2) Variable must be changed (D$ → E$) for second loop
(3) Segment count (N TO N + 8) must be correct for recognised word (YESTERDAY)

(4) In line 10, a count of 13 from four spaces used in LEN D$ in lines 100 and 130

Comparing strings

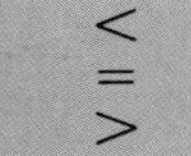

Numbers in strings can obviously be compared to find which is the greater or the lesser of any two numbers. The operators used to test the numbers are <, =, >. The computer has an ASCII code (*page* 57) in numbers for each character, and the number codes for the letters are in ascending order. Two letters can thus be compared numerically using the machine code; with the letter A having the least numerical value and the letter Z the biggest numerical value. When two words are compared, each letter is compared in turn for each of the words. When two different letters are reached, the words are sorted into alphabetical order. This can be seen in the example of WOMAN and WOMEN. The first three letters compared, W, O, and M, are the same for each word. The fourth letter of each word differs so WOMAN is listed in order before WOMEN. This technique of comparison is used in compiling lists in alphabetical order.

Program 6.15

```
5    REM    COMPARING STRINGS
10   INPUT  A$
20   PRINT  A$
30   IF     A$ = "?" THEN GOTO 150
40   INPUT  B$
50   PRINT  B$
60   IF     A$ < B$ THEN GOTO 130
70   IF     A$ = B$ THEN GOTO 110
80   PRINT  A$; "sp IS GREATER THAN sp"; B$
90   GOTO   10
100  REM    TRY SINGULAR AND PLURAL
110  PRINT  A$; "sp"; "IS EQUAL TO"; "sp"; B$
120  GOTO   10
130  PRINT  A$; "sp IS LESS THAN sp"; B$
140  GOTO   10
150  STOP
```

Input

A$	B$
AB	AC
FATHER	MOTHER
HOPE	FAITH
WOMAN	WOMAN
ZYX	XYZ
DATE	DATE
DATES	DATE
FAIRIES	FAIRY

Result

```
AB
AC
AB IS LESS THAN AC
HOPE
FAITH
HOPE IS GREATER THAN FAITH
DATE
DATE
DATE IS EQUAL TO DATE
```

Notes

(1) For an alphabetical string, 'less than' does not mean 'shorter than'.

(2) One letter is less than another if it comes before it in the alphabet, e.g. A is less than B.

(3) If the words CRUMBLE and CRUMPLE are compared then CRUMBLE is less than CRUMPLE as B is less than P.

(4) For plurals in which the letter 's' is added, the plural is greater than the singular as S is greater than the space after the singular word.

Naming strings

Most computers name strings with a letter followed by the $ sign and any letter from A to Z can be used. Some computers limit the number of letters that can be used. Acceptable string names are A$, B$, . . . Z$, for all computers using $ after a letter. Some systems use $A, $B, etc., with $ in front of the letter.

Most computers allow the use of more than one letter to name a string, for example AA$, CG$, etc., and then recognise these as individual strings. With such a system longer strings of letters, or numbers, can be used to name a string, but each computer has a limit to the number of characters it can recognise to differentiate between two strings. For example, one string can be named ABCDEF$ and another ABCDEFG, but a system that recognises only two or even three letters will not differentiate between the two strings.

Arranging strings in alphabetical order

Program 6.16 arranges two words in alphabetical order. The important steps are in lines 40, 50, and 60. The conditional statement in line 30 refers the three words, which are not in alphabetical order, to the sorting process in the next three lines. In order to understand this process, the principle can be illustrated by using two numbers, 4 and 3,

Program 6.16

```
5   REM    ARRANGING IN ALPHABETICAL ORDER
10  INPUT  A$
20  INPUT  B$
30  PRINT  A$, B$
40  IF     A$ < B$ THEN GOTO 70
50  LET    C$ = A$
60  LET    A$ = B$
70  LET    B$ = C$
80  PRINT  "ORDER IS:1.sp"; A$; "sp 2.sp"; B$
90  GOTO   10
```

Input

A$	B$
MOTHER	FATHER
WOMEN	WOMAN
CURRENT	CURRANT

Result

```
MOTHER    FATHER
ORDER IS:
1. FATHER 2. MOTHER
```

Notes

(1) Line 30 determines whether A$ is above B$ alphabetically. If it is, then the list remains as it is. If not, then the program goes to line 40.

(2) Lines 40, 50, 60 interchange A$ and B$. This technique is used frequently in all types of rearranging lists.

which are in the wrong sequence and then following the working of the computer in each line.

LINE	A$	B$	C$	
30	4	3	—	
40	4	3	4	(LET C$ = A$)
50	3	3	4	(LET A$ = B$)
60	3	4	4	(LET B$ = C$)

The two numbers are now arranged as 3 and 4.

Finding the smallest or the greatest number

In program 6.17 a numeric string is given the name SMALLEST, and in line 40 the initial input is the smallest, as it is the only one. Successive inputs, in line 50, are compared with the SMALLEST, and if it is greater than the input, then the new input becomes the smallest. By changing 'greater than' into 'less than', the biggest number can be found.

Program 6.17

```
5   REM     FINDING THE SMALLEST NUMBER
10  PRINT   "NUMBER", "SMALLEST IN LIST"
20  INPUT   A
30  LET     SMALLEST = A
40  PRINT   A, SMALLEST
50  INPUT   A
60  IF      SMALLEST > A THEN LET SMALLEST = A
70  GOTO    40
```

Input

43	−4
21	36
79	−26
5	19

NUMBER	SMALLEST IN LIST
43	43
21	21
79	21
5	5
−4	−4

Notes

(1) SMALLEST is the name of the string number.

(2) GOTO in line 70 runs the program without clearing the screen.

Exercises

(1) In the following program:

```
10 INPUT P$
20 LET N = LEN P$
30 LET Q$ = P$ (TO (N − 3))
40 LET R$ = P$ ((N − 2) TO)
50 PRINT P$; TAB 10; TAB 20 R$
```

replace lines 30 and 40 using any of LEFT$, MID$, RIGHT$.

(2) Write a program to recognise words ending in -ING, and list the root word and the ending, suitably spaced.

(3) Write a program to change the following dates: 1.4.81; 12.3.81; 16.10.81; 3.11.81 to the corresponding dates in 1982.

(4) A program has to print the following statement:
MR. . . . .(A) Your renewal date is the 1st of . . (month). . 1983.
The data are: Jones – March; Smith – June; Brown – February.
Write the program to receive the necessary inputs.

(5) Rewrite program 6.15 to compare two numbers, and to print whether one number is greater than, equal to, or less than a second number.

(6) What is the effect in program 6.16 of changing the 'less than' symbol in line 30 to a 'greater than' symbol?

(7) Rewrite program 6.17 to find the highest word in alphabetical order from a list of words (e.g. RAT is higher than CAT). (*HInt*: use H$ in place of SMALLEST).

Using strings

Program 6.18 shows a successive increase in the length of a string. For each value of J, an initial character is added to the string. The effect of A$ = A$ (3 TO) and other slices can be tried. The string can be sliced the other way by A$ = A$ (TO (20 – J)). The input U$ is not printed in the original program, so the INPUT is immaterial, even an empty string continues the program. Both lines 50 and 60 can be deleted, and the program then runs continuously.

The replacement of RUN by GOTO 30 in line 80 shows one way of controlling the printing. If one line only is needed, then CLS can be written into the program.

Program 6.18

```
5  REM    EXERCISE WITH STRINGS
10 LET    A$ = "12345678901234567890**"
20 FOR    J = 1 TO 20
30 LET    B$ = A$((22–J)TO)
40 PRINT  B$
50 INPUT  U$
60 IF     U$ = "/" THEN STOP
70 NEXT   J
80 RUN
```

Input

ANY CHARACTER
OTHER THAN "/"
OR NO CHARACTER
i.e. JUST PRESS
KEY

Result

```
2345678901234567890**
345678901234567890**
↓
890**
90**
0**
**
2345678901234567890**
```

Notes

(1) The string A$ is progressively increased by slicing in the next character.

(2) When J = 20, the string becomes empty and the cycle of printing, for J = 1 to 20, is repeated.

(3) There is no need to input any character for U$, an empty string activates the program by keying RETURN.

Variations

(1) Replace line 80 by (*a*) GOTO 20 and (*b*) GOTO 10. With (*a*) the cycle is printed once only. (*b*) has the same effect as RUN. Add line: 65 CLS. This clears the screen, and each string is printed at the top of the screen, in succession as U$ is put in.

(2) Go back to the original program, then add or replace the following lines.

```
15  LET U$ = "ABCDEFGHJK"
40  PRINT AT (21 – J), 0; B$
50  INPUT C$
60  PRINT AT J, (22 – J); U$
65  IF B$ = "45678901234567890
    **" THEN STOP
```

This will give a variety in printing and show the effect of the PRINT AT statements. When the program stops, use CONT.

The variations show control of the printing by using PRINT AT statements. Notice that a PRINT AT statement can include a variable to change the position of printing the result. Notice that careful use of the variable J allows the two sets of print to join up accurately.

Exercises

(1) Input a string "123456". Write a program to print out 654321.

(2) Write a program to produce the cube of numbers 1 to 12. Use a print statement to produce an entry such as: 2 CUBED IS 8.

(3) Admission for a competition is limited to children over the age of 14. Here is a list of names and ages: BROWN – 12; SMITH – 18; JONES – 17; BROWNE – 14; PINTER – 19; DREW– 13. Write a program which prints on the left-hand side of the screen ADMIT, and on the right-hand side DO NOT ADMIT and lists only the names in the correct column.

Definitions

letter any letter of the alphabet.

figure any of the figures 1, 2, 3, 4, 5, 6, 7, 8, 9, 0 which represent one, two, etc. Note that the figure 0 needs distinguishing from the letter O.

number a group of figures with a numerical meaning in decimal notation, e.g. 536, 4072 are numbers. Other notations must be specified.

digit the value of a figure in its place in a number, e.g. the number 536 has three digits and the digit 5 stands for 500 in decimal notation. In hexadecimal notation, letters are used as digits.

notation a method of recording information. Applied to numbers it indicates the base used for counting, e.g. 10 in decimal notation.

function A function returns a result when given an argument, e.g. trigonometrical functions such as sine, cosine, arcsine, arccosine, etc.; mathematical functions such as log, square root, modulus, integer, exponential, etc.; other functions such as VAL, LEN MID$, etc.

power the number of times a number is multiplied by itself, e.g. $(3.6)^2$ is 3·6 to the power of 2.

character Any figure, letter, symbol, or a space, in a statement.

symbol a mark describing a mathematical operation or statement, e.g. +, ×, −, =, /, >, <, >=, <=, ↑, are symbols.

standard form any number between 0 and 10, including decimal fractions, multiplied by 10 to any given power, e.g. $1{\cdot}327 \times 10^3$; $7{\cdot}48967 \times 10^5$; $3{\cdot}1014 \times 10^{-4}$; $3{\cdot}01 \times 10$ are in standard form.

constant any value that does not change during the execution of a program, for example the value of π, the value of a deductable or additional percentage factor, e.g. VAT at 15%.

variable — any value, or word, or group of letters, that is subject to change during the course of working through a program.

Summary

A **string** consists of a group of characters (letters, figures, signs, spaces, operators).

A **string** is designated by $ (dollar sign).

Strings can be numeric, alphabetical, alphanumeric, or empty.

VAL evaluates a numeric string.

LEN gives the number of characters in a string.

STR$ converts a number into a string.

Strings can be joined by a plus (+) sign; this is **concatenation**.

Strings can be divided into substrings; this is **slicing**.

LEFT$, MID$, RIGHT$, TL$, SEG$ are used to slice strings.

Quotes (") enclose a string of characters for a **PRINT** statement.

Strings can be compared using the operators =, $<$, $>$.

CHAPTER 7

Arrays and logic

Numeric arrays

A numeric array is an array of numbers in rows and columns. The simplest array has only one column.

The DIM statement

All programs using arrays start with a DIM (for dimension) statement; it lists the arrangement of rows and columns and signals to the CPU to set aside sufficient space in RAM to store the data. The simplest array, of one column, uses a statement such as: DIM A (12) showing a single column of twelve rows, that is a list of twelve numbers. A loop is used to input data, the simplest using the INPUT statement.

DIM

Program 7.1

5	REM	PUTTING AN ARRAY INTO RAM
10	DIM	A (5)
20	FOR	N = 1 TO 5
30	INPUT	A(N)
40	PRINT	A(N)
50	NEXT	N
60	END	

Input

2, 6, 8, 4, 7

Result

2
6
8
4
7

Notes

(1) The loop counter, N, executes the number of loops required by the DIM statement.

(2) The PRINT statement must be enclosed within the loop, otherwise a separate loop is needed for printing.

(3) Fewer numbers than are in the list can be entered, but zeros must then be entered to complete the loop; dashes or spaces cannot be entered in a numeric array.

A two-dimensional numeric array

The DIM statement has two figures in brackets, the first shows the number of rows, the second the number of columns, for example: DIM (rows, columns).

Using the statement DIM A (3, 6) there will be three rows in six columns which can be printed as:

A(1, 1) ..... A(1, 6)
A(2, 1) ..... A(2, 6)
A(3, 1) ..... A(3, 6)

In order to print this array, two nested loops will be needed. The inner loop will print successive data along a row, and the outer loop will descend the columns. If the counters are N for the outer loop and M for the inner loop, then M will loop from 1 to 6 and N from 1 to 3. A sample program is:

Program 7.2

```
5  REM    TWO-DIMENSIONAL ARRAY
10 DIM    A(3, 5)
20 FOR    N = 1 TO 3
30 FOR    M = 1 TO 5
40 INPUT  A(N, M)
50 PRINT  TAB (6*M,3*N);A(N, M);
60 NEXT   M
70 PRINT
80 NEXT   N
90 END
```

Input

```
1    23    3444
2    24    3555
3
4    25
5    3111
21   3222
22   3333
```

Result

```
1    2    3    4    5
21   22   23   24   25
3111 3222 3333 3444 3555
```

Notes

(1) PRINT in line 70 prevents the run-on after the semi-colon in line 50. Try the program without the semi-colon.

(2) In line 50, the numbers in a row are spaced apart by the TAB statement. If TAB is not accepted, use: PRINT AT 3*N, 6*M.

(3) The input can be any number of figures, a numeric array does not restrict the length of the input.

(4) In printing, the TAB statement must allow space for the maximum number of digits.

Two-dimensional array with headings

The data to be entered are:

Rainfall in mm

	JAN	FEB	MAR	APR	MAY	JUN
Paris	18	21	14	6	3	0
Rome	24	13	10	3	0	0
Berlin	16	18	15	23	5	7

The headings for the months will be a PRINT statement with carefully calculated TAB positions for each column. The headings for the towns will be dependent on the N counter, assuming A(M, N) for the dimensioned array. The flowchart for the process is shown in the diagram; from it is produced the program.

Program 7.3

```
5   PRINT  "RAINFALL IN MM"
10  PRINT  TAB (9); "JAN"; TAB (13); "FEB"; TAB (17); "MAR";
           TAB (21); "APR"; TAB (25); "MAY"; TAB (29); "JUN"
20  DIM    A(3, 6)
30  FOR    N = 1 TO 3
40  IF     N = 1  THEN GOTO 70
50  IF     N = 2  THEN GOTO 90
60  IF     N = 3  THEN GOTO 110
70  PRINT  TAB (0, 3*N + 8) "PARIS";
80  GOTO   120
90  PRINT  TAB (0, 3*N + 8) "ROME";
100 GOTO   120
110 PRINT  TAB (0, 3*N + 8) "BERLIN";
120 FOR    M = 1 TO 6
130 INPUT  A(N, M)
140 PRINT  TAB (4*M + 5); A(N, M)
150 NEXT   M
160 NEXT   N
170 END
```

Notes

(1) Line 140 spaces the data beneath its suitable heading.

(2) Lines 40-60 control the printing of headings for each row.

(3) After each heading is printed for a row, there is an unconditional jump to the start of the M loop. The printing of the heading is inside the N loop.

(4) If TAB is rejected, then use:

140 PRINT AT 3*N + 8, 4*M + 5; A(N, M)

and replace TAB (0, 3*N + 8)

by PRINT AT 3*N + 8, 0; for all three towns.

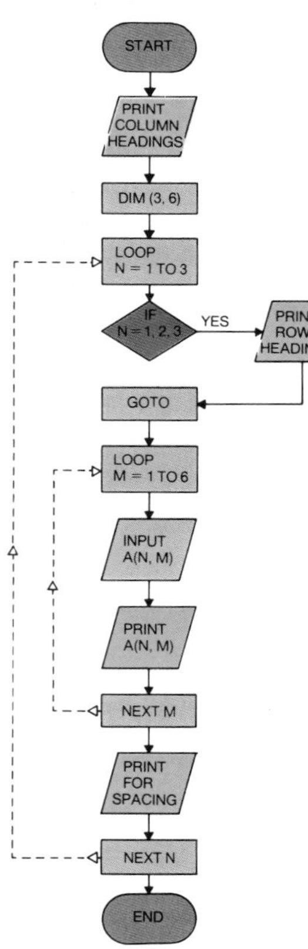

Flowchart for an array of numbers

Aphanumeric arrays (string arrays)

These are arrays which use either letters or figures or both. The capabilities of microcomputers entering string arrays varies considerably. One or two microcomputers will not input a string unless it has a DIM statement entered before the input. Other computers accept one, ten, fifty, or more characters in a dimensioned string. To test a computer, enter the following program:

Program 7.4

```
5  REM    TESTING DIM STATEMENTS
10 DIM    A$ (3)
20 FOR    N = 1 TO 3
30 INPUT  A$ (N)
40 PRINT  A$ (N)
50 NEXT   N
60 END
```

ABCDE6GH9ØABCDE

The anticipated results are shown in the diagram. Check with your manual the string array capabilities of your microcomputer, and the method of handling string arrays. Check particularly whether the number of characters in a row can be controlled by a DIM statement. The programs on string arrays will assume that the number of characters in a string array can be controlled by the last figure in a DIM statement, for example DIM A$(3, 6) assumes that there will be three strings each of which contains six characters, and no more are allowable. Some microcomputers using the $ sign in front of a string do the same for an array. Some microcomputers need two letters to describe a string, for example AA, ZZ. Other micro-

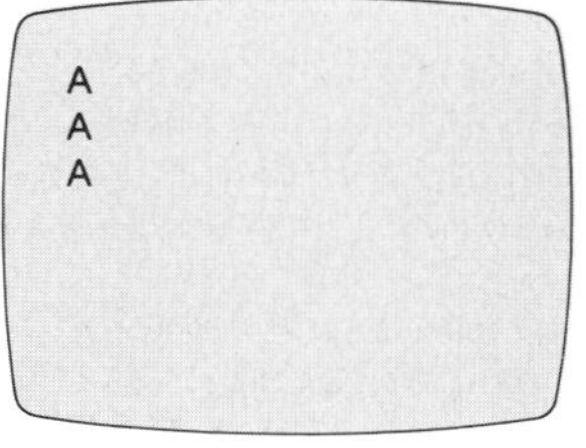

Accepts one character only

Accepts 10 characters only

ABCDE6GH9ØABCDE
ABCDE6GH9ØABCDE

Accepts more than 10 characters

computers allow figures to be used after an initial letter, for example A3$. Check with your manual the limitations on string array descriptions.

Input

THIS
DEMONSTRATES
STRING
ARRAYS
ARE
USEFUL

Using string arrays

The following program shows the effect of printing string arrays in columns and rows when the length of the string is given a dimension.

Program 7.5

```
5   REM    STRING ARRAYS IN PRINT
10  DIM    A$ (6)
20  FOR    N = 1 TO 6
30  INPUT  A$(N)
40  PRINT  A$(N)
50  NEXT   N
60  PRINT  A$(1) + A$(2) + A$(3) + A$(4)
70  PRINT
80  PRINT  A$(3); A$(4); A$(5); A$(6)
90  PRINT  A$(4); "ARE"; A$(6)
100 IF     INKEY $ = "X" THEN GOTO 120
110 GOTO   100
120 PRINT  A$(2); "sp PRINTING"
130 END
```

Result

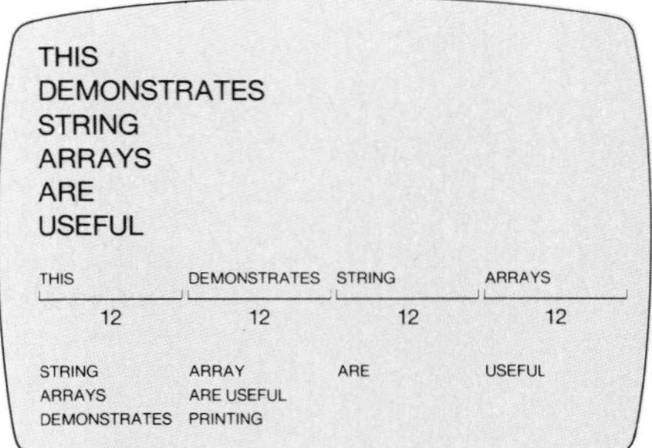

The results are shown in the diagram.

Notes

(1) Line 30 dimensions N for the string. If it is necessary to dimension the length in the DIM statement, then DIM A$(6,12) is used and the remainder of the program is the same. If the string length needs dimensioning, use A$ (6,12).

(2) Line 40 prints the strings as a list in one column. This can be considered as similar to a two-dimension numeric array, with each letter occupying one place in the tabular array.

(3) The numbers 1-6 are **subscripts**. Each subscripted string can be joined in a chain by a plus (+) sign. Putting a semicolon between each subscripted string has the same effect.

(4) When the subscripted strings are put in a row, they are connected without a space if the length has not been defined in the DIM statement. If the string length is given as 12, then each string will have spaces to make up this number.

(5) When subscripted strings come after alphabetical inputs, separated by a semicolon, the usual print rule holds true; line 90 shows this feature.
(6) Line 100 contains the statement INKEY$. When the program reaches this line, the microcomputer waits for the X key to be pressed before continuing; only the X key will make the program continue.
(7) Line 110 has to follow line 120, otherwise the program may crash and the screen become blank. This keeps the CPU circling waiting for the INKEY$ key to be pressed, otherwise the microcomputer does not wait as it does for INPUT.
(8) A further line can be added to the program:

    125 PRINT A$(1), A$(2)

With the comma between the two subscripted strings, the second string is printed in the second zone of the screen, that is in the seventeenth position for some computers, at the fifteenth for others. This is dependent on the string length being limited to twelve spaces.

Slicing string arrays

A subscripted string can be sliced in the same way as an ordinary string. If it contains numbers, the value of a slice can be used in a calculation. The slice can be found from LEFT$, MID$, RIGHT$; some microcomputers also use the statement SEG$, which can replace any of them.

Program 7.6

```
5   REM    SLICING SUBSCRIPTED STRINGS
10  DIM    A$(3)
20  FOR    N = 1 TO 3
30  INPUT  A$(N)
40  PRINT  A$(N)
50  NEXT   N
60  PRINT
70  PRINT  LEFT$(A$(2), 4)
80  PRINT  RIGHT$(A$(1), 4)
90  PRINT  MID$(A$(3), 4, 3)
100 PRINT  SEG$(A$(3), 2, 4)
110 LET    B = VAL SEG$(A$(2), 2, 2)
120 PRINT  "B*10 = sp"; B*10
130 PRINT  MID$(A$(1), 3, 1);LEFT$(A$(1), 1);RIGHT$(A$(3), 1)
140 END
```

Input

```
ABCDEFGH
12345678
IJKLMNOP
```

Result

```
ABCDEFGH
12345678
IJKLMNOP
1234
EFGH
LMN
JKLM
B*10 = 230
CAP
```

Notes

(1) The slicing statements, that is MID$, etc., treat the subscripted strings, e.g. A$(2), as an ordinary string.
(2) The statement, SEG$, functions as for MID$.

The use of sliced subscripted strings

A string can be used to carry coded information. For example, the number of an insurance policy can provide all the information needed about any one particular policy. Here is a simple example of coded information and a subsequent program on its use.

A person has an insurance policy number of L2413621; the information provided is:

- L shows it is a policy on the person's life.
- 2 shows the area in which the person lives.
- 4 indicates the agent in the area who sold the policy; this is useful in paying annual commission when premiums are received.
- 1 the method of payment is monthly.
- 36 gives the year of birth.
- 21 a personal number for that particular policy.

The code would thus allow for ten areas to have ten agents and each agent to have one hundred clients. There is thus room in the code for 10,000 policies of a particular type. The code, described here, is very simple compared with the codes used by business firms. In addition to the code number of the policy, the amount payable can also be added, say $310 per month. It is useful in a small system to keep sections of the code at a fixed length. If four figures are allowed for the amount payable, that is a maximum of $9999, then the code number can be extended to L24136210310, where 0310 is the amount payable.

In the following program, the number of policies has been limited to ten. The information required for presentation in tabular form is (*a*) area (*b*) year of birth (*c*) method of payment (*d*) total annual payment. The method of payment is coded as: 1 – monthly payment; 2 – quarterly payment; 3 – annual payment.

Program 7.7

```
5   REM     CODED INFORMATION, INSURANCE POLICY
10  DIM     B$(10) (see footnote*)
20  FOR     N = 1 TO 10
30  INPUT   B$(N)
40  PRINT   LEFT$(B$(N), 8)
50  NEXT    N
60  PRINT
70  PRINT   "AREA";TAB (16);"YEAR";TAB (20); "PAY";TAB (26);
            "AN.TOT"
```

*If the string length has to be dimensioned, then use B$ (10,12)

Input

```
L 24136210310
M 34132360110
P 44229430450
A 12341231830
P 61353762500
L 53255980350
L 52139140200
M 45232540900
A 32336683500
P 34332824000
```

The following codes are used: L = life policy; M = mortgage policy; P = pension policy; A = annuity premium.

```
80  FOR     N = 1 TO 6
85  REM     THIS LOOP COVERS THE 6 AREAS
90  PRINT   N;
100 FOR     M = 1 TO 10
105 REM     THIS LOOP COVERS THE 10 POLICIES
110 IF      VAL MID$(B$(M), 2, 1) = N THEN GOSUB 200
115 REM     THIS LINE CHECKS THE AREA OF THE POLICY
120 NEXT    M
125 PRINT
130 NEXT    N
140 END
200 LET     C = VAL (RIGHT$(B$(M), 4)
210 IF      VAL MID$(B$(M), 4, 1) = 1 THEN GOTO 250
220 IF      VAL MID$(B$(M), 4, 1) = 2 THEN GOTO 240
230 LET     T = C
235 GOTO    260
240 LET     T = 4*C
245 GOTO    260
250 LET     T = 12*C
260 PRINT   TAB (10);"19";TAB (12);MID$(B$(M), 5, 2);TAB (20);
            MID$(B$(M), 4, 1);TAB (25);"$";TAB (26);T
270 RETURN
```

Notes

(1) Lines 10-50 inclusive load the data into memory in the order of the input, i.e. subscript 10 is policy P3433282. Note that twelve characters are needed.

(2) Only the policy number, not the amount, is printed from line 40, as the left eight characters are sliced.

(3) The loop lines 80 to 130 use line 110 to search for the areas in consecutive numerical order 1-6. For each value of N, the second loop, M = 1 to 10, searches through the list for the area number.

(4) On finding the area number, the subroutine, signalled by GOSUB, is called.

(5) The subroutine (see p. 49) executes the following procedures: (*a*) finds the payment from line 200 for a policy; (*b*) uses lines 210, 220 to determine the method of payment; (*c*) uses lines 230, 240, 250 to calculate the annual payment from the method of payment.

(6) After each calculation of annual payment, an unconditional jump is necessary to line 260, so that the data can be printed. Without it consecutive execution of the program would produce more than one value of T.

(7) Line 270 ends the subroutine with RETURN. The program is resumed at the line after the GOSUB statement, that is line 115, which is ignored, passing on to line 120.

Result

AREA	YEAR	PAY	AN.TOT.
1	1941	3	$1850
2	1936	1	$3720
3	1932	1	$1320
	1936	3	$3500
	1932	3	$4000
4	1929	2	$1800
	1932	2	$3600
5	1955	2	$1400
	1939	1	$2400
6	1929	2	$2500

Coded information, insurance policies

Two-dimensional string arrays

A two-dimensional string array is similar to a two-dimensional numeric array. In the DIM statement, there will be three figures instead of two for those microcomputers which need the string length to be dimensioned. For example, DIM A$(3, 6, 5) will give the dimension for a table containing three rows of six columns, with each item containing a maximum of five characters. If the length of a string is not essential for input in a microcomputer, then the last number can be omitted leaving A$(3, 6) as the array. With such arrays, RIGHT$ is not always usable as the string length may be indeterminate.

A typical tabulated form of data can be used with a two-dimensional string array, as both alpha and numeric characters can be entered. This allows headings to be part of the array and the numeric data the other part.

Here is a typical problem. The number of fatal road accidents is recorded for each month for a particular area. In order to keep the program simple, four roads and six months are provided with data. The processed information required is (*a*) total number of accidents for each month; (*b*) the average number of accidents for each area. These two problems illustrate the main applications of processing. The data are shown in boxes, each box being one entry for the input.

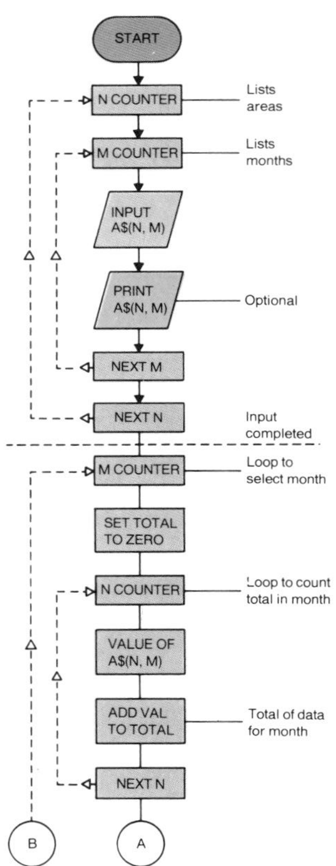

Fatal accidents by area and month

sp	sp	JAN	FEB	MAR	APR	MAY	JUN
EAST	sp RD sp	4	3	1	2	1	1
WEST	sp ST sp	6	2	0	1	0	0
N'TH	sp AV sp	2	0	0	2	1	1
S'TH	sp RD sp	2	2	3	1	1	4

In planning the printing, the use of fixed length strings provides suitable spacing of columns. On a 32-character screen, each column can have four characters; this spacing is given in the table above. For a 64-character screen, each column could be eight characters long. This does not permit a full printing of each month as there must always be at least one space after the word to avoid running into the next word. If fixed length strings are not used, or are not available, then a TAB statement has to be used, as in program 7.2.

A flowchart to show the construction of the program is given in the diagram. As variations in the use of strings are found in different microcomputers, a revised program can

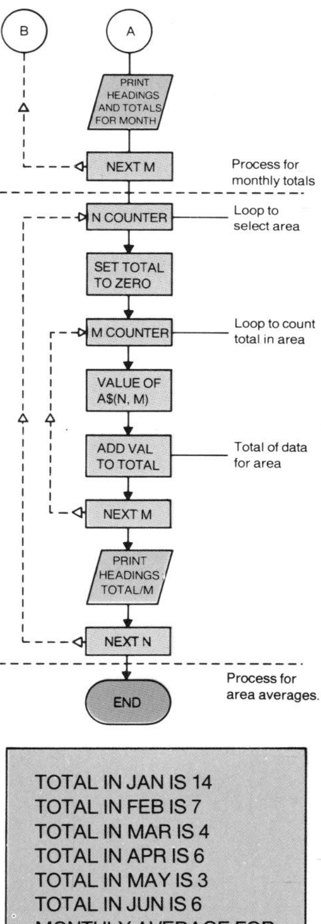

be constructed from the flowchart. There are three processes: (*a*) input of data assigning headings and numerical values to subscripted strings; (*b*) looping to determine the totals for each month; (*c*) looping to determine the totals for each area and hence the monthly average rate of occurrence. The data can be printed or omitted; printing does show that the data have been entered correctly.

Program 7.8

```
5   REM    PROCESSING DATA ON FATAL ACCIDENTS
10  DIM    A$(5, 8) (see footnote*)
20  FOR    N = 1 TO 5
30  FOR    M = 1 TO 8
40  INPUT  A$(N, M)
50  PRINT  A$(N, M);
60  NEXT   M
65  PRINT
70  NEXT   N
75  REM    SUBSCRIPTED DATA NOW ENTERED
80  FOR    M = 3 TO 8
85  REM    THIS LOOP SELECTS THE MONTH
90  LET    T = PI – PI
100 FOR    N = 2 TO 5
105 REM    THIS LOOP COUNTS TOTAL FOR MONTH
110 LET    C = VAL (A$(N,M))
120 LET    T = T + C
130 NEXT   N
140 PRINT  "TOTAL IN sp";A$(1,M); "sp IS sp"; T
150 NEXT   M
155 REM    COMPLETION OF TOTAL FOR EACH MONTH
160 FOR    N = 2 TO 5
165 REM    THIS LOOP SELECTS THE AREA
170 LET    S = PI – PI
180 FOR    M = 3 TO 8
185 REM    THIS LOOP COUNTS TOTAL FOR AREA
190 LET    D = VAL (A$(N,M))
200 LET    S = S + D
210 NEXT   M
220 PRINT  "MONTHLY AVERAGE FOR sp"; A$(N,1); "sp IS sp";
           INT((S/6)*10 + 0.5)/10
230 NEXT   N
240 END
```

```
TOTAL IN JAN IS 14
TOTAL IN FEB IS 7
TOTAL IN MAR IS 4
TOTAL IN APR IS 6
TOTAL IN MAY IS 3
TOTAL IN JUN IS 6
MONTHLY AVERAGE FOR
EAST IS 2
MONTHLY AVERAGE FOR
WEST IS 1.5
MONTHLY AVERAGE FOR
N,TH IS 1
MONTHLY AVERAGE FOR
S,TH IS 2.2
```

The printed result, with data omitted, is shown in the diagram. The data are entered, row by row, from the table given previously.

*If the string length has to be dimensioned then use A$ (5,8,4)

Notes

(1) The semicolon in line 50 produces print along a row and the blank PRINT line in line 65 prevents one row following on the row above (try deleting line 65).

(2) In lines 90 and 170, both T and S are made equal to PI – PI; this is putting them both equal to zero, but on a small computer this expression saves space in RAM. If PI is not on your microcomputer, use T, S = Ø.

(3) In line 220, the result of S/6 could be expressed by eight digits. This is not desirable, so the result is multiplied by 10, then truncated to an integer, then divided by 10. This gives the answer in two digits, sufficient for the present problem. The 0.5 is added, as explained on p. 71 to round up as well as down. Without the 0.5, one answer is 2.1. As the fuller answer is 2.16, the correct answer is 2.2.

Logical operators

A microcomputer has three logical operators: AND, OR, NOT. These connect statements which operate on variables called **Boolean variables**. A Boolean variable has only two states, *true* and *false*, and can be represented by the digits 1 and Ø. Electronic circuits in computers use Boolean variables in processing information as will be seen in later chapters.

Boolean variables

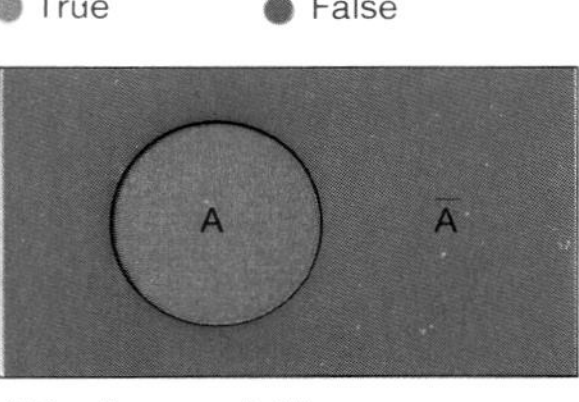

A Boolean variable

Let us take a statement such as 'All Danes have blond hair', and let it be a true statement. Represent the statement by the letter A. The opposite statement 'No Dane has blond hair' is false if A is true. The false statement is called an **inverse** of the true statement and given the symbol Ā. A diagram can be used to represent these facts, as shown, that is A is true and Ā is false. The rectangular shape is called a **'universe'** and represents a false statement of A. This is most easily seen by the statement 'Let A = 5', a true statement; then A = 6, 1000, or any other number, is false. This gives an idea of the universe outside the true statement.

The AND statement

AND

This word joins two statements so that both have to be true. Take the two statements 'All Danes have blond hair' and 'All Danes have blue eyes'. Then a Dane has both blond hair and blue eyes; if a person is without one of these features, then he cannot be called a Dane. Put this into a diagram as shown below, where A represents the first statement and B the second statement. The diagram (*below, left*) shows both statements to be true for **A AND B** to be true.

The OR statement

OR

This word joins two statements, either of which can be true. For example, let A be 'Women are kind' and B be 'Women are beautiful', then some women can be both kind and beautiful. This is represented by **A OR B** in the diagram (*below, right*). **A** represents kind women, **B** represents beautiful, $\bar{\mathbf{A}}$ represents ugly women, $\bar{\mathbf{B}}$ represents unkind women, and $\bar{\mathbf{A}}$ and $\bar{\mathbf{B}}$ are false. The intersection of **A** and **B** represents women who are both kind and beautiful.

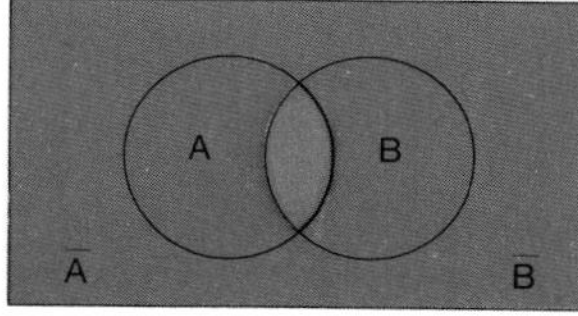

The AND statement

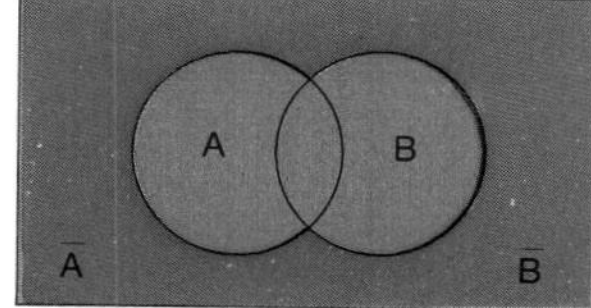

The OR statement

The NOT statement

NOT

This statement reverses the original statement; it changes a true statement into a false statement and vice versa. It changes a statement A into the inverse statement $\bar{A}$. A NOT statement can operate on an AND statement and on an OR statement. NOT and AND form a NAND statement. NOT and OR form a NOR statement.

The NAND statement

This word joins two statements which cannot both be true. For example 'Some men are fat'; 'Some men are thin'. A man cannot be fat and thin at the same time, so a man is fat NAND thin. The diagram shows fat men, thin men, not fat men not thin men (i.e. the inverses) all exist, that is the statement is true, but the statement 'a man is fat AND thin' is false.

The NAND and NOR statements

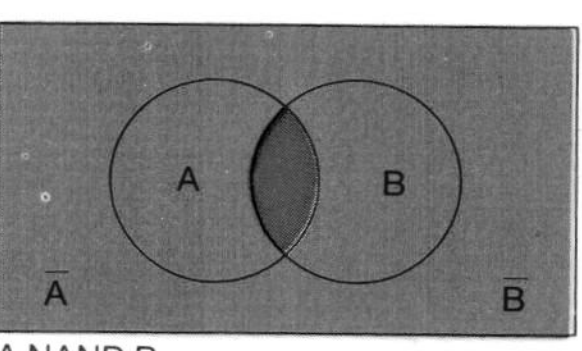

A NAND B

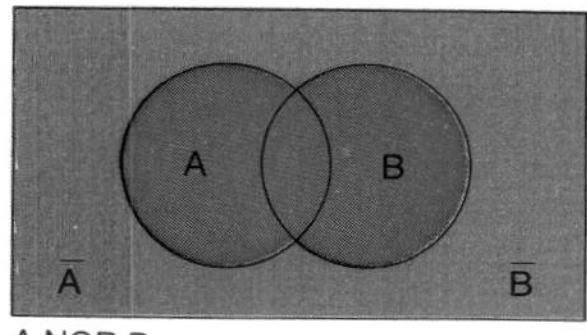

A NOR B

The NOR statement

If the two statements used for the OR example on page 105 are false, then the truth is 'Women are neither good nor beautiful'. This is shown in the diagram, with statement A being false, statement B being false and A AND B being false. Notice that the NAND and NOR diagrams are the complete opposites of the AND and OR diagrams.

The XOR statement

This statement is an exclusive OR, that is either of two statements can be true, but they cannot both be true. For example 'An integer represents a magnitude'; 'A real number represents a magnitude'; but a magnitude cannot be both an integer and a real number. The diagram illustrates the result of the XOR statement; it is also called the 'non-equivalence' statement. Integers show equivalence of properties, but equivalence for both is false. Magnitudes other than integers or real numbers (e.g. complex numbers) also have non-equivalent properties to integers and real numbers.

The NOT XOR statement

This statement is the opposite of exclusive OR. To use the two statements from the OR example, women are good and beautiful or bad and ugly. A woman cannot be good and ugly or bad and beautiful in a NOT XOR statement.

Remaining simple logical statements

The diagrams in the previous five illustrations can be used to make rules concerning the use of logical operators. These rules depend on the operation of AND, OR and NOT. For AND both A and B must be true; for OR A, B, or A and B can be true; with NOT the inverse of whichever of A and B is negated becomes the inverse.

In the diagram, four more simple Boolean expressions are illustrated. NOT A AND NOT B means that $\bar{A}$ and¯ must both be true. For example, if A represents females and B represents people under eighteen years old, then only NOT A AND NOT B can enter an infantry unit in the army, being neither A or B disqualifies a person. Hence this is the opposite case to A OR B. Check the two diagrams to show this is true. The same reasoning can be applied to NOT A OR NOT B. Let A represent a failure in one subject of an examination and B a failure in another subject. A candidate can be referred for one failure, but fails the whole examination with two failures. In this case A and¯

Non equivalence

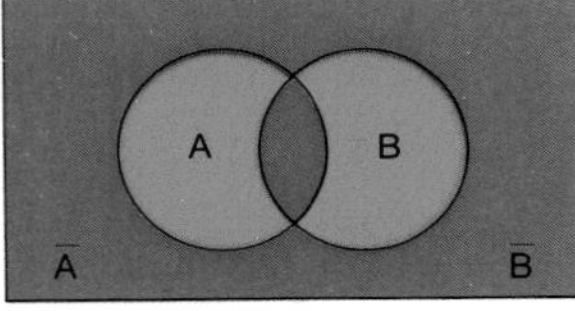

A XOR B

Equivalence

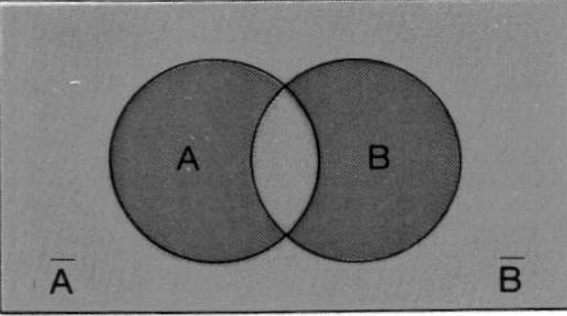

NOT (A XOR B)

The XOR and NOT XOR statements

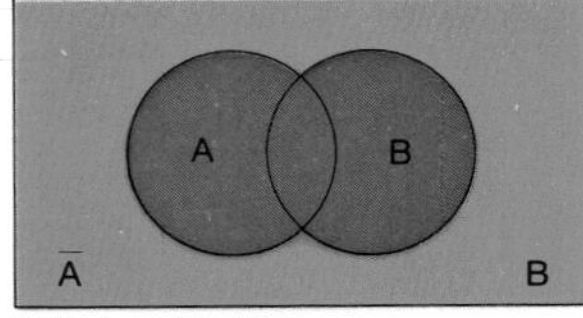

NOT A and NOT B

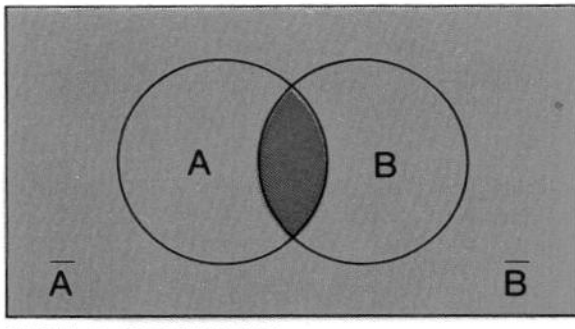

NOT A OR NOT B

Simple Boolean statements

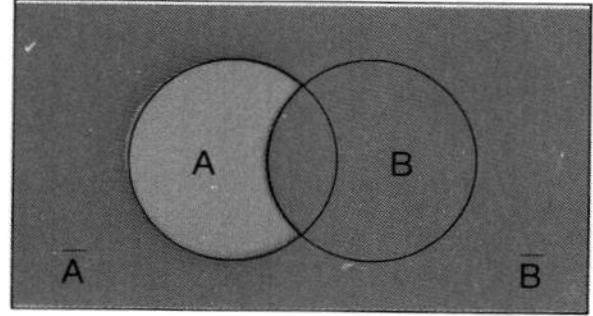

A AND NOT B

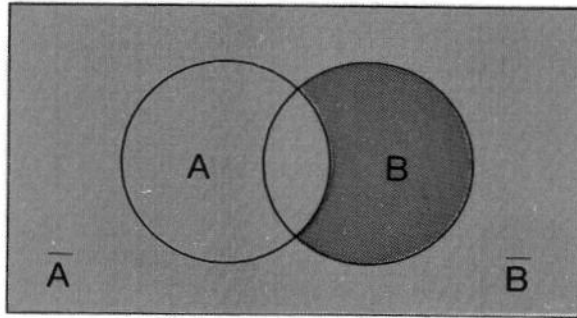

A OR NOT B

represent passes in the subjects. So two passes, or a pass in either subject, A or B, represents a person not failing, that is it is true he does not fail. In the statement A AND NOT B, the part of A outside B is the only part that is true. In the statement A OR NOT B, B excludes if not part of A. For example, let A represent physical fitness and B weak eyesight, then a fit person with weak eyesight will be accepted, an unfit person with good eyesight will be accepted, but an unfit person with weak eyesight will be rejected. The statement 'The person is accepted' is true or false according to the conditions.

Notice from the last two diagrams in the illustration, that B OR NOT A will be the opposite of A AND NOT B. Also that NOT A OR NOT B is the same statement as A NAND B, and NOT A AND NOT B is the same statement as A NOR B.

Gates

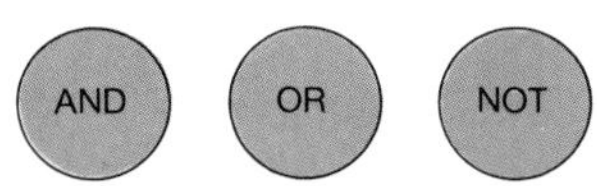

Symbols for logic gates

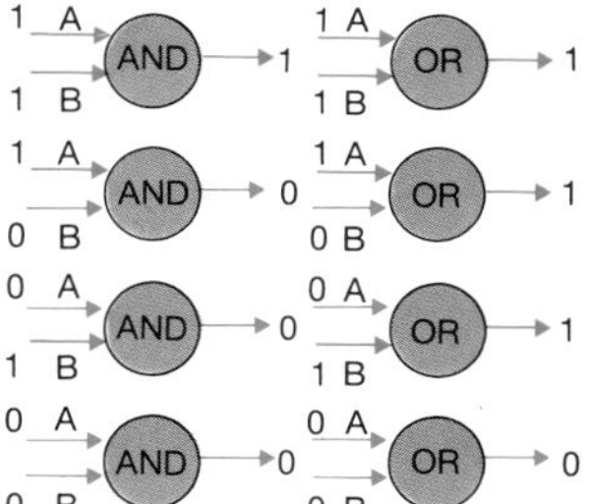

Results from AND/OR gates

Electronic circuits can be used to produce the results of Boolean expressions. Previously transistors were used in such circuits. Transistors have three connections but they provide one input and one output as the third connection is a common ground reference voltage. Two inputs, representing the A and B of Boolean expressions need two transistors, or a parallel input to one transistor, to produce the result as an output. In microcomputers, solid-state transistors are used in gates, and a silicon chip has many hundreds of parts functioning as gates. Simple symbols used to represent gates are shown in the diagram.

The AND and OR gates

The input for A can represent true or false. In microcomputer circuits, using binary code, 1 represents true and Ø represents false*. Now apply the statements considered for AND (p. 104). 'Has the person blue eyes?' Yes = true; No = false. 'Has the person blond hair?' There are four categories of persons from these questions which can be represented on the binary code as 11, 1Ø, Ø1 and ØØ. These four categories are made inputs for an AND gate in the diagram. In one case only, that of 11, is the result true, i.e. a result of 1. Now look at the results for the OR gate. In one case only, that of a ØØ input, is the output false, i.e. Ø.

The NOT gate

A NOT gate has only one input and one output. If the input is 1 the output is Ø; if the input is Ø the output is 1†. A NOT

*Many microcomputers use −1 for true and Ø for false. The results of 11, 1Ø and Ø1 need to be changed correspondingly.

†Ø is changed to −1 and −1 to Ø if the microcomputer uses −1 for true.

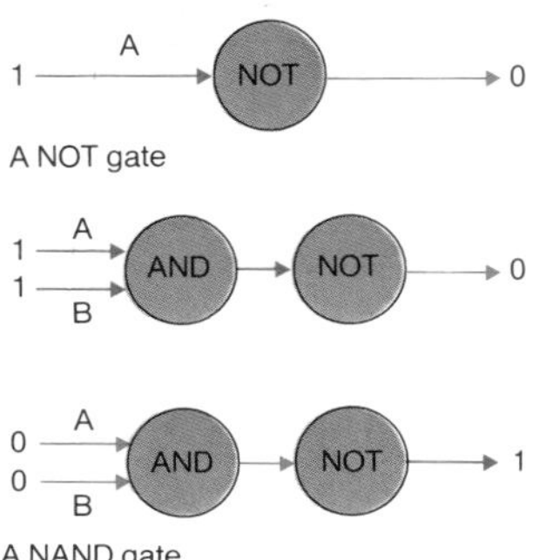

Results from NOT and NAND gates

gate is used to make a NAND gate, as shown in the diagram. Two cases, those of 11 and ØØ, are shown. Draw the cases for Ø1 and 1Ø and verify the result from the diagram for the Boolean expression. A NOT gate is combined with an OR gate to form a NOR gate; the result for an input of Ø1 is shown in the diagram. A NOT gate can be

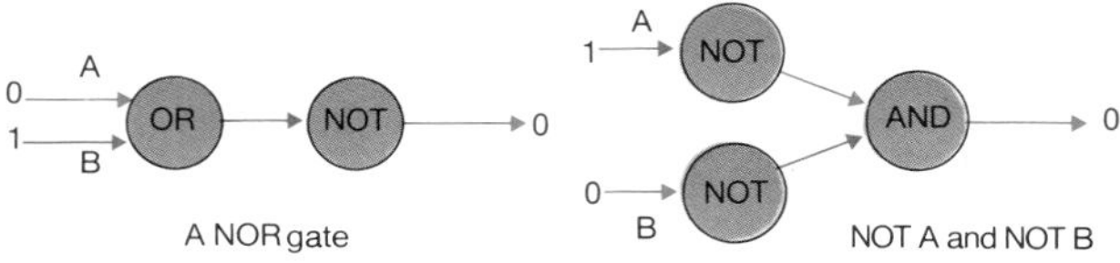

used for both inputs as shown in the diagram for NOT A AND NOT B. In these, and more complicated gate circuits, the rules for AND, OR, and NOT gates are followed from the simple result of one gate. In complicated circuits, there will always be four cases for the input, represented in binary code by 11, 1Ø, Ø1 and ØØ. Try to use all four cases to determine the final result of a system of gates*.

Make the following inputs*:

```
PRINT 1 AND 1
PRINT 1 AND Ø
PRINT Ø AND Ø
PRINT 1 OR 1
PRINT Ø OR 1
PRINT Ø OR Ø
PRINT NOT 1
PRINT NOT Ø
PRINT NOT 1 AND NOT Ø
PRINT NOT Ø AND NOT Ø
PRINT NOT 1 OR NOT 1
```

Truth tables

The results determined from the logic gates can be presented as a truth table. Two variables, A and B, are given the values true (T) and false (F), with inputs of TT, TF, FT, FF. The corresponding result for AND, OR, NAND, NOR, XOR are shown in the table. A microcomputer

A	B	A AND B	A OR B	A NAND B	A NOR B	A XOR B
T	T	T	T	F	F	F
T	F	F	T	T	F	T
F	T	F	T	T	F	T
F	F	F	F	T	T	F

usually has the logic statements of AND, OR and NOT only, so the other logic statements have to be derived by using combinations of these three. The combinations are:

A NAND B is NOT(A AND B); **A NOR B** is NOT(A OR B).

The exclusive OR statement, written as XOR, but usually described as an EOR gate, has to be made from a combination of gates. The circuit used for the combination is shown in the diagram, with the results of operating on two expressions, one for an input of 11 and one for an input

*If your computer uses −1 for true, then the inputs are −1 −1, 1Ø, Ø−1, ØØ, etc.

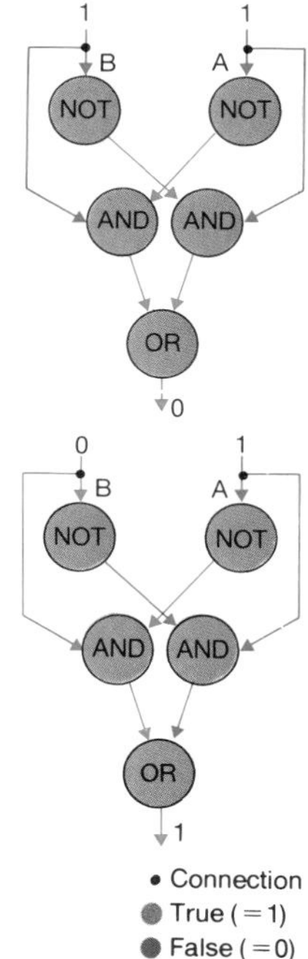

The EOR gate also called a comparator

of 1Ø. The result agrees with the truth table. Test the gate with inputs of Ø1 and ØØ. How is this gate interpreted on the microcomputer keyboard? Two expressions are to be connected by OR. The input from one is A AND NOT B, the other is B AND NOT A. So the computer statement will be (A AND NOT B) OR (NOT A AND B). This gate is also called a **comparator** as it indicates with Ø if two inputs are alike, for example both true or both false, and indicates with a 1 if two inputs are unlike.

Logic statements on a computer

Here is a program to test logic statements:

Program 7.9

```
5    REM    TESTING LOGIC STATEMENTS
10   DIM    A(4)
20   DIM    B(4)
30   PRINT  "A", "B"
40   FOR    N = 1 TO 4
50   INPUT  A(N)
60   INPUT  B(N)
70   PRINT  A(N), B(N)
80   NEXT   N
85   PRINT
90   FOR    N = 1 TO 4
100  LET    C = A(N) AND B(N)
110  LET    D = A(N) OR B(N)
120  PRINT  "C = sp";C, "D = sp";D
130  NEXT   N
135  PRINT
140  FOR    N = 1 TO 4
150  LET    E = NOT(A(N) AND B(N))
160  LET    F = NOT(A(N) OR B(N))
170  PRINT  "E = sp";E, "F = sp";F
180  NEXT   N
190  END
```

Input*

A	B
1	1
1	Ø
Ø	1
Ø	Ø

Result

A	B
1	1
1	0
0	1
0	0
C = 1	D = 1
C = 0	D = 1
C = 0	D = 1
C = 0	D = 0
E = 0	F = 0
E = 1	F = 0
E = 1	F = 0
E = 1	F = 1

Notes

The computer has to take one value for each of A and B at a time. Any number other than 1 or Ø causes confusion in testing simple logic statements. The next program tests the statement for an EOR gate.

*Replace 1 by −1 in all inputs if your computer uses −1 for true.

Program 7.10

```
5   REM    TESTING AN EOR GATE
10  DIM    A(4)
20  DIM    B(4)
30  PRINT  "A", "B"
40  FOR    N = 1 TO 4
50  INPUT  A(N)
60  INPUT  B(N)
70  PRINT  A(N), B(N)
80  NEXT   N
90  PRINT
100 FOR    N = 1 TO 4
110 LET    C = (A(N) AND NOT B(N)) OR (NOT A(N)
           AND B(N))
120 PRINT  "C =    ";C
130 NEXT   N
140 END
```

Input *

```
A    B
1    1
1    Ø
Ø    1
Ø    Ø
```

Result

```
A    B
1    1
1    0
0    1
0    0
C = 0
C = 1
C = 1
C = 0
```

The execution of this program is similar to that of the previous program.

Logical statements with values other than 1 or Ø

Most microcomputers apply a logical statement to each bit of a numeric variable; this produces the values of −1 and Ø representing true and false, as NOT (−1) = Ø and NOT Ø = −1.

```
    ØØØØØØØØ...........(Ø)        ØØØØØ1Ø1..........(5)
NOT 11111111.......(−1)      NOT 11111Ø1Ø.......(−6)
```

Taking Boolean expression A AND B, the same result should be obtained for B AND A. This can be tested on your computer by an input of:

(1) . . . PRINT 5 AND 7 (result = 5)
(2) . . . PRINT 7 AND 5 (result = 5)

Some computers do not give this result, instead the output of (1) is 5 and of (2) is 7. In this case, read your computer manual to find out exactly the method used by the computer to deal with logical statements acting on numbers.

By putting P and Q equal to 1† or Ø for all possible combinations, it can be checked that the set of statements reproduces the truth table on p. 108. A program to check these statements can be used to test a microcomputer.

BOOLEAN OPERATORS ACTING ON NUMBERS

```
    00000101  . . . (5)
AND 00000100  . . . (4)
    00000100  . . . (4)

    00000101  . . . (5)
AND 11111111  . . . (−1)
    00000101  . . . (5)

    00000101  . . . (5)
 OR 00000100  . . . (4)
    00000101  . . . (5)

    00000101  . . . (5)
 OR 11111111  . . . (−1)
    11111111  . . . (−1)
```

*Replace the values of 1 by −1 if your computer uses −1 to represent true.

†If your computer uses −1 for true, then the inputs for P and Q are −1 and Ø.

Program 7.11

5	REM	NUMBER VALUED LOGICAL STATEMENTS
10	LET	P1 = 5
20	LET	P2 = Ø
30	LET	Q1 = −1
40	LET	Q2 = 7
50	LET	Q3 = Ø
60	PRINT	P1;"AND";Q1; "=";P1 AND Q1, P1; "AND"; Q2; "=" P1 AND Q2
70	PRINT	P1; "AND"; Q3; "="; P1 AND Q3
80	PRINT	P2; "AND"; Q1; "="; P2 AND Q1, P2; "AND"; Q3; "="; P2 AND Q3
90	PRINT	P1; "OR"; Q1;"="; P1 OR Q1, P1 "OR"; Q3; "="; P1 OR Q3
100	PRINT	P2; "OR"; Q1; "="; P2 OR Q1, P2; "OR"; Q3; "="; P2 OR Q3
110	PRINT	"NOT"; P1; "="; NOT P1, "NOT"; P2; "="; NOT P2
120	END	

Result

```
5 AND −1 = 5     5 AND 7 = 5
5 AND Ø = Ø
Ø AND −1 = Ø     Ø AND Ø = Ø
5 OR −1 = 1      5 OR Ø = 5
Ø OR −1 = 1      Ø OR Ø = Ø
NOT 5 = Ø        NOT Ø = 1
```

A fuller program can be written using values of Q2 as well as Q1 and Q3 in all the expressions.

Program 7.12

5	REM	LOGICAL CONDITIONAL STATEMENTS (1)
10	LET	X = 2
20	LET	Y = −1
40	IF	X + 2*Y THEN GOTO 70
50	PRINT	"2 + (−2) IS FALSE"
60	GOTO	80
70	PRINT	"2 + (−2) IS TRUE"
80	IF	NOT (X OR Y) THEN PRINT "NO"
90	PRINT	"2 AND NOT (−1) = "; X AND NOT Y
100	END	

Result

```
2 + (−2) IS FALSE
2 AND NOT (−1) = 0
```

*If your computer uses −1 for true, then the value of 1 is replaced by −1.
Also try X = 4, Y = −2.

The next two programs demonstrate the results from using logic statements with conditional statements.

Notes

(1) When a condition is realised, then the command following the condition is obeyed; if the condition is not realised, the program goes to the next line in sequence.

(2) A condition is realised when it is true and thus given the value of 1*. In line 40 the value is Ø so the condition is not realised and the program goes to line 50.

(3) In line 80, the expression NOT(X OR Y) IS NOT(2 OR −1), that is NOT(1)* which is Ø, hence the condition is not realised and the program proceeds to line 90.

(4) In line 90, 2 AND NOT(−1) becomes 2 AND Ø, which has the value of Ø.

Program 7.13

```
5   REM    LOGICAL CONDITIONAL STATEMENTS (2)
10  LET    X = 2
20  LET    Y = -1
30  LET    Z = Ø
40  IF     Z < Y AND Y < = ABS(Y) THEN GOTO 200
50  LET    X = 5
60  IF     X < Z OR (X + Y) < (X - Y) THEN GOTO 200
70  LET    X = 9
80  IF     (X = Y + 6 AND X = 3) OR (X = 5 OR Y = -1) THEN
           GOTO 200
90  LET    X = 1Ø
200 PRINT  X + 3*Y, "X =    "; X
210 IF     X > = 9 THEN STOP
220 GOTO   70
```

Result

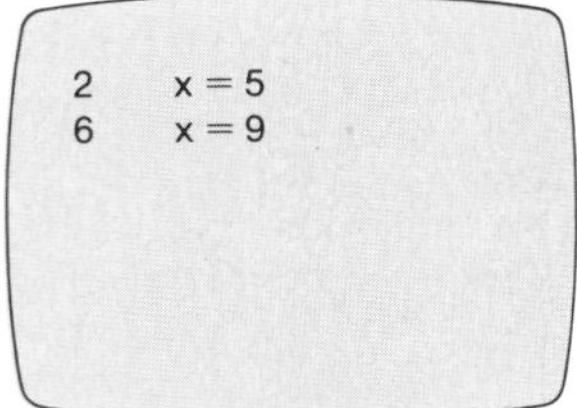

Notes

(1) In line 40, the values are Ø< −1 AND −1 < = 1; as only the latter is true, the final result is false; the program goes to line 50.

(2) In line 60, the values are 2 < Ø OR 1 < 3; the latter is true so the condition is realised; and the program goes to line 200.

(3) In line 80, the values are (9 = 5 AND 9 = 3) OR (9 = 5 OR −1=−1). The only true statement is −1=−1, which makes the second expression true, making the whole expression true, hence the program goes to line 200.

(4) Line 210 stops the program as X = 9.

Using logic statements in analysis

Codes can be used for descriptions and values of 1 or Ø assigned to give the description. Take the case of three people, numbered 1, 2 and 3, and use a number code to describe them. Let A represent blond hair and B represent male. Then $\bar{A}$ can be taken as brown/black hair and $\bar{B}$ as female. A truth table, from information supplied, can be constructed as shown:

Person 1 is a blond female (A, $\bar{B}$)
Person 2 is a blond male (A, B
Person 3 is a brown-haired m
($\bar{A}$, B)

	1	2	3
A	1	1	Ø
B	Ø	1	1

Taking a larger group of eight people, let them be put into three categories, tall, thin and male. The opposites of these will be short, fat and female. From data supplied, a truth table can be constructed as follows*:

NUMBER	1	2	3	4	5	6	7	8
TALL	Ø	1	Ø	Ø	Ø	1	1	Ø
THIN	1	Ø	Ø	1	1	1	Ø	Ø
MALE	Ø	1	1	1	Ø	1	Ø	Ø

*For computers using −1 to represent true, replace all values of 1 by −1.

From the table, person number 3 is short, fat and male. Persons 1, 5, 7 and 8 are female. Now let A, B and C represent tall, thin and male respectively, and let the table be searched for all people who are tall, fat and male. In Boolean variables this expression will be: A AND NOT B AND C. Arrays are set up for A(N), B(N) and C(N); in this example, N = 8 and the array is given the headings shown in the table.

Program 7.14

```
5   REM    CLASSIFYING PEOPLE, TRUTH TABLE
10  DIM    A(8)
20  DIM    B(8)
30  DIM    C(8)
40  PRINT  "NUMBER";
50  FOR    N = 1 TO 8
60  PRINT  TAB (3*N + 5); N;
70  NEXT   N
75  PRINT
80  PRINT  "TALL";
90  FOR    N = 1 TO 8
100 INPUT  A(N)
110 PRINT  TAB (3*N + 5); A(N);
120 NEXT   N
125 PRINT
130 PRINT  "THIN";
140 FOR    N = 1 TO 8
150 INPUT  B(N)
160 PRINT  TAB (3*N + 5); B(N);
170 NEXT   N
175 PRINT
180 PRINT  "MALE";
190 FOR    N = 1 TO 8
200 INPUT  C(N)
210 PRINT  TAB (3*N + 5); C(N);
220 NEXT   N
225 PRINT
230 PRINT
240 FOR    N = 1 TO 8
250 LET    P = A(N) AND NOT B(N) AND C(N)
260 IF     P = 1 THEN GOTO 280 (see footnote*)
270 GOTO   290
280 PRINT  "TALL, FAT AND MALE: NO.   "; N
290 NEXT   N
300 END
```

*If the computer uses −1 to represent true, then use P = −1.

The result could be easily read from the table of data; if there were several hundred people, and five or six categories, the program would work equally well, but it would be very difficult to search by eye through the table.

The next program searches for items in particular categories and then counts the number in those categories. This type of program is useful in searching through data on scientific experiments, particularly biological experiments. The experiment used for illustration has rats in a maze, starting from a fixed point and finding their way to food in a given period of time. The success rate is observed for each rat. The experiment uses seven rats each given three attempts. The rats are labelled 1 to 7 and the attempts A, B and C.

Result

```
TALL, FAT AND MALE:
NO 2
```

Program 7.15

```
5   REM    COUNTING SUCCESS RATE
10  DIM    A(7)
20  DIM    B(7)
30  DIM    C(7)
35  DIM    X(7)
40  PRINT  "A";
50  GOSUB  500
55  FOR    N = 1 TO 7
60  LET    A(N) = X(N)
65  NEXT   N
70  PRINT  "B";
80  GOSUB  500
85  FOR    N = 1 TO 7
90  LET    B(N) = X(N)
100 NEXT   N
110 PRINT  "C";
120 GOSUB  500
125 FOR    N = 1 TO 7
130 LET    C(N) = X(N)
140 NEXT   N
150 LET    Y = 0
160 FOR    N = 1 TO 7
170 LET    P = A(N) AND B(N) AND C(N)
180 IF     P = 1 (see footnote*) THEN GOTO 200
190 GOTO   210
200 LET    Y = Y + 1
205 PRINT  "NUMBER sp"; N
210 NEXT   N
220 PRINT  "3 SUCCESSES –"; Y
230 STOP
```

*If your computer represents true as −1, then use P = −1 in line 180.

```
500 FOR    N = 1 TO 7
510 INPUT  X(N)
520 PRINT  TAB (3*N + 4);X(N);
530 NEXT   N
540 PRINT
550 RETURN
```

Input

```
A Ø11ØØ11
B 1Ø11Ø1Ø
C Ø111Ø1Ø
```

Result *

```
A Ø11ØØ11
B 1Ø11Ø1Ø
C Ø111Ø1Ø
NUMBER 3
NUMBER 6
3 SUCCESSES -2
```

Notes

(1) A GOSUB technique is used to load the input. With few rows, the gain is little, but with many rows, some gain is made in the length of the program.
(2) A heading for each column has been omitted.
(3) Line 170 gives the conditions for a rat to have three successes in three attempts.

Alternative questions

The questions and their translation into Boolean expressions are as follows: If P = 1*, then the sum of Y = Y + 1 (line 200) will answer each question.

(1) 'How many rats had at least one success?'
P = A(N) OR B(N) OR C(N)

(2) 'How many rats did not succeed all three times?'
P = NOT (A(N) AND B(N) AND C(N)

(3) 'How many rats were never successful?'
P = NOT A(N) AND NOT B(N) AND NOT C(N)

(4) 'How many rats succeeded on the final try?'
P = C(N)

(5) 'How often was a success followed by a success?'
P = (A(N) AND B(N) AND NOT C(N)) OR (NOT A(N) AND B(N) AND C(N)) OR (A(N) AND NOT B(N) AND C(N))

The table of data can be printed by using a heading, followed by a numeric single-dimension array for each line, using a TAB statement to space out the data. This may be an easier method on some microcomputers. An array is needed in order to get the value of N for each rat. Alternatively, if the table is not printed, then a two-dimensional numeric array can be used for the data alone.

Exercises

In the following exercises, use the method most suitable to your microcomputer. Print the table of data (including those for true and false) if possible.

*If your computer represents true as −1, then all values of 1 are replaced by −1 in the input and output.

(1) The number of pairs of jeans sold in five different stores for the months of January to June were as follows:

	JAN	FEB	MAR	APR	MAY	JUN
Bradley	36	28	54	47	39	26
Zenith	131	106	184	165	115	129
Topon	54	68	71	39	46	88
Lucky	201	194	238	222	69	104

Find (*a*) total sales in each month; (*b*) total sales for all six months; (*c*) average sale per month for all stores; (*d*) average sales per month for each store.

(2) A firm has five salesmen, each with a works number. The salesmen are grouped into three areas. A record is kept of the number of sales they make, and the total sum of money received, in one week. The data are:

Salesman No.	*Area*	*No. of sales*	*Receipts*
28	1	5	$1200
74	3	15	$3900
86	2	12	$4200
92	2	4	$600
108	1	21	$6700

(*a*) Devise a simple code to list the salesmen, and construct a table to show the number of sales, the total receipts and the commission for each salesman calculated by the following rule. For receipts under $3000, a 5% commission is paid; for receipts of $3000 and over the commission is 7½%.

(*b*) (*i*) Make a table to show the average sum received per sale for each salesman. (*ii*) Find the average receipt per sale for the whole sales force.

(3) An experiment is conducted on the degree of salinity that can be withstood by a selection of estuarine animals. The degree of salinity is expressed as a percentage of the salinity of sea water, for example 0% is fresh water, 100% is sea water. The statement is 'The animal can withstand the degree of salinity'. True statements are represented by 1, false statements by Ø. The data for the animals are:

Salinity	0%	10%	30%	50%	70%	90%	100%
Oyster spp	1	1	1	Ø	Ø	Ø	Ø
Ragworm spp	Ø	1	1	1	Ø	Ø	Ø
Crab spp	Ø	1	1	1	1	1	Ø
Worm spp	Ø	Ø	1	1	1	1	1
Barnacle spp	Ø	Ø	Ø	1	1	1	1

Construct a program to input the data and then to provide an answer to the following: (*a*) List the animals that can live in a salinity of 10% to 30%. (*b*) List the animals that cannot live in a salinity below 50%.

Summary

A **DIM** statement, at the start of a program, is needed to dimension an array.

Using an input and a loop the array can be entered into RAM.

The print statement of data must be enclosed in the loop.

A one-dimensional numeric **array** is shown by A(N) and a two-dimensional numeric **array** by A(N,M) where N gives the number of rows and M the number of columns.

Numeric arrays can contain any number of figures for one entry; alpha, or string, arrays, may need the length of each item to be entered as a further dimension, for example A$(3,6,6) is an array of three rows with six columns, each entry containing six characters or spaces. Most microcomputers do not need the number of characters in a string to be dimensioned.

The numbers in brackets for the DIM statement or array statement are **subscripts**.

Subscripted arrays, numeric or string, can be sliced using LEFT$, MID$, RIGHT$, or SEG$.

True statements are represented by the figure 1* and false statements by the figure Ø. **Logical statements**, AND, OR NOT, are illustrated by two facts, A and B.

For **AND** statements, both A and B must be true.

For **OR** statements, either A or B or both can be true.

NOT statements change 1* to Ø and Ø to 1*, that is true to false and vice versa.

For **NAND** statements, both A and B cannot be true.

For **NOR** statements, neither A nor B nor both can be true.

For **XOR** statements, either A or B, but not both, are true; the XOR statement compares two variables A and B; if they are alike, the result is Ø, if unlike, the result is 1*.

Logical statements can be joined in an expression.

Gates are electronic circuits which produce the results of Boolean expressions containing logical statements.

There are AND, OR, NOT, NAND and NOR gates.

Truth tables use the values of 1* and 0 to show the result of logical statements acting on two or more Boolean variables.

Logical statements can execute number valued operations; they are;

P AND Q applies the operator AND to each bit, so that 5 AND 7 = 5.

P AND Q = Q AND P

P OR Q applies the operator OR to each bit so that 5 OR 7 = 7.

P OR Q = Q OR P

NOT Q = 1*; NOT 1* = Q

Logical statements can be used with arithmetical operators.

*Many computers use the value of − 1, and not the value of 1 to represent true.

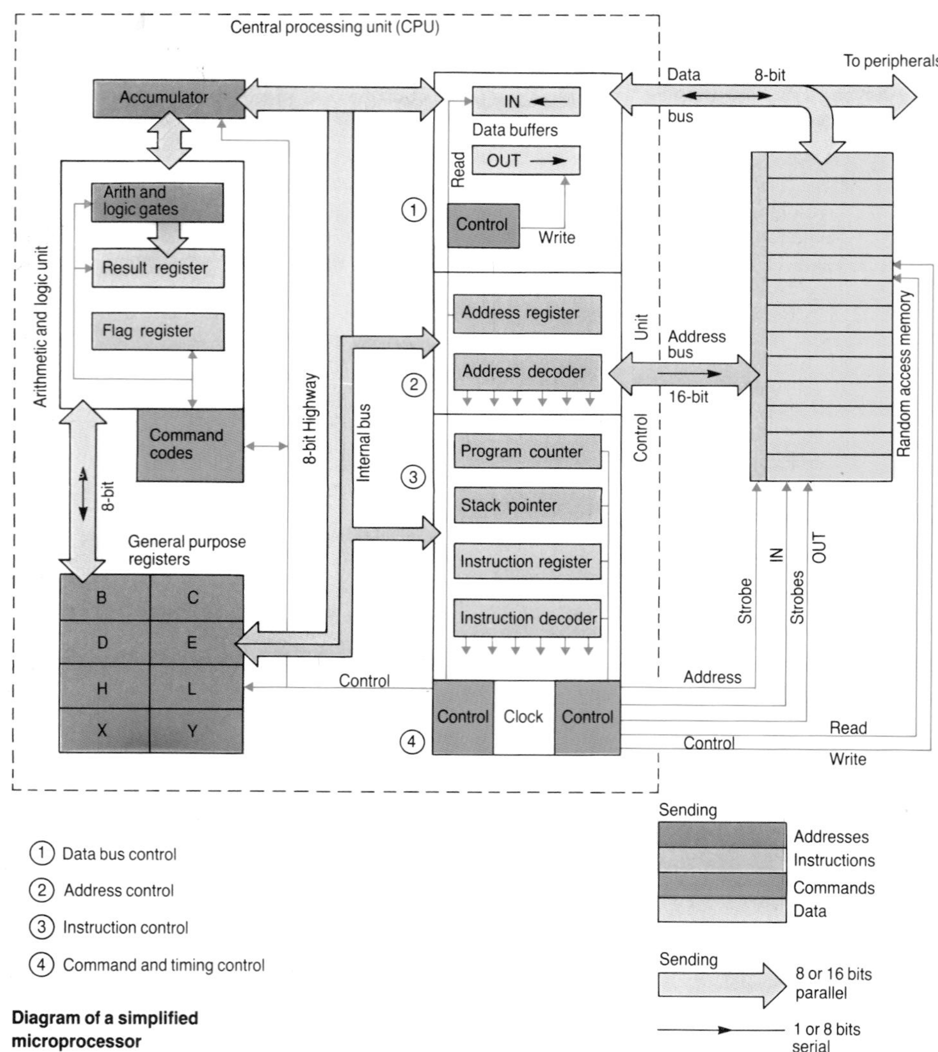

(1) Data bus control

(2) Address control

(3) Instruction control

(4) Command and timing control

Diagram of a simplified microprocessor

CHAPTER 8

Central processing units

The central processing unit (CPU) is that part of a computer which directs its operations, so it is obviously a very complicated system of electronic circuits. It is the aim of this chapter to give as simple an explanation as is possible of the way in which a CPU executes a program in machine code (see p. 141), and of the interaction between the CPU and the machine code. Using a microcomputer is similar to using a motor car; it is not essential to know how either machine functions in order to use it. Having some knowledge of the way in which either machine functions, however, improves one's ability to use it.

Microprocessor architecture

A CPU in a microcomputer is a microprocessor, and is a silicon chip. Its architecture is its design and the method of assembling the different components on the chip. Different chips have different designs, but all contain standard features. These standard components are illustrated in the diagram, which shows the connections between the different parts of a simplified microprocessor. The function of the different components is as follows.

Instruction control unit

This consists of three registers and a decoder.

Program counter (PC). This is a 16-bit register which stores the address of the *next* instruction of a machine code program. When an instruction is executed, 1 is added to the PC, so it than contains the next sequential step in the program. If an instruction consists of more than one byte, then 2 or 3 has to be added to the PC. An exception to this is a **jump** instruction which indicates the program jumps to an instruction other than the next sequential instruction. The jump instruction then includes a command to add the correct number of steps to the PC so that it indicates the correct instruction signalled by the jump. Many jump instructions replace the contents of the PC with the new address. The address of the return location must also be stored in the memory.

Stack pointer (SP). This is a 16-bit register which stores the **next** available empty memory location in RAM for use by the machine code instructions. The most common use is for storing information concerning subroutines (p. 49). The stack in RAM can be added to, or reduced by, two bytes at a time. These bytes come from the general registers. Each time a transfer is made to the stack, the SP is updated.

Instruction register. An 8-bit register into which the program instruction is loaded. Some instructions consist of words of two, three, or four bytes, each of eight bits. Each byte is loaded into the register and dealt with separately.

Instruction decoder. A circuit which switches on the necessary electrical connections for an instruction to be executed. Its operation will be explained more fully.

Command control unit. This unit operates in conjunction with a quartz-controlled clock delivering pulses at the rate of 1 to 4 MHz. These pulses act as commands for switch gates, switching them on and off, allowing coded data to pass from one section of the computer to another. Control and timing will be mentioned again under the description of particular devices. This completes the description of the essential parts of the instruction control unit, and the command and timing unit.

Address control unit

This consists of an address register and an address decoder.

Memory address register (MAR). This is a 16-bit register which holds the address of a location in RAM. Sixteen bits can represent, in binary notation, any number between 0 and 65,535 in decimal notation. This allows 65,536 locations to be addressed. Part of an instruction can be an address, for example load the data in the accumulator into location 1A4Ch, where 1A4C is a hexadecimal number and the h indicates it is in hexadecimal notation. The address part of an instruction is transferred from the instruction register to an address decoder.

Address decoder. This device switches on electrical connections to a particular location in RAM or to a particular register. Its operation will be explained later. These two components of the address control unit are connected directly to the random access memory (RAM) by a 16-bit address bus. Transmission of the location address number is in parallel (p. 59) for the sixteen bits, so is quick. This bus is uni-directional, passing address information only into RAM. The location in RAM is activated to pass data out to the data control unit.

Data control unit

This consists of two **buffers**, one for data in and the other for data out. A buffer is a register for the temporary storage of a binary number until the data is needed by the next device or component. Data enters the 'in' buffer or leaves the 'out' buffer by an 8-bit data bus to the RAM. This bus is bi-directional, passing data either way. The data control unit also uses the data bus to pass data to peripheral devices such as a VDU, a printer, a cassette, etc. More information will be given on this topic.

The accumulator (ACC)

In the majority of microcomputers this is an 8-bit register. In larger microcomputers, 16-bit accumulators are used. For the purpose of this book, an 8-bit register will be assumed. The accumulator is the most important register of the CPU; it is connected directly to the internal data highway. All data from RAM can be loaded into the accumulator; and similarly all data from the general purpose registers can also be loaded into it. Arithmetic and logic operations are executed using one **operand** in the accumulator and the other **operand** fetched from the RAM. An **operand** is a data item which is the subject of a program instruction, for example in 3 × 6, the two numbers are each operands. Results from the arithmetic and logic unit are sent back to the accumulator. Various operations can be executed only on the accumulator contents, they include complementing, incrementing, decrementing, shifting and comparing data. Different microcomputers use their accumulators, however, in different ways.

The arithmetic and logic unit (ALU)

This consists of three arithmetic registers (ADD, SUBTRACT and the SHIFT register), and three logic gates (AND, OR, XOR gates). The XOR gate is usually called a comparator (CP) gate. The function of these gates will be described later. An instruction can be used to complement the accumulator, and then by adding 1, to get the true complement. The ALU is connected by data buses to the data control unit and to the registers.

The registers

A register in a microcomputer stores data items, usually of length eight bits. Registers can be made to work in pairs, allowing for the storage of sixteen bits. Storage registers consist of devices called flip-flops, described on page 124. The accumulator is a storage register, usually associated with the general purpose registers. Other registers include the program counter, stack pointer, instruction and address registers, and the buffers. A buffer stores data until activated by a command to release the data to another part of the computer. Such a device is needed, as different processes have different periods of time for the execution of their processes. A buffer holds the information until the next device is ready to receive it. A common register arrangement consists of general purpose registers B, C, D, E which can be paired to form BC and DE as 16-bit registers. In addition, there are the H and L registers, usually restricted to holding addresses, and the X and Y registers used for addressing indexed instructions. In an **indexed instruction,** the program is directed to a location, not included in the program sequence; this index is capable of being altered by instructions in further program steps.

The central processing unit

The CPU has three main sections, as described above, connected internally by an 8-bit **highway**. The highway transmits data and instructions, which include register addresses, and is multi-directional. In addition, control lines pass signal pulses to all parts of the CPU, and receive signal pulses back. The CPU is connected to peripheral devices by an 8-bit data bus, a 16-bit address bus, and by control lines transmitting commands. The control lines can also transmit some data bits serially. This gives an overall picture of the CPU. More detail is needed to explain the working of individual devices, and how these devices respond to machine code instructions.

Electronic devices

Electronic devices consist essentially of switches, diodes and resistors. A silicon chip contains hundreds of such devices made from two different types of semiconducting silicon, called p-type (positive type) and n-type (negative type) silicon, and silicon dioxide, the latter being used to provide resistance. The devices are **integrated** on the chip, that is, each device is in contact with one or more devices and no wires are used to connect them.

Transistors

This is the most common device, formed from layers of p-type and n-type silicon. It functions as a switch. A

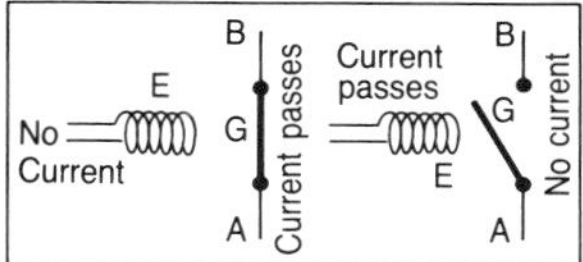

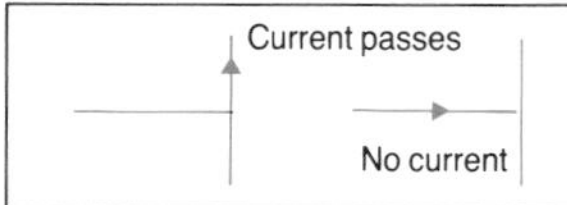

mechanical example of a switch is shown in the diagram with an arm, labelled G, which can swing from open to shut. It is attracted by an electromagnet, labelled E, when current passes through the coil of E. With no current in the electromagnet, current passes from A to B. With current in the electromagnet, no current passes from A to B. The current from A to B can thus be switched on and off, by using E.

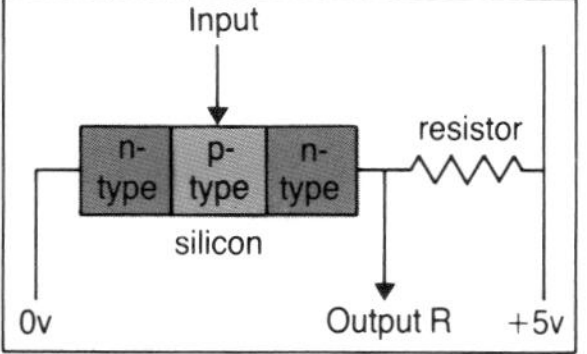

A transistor

A transistor operates in a similar fashion. The diagram illustrates a transistor with an input of 0 volts producing an output of current at +5 volts. The voltage is applied to the p-type portions of the transistor by a pulsating voltage, each **pulse** being timed by the clock in the CPU. The input is similarly timed by the clock, giving a series of inputs at a potential of 0 volts or +5 volts. This pulsating input produces a pulsating output, as shown in the diagram. The

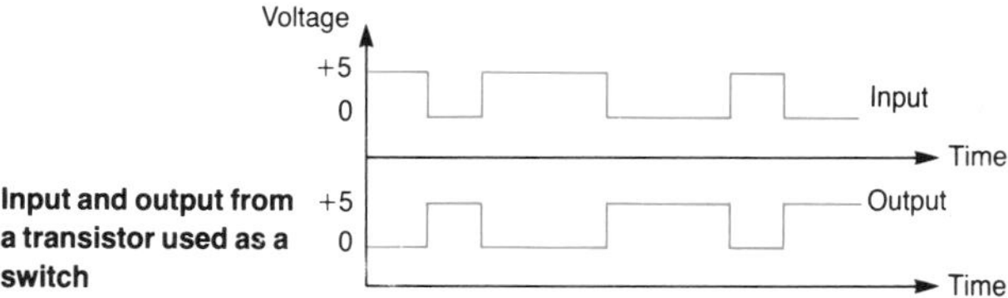

Input and output from a transistor used as a switch

output is opposite in voltage to the input; so the transistor, used in this fashion, is equivalent to a NOT gate. The symbol for a NOT gate and its result is shown in the diagram.

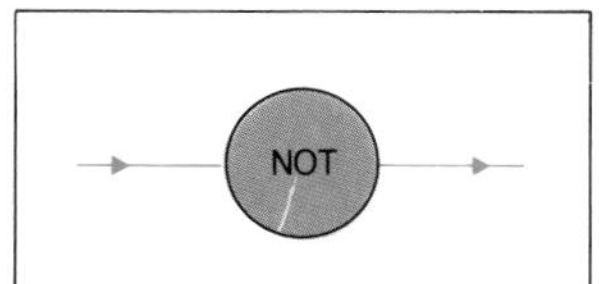

A NOT gate

Combinations of transistors can be made in an integrated circuit, as seen in the diagram for an AND gate.

An AND gate

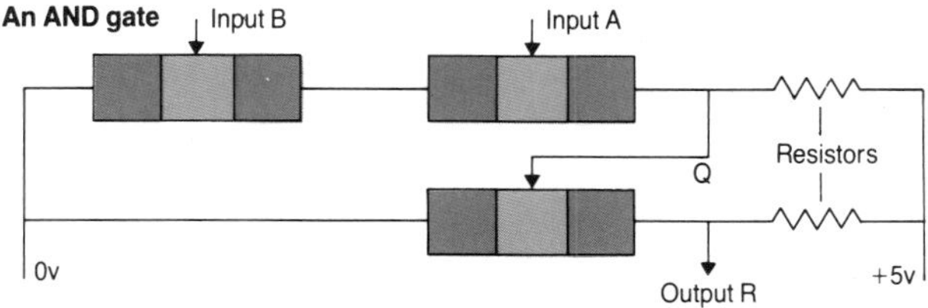

Without the third transistor (producing the output R), the combination would be a NAND gate with an output from PQ. The diagram gives the result for two inputs each of +5 volts. If +5 volts is taken to represent 1 and 0 volts to represent Ø, then the truth table for the AND gate can be compiled as illustrated, with the table showing the intermediate values of P and Q.

A	B	Q	R
1	1	0	1
1	0	1	0
0	1	1	0
0	0	1	0

AND gate results

A combination of two transistors produces an OR gate. The diagram shows the output, R, from two inputs A and B, where A = 1, and B = Ø. The intermediate output, P, is converted by the second transistor to the output R. Without the second transistor, a NOR gate is formed. Write out and complete a truth table for different values of A and B producing results P and R. The values of A and B should be 11, 1Ø, Ø1, and ØØ.

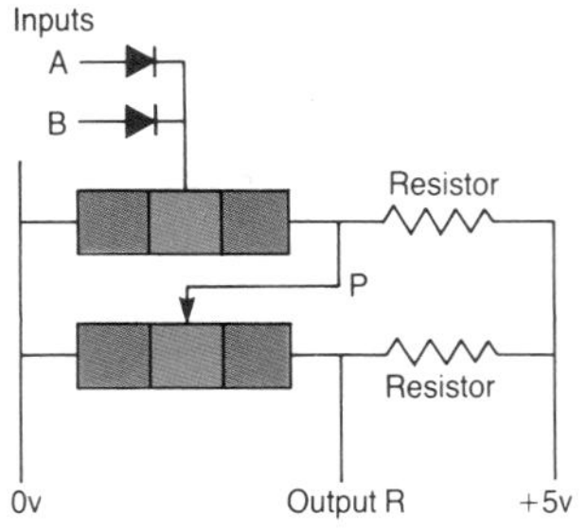

An OR gate

Flip-flops

A flip-flop consists of two transistors connected with the input or one connected to the output of the other and vice versa. The circuit also contains resistors and diode rectifiers (a diode permits current in one direction only). A flip-flop can take either one of two possible states, which can be identified as Ø or 1. That state is held until changed by a suitable input. The input and output terminals are shown in the diagram, together with a third terminal supplied with a regular pulse controlled by the clock in the CPU.

The input is delivered to a terminal marked S for set. The pulse is delivered to a terminal marked R for reset. The flip-flop is **set** when its value is 1 and **reset** when its value is Ø. The flip-flop's output is derived from its initial state before the input acts. The four possible combinations of input and flip-flop states are shown in the diagram, and summarised in the table.

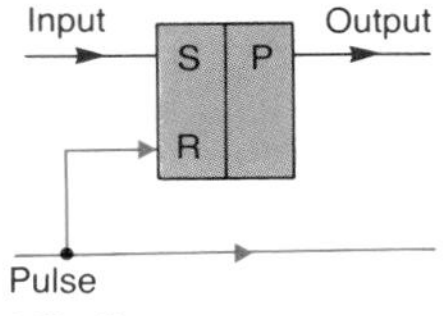

A flip-flop

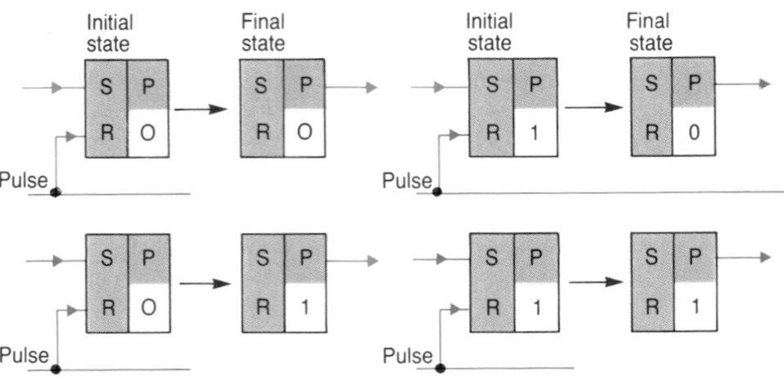

Results from flip-flop operations

INITIAL STATE	INPUT	FINAL STATE	OUTPUT
Ø	Ø	Ø	Ø
Ø	1	1	Ø
1	0	0	1
1	1	1	1

→ 1

→ 0

The operation pattern of a flip-flop is:

(1) The input is activated to deliver 0 volts or +5 volts (Ø or 1), there is no action.

(2) The pulse arrives at terminal R. This activates the transistors so that its final state is reached and the output assumes the correct value.

This action takes time, and the timing is controlled by, and depends on, the clock in the CPU.

Registers, gates and buffers

The most common register consists of flip-flops, with an 8-bit register consisting of eight flip-flops. Registers and memory locations in microcomputers usually hold a byte of eight bits. All transfers take place on an 8-bit bus, that is, in parallel. Before a register can be used, it has to be cleared, that is, all the flip-flops reset to zero, making the register empty. The command line, connected to the clock, is connected to the reset terminal of the flip-flop. When a pulse is sent along this command line and there is no input, the flip-flop is reset to zero. The diagram shows the circuit for this operation, with each flip-flop connected to the command line. A pulse passed along the line clears all the flip-flops in the register at the same time.

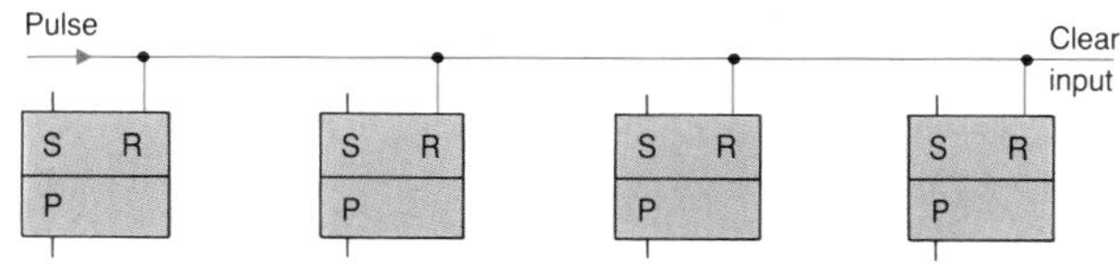

Clearing a register

Transferring the contents of one register to another is carried out by the circuit illustrated. A pulse along the clear line empties register C. At the same time the outputs of register B are connected to the individual AND gates, but nothing happens as the gates require two inputs. A pulse along the transfer line supplies this second input to all the flip-flops at the same time. This command pulse activates the AND gates, so there is an output from each gate. In the diagram, register B holds the binary number 1001. After the clear and the transfer commands, register C holds the number, as indicated, of 1001. The number still remains in register B. The register illustrated is for a 4-bit item of data. An 8-bit register has eight flip-flops instead of four and the principle of operation is identical.

Transfer of data from register B to register C

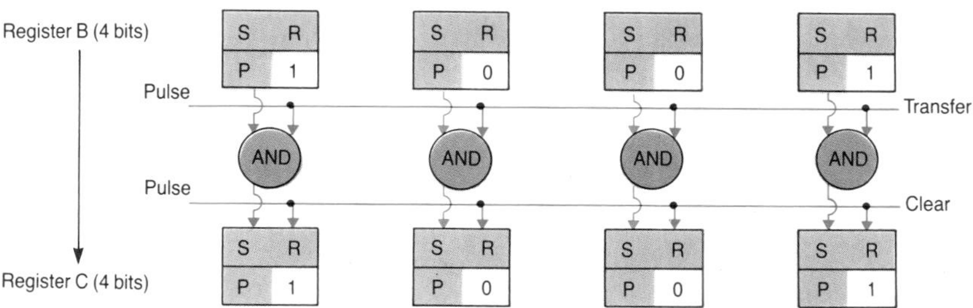

Memory locations, as well as registers, can use flip-flops, so the transfer of data from memory to register is exactly the same as the transfer from register to register.

The arithmetic and logic unit (ALU)

The architecture of an ALU varies from computer to computer. The ALU discussed in this book represents the circuits necessary for most operations carried out by a microcomputer.

The diagram shows a simplified circuit for an ALU, with the accumulator as part of the ALU. The circuit has 16-bit registers and logic gates, with a result register acting as a buffer. Data can be fed in from the CPU highway into the accumulator, or from the registers. The mode of action is that one **operand** is put in the accumulator, the other operand in one of the registers or gates, and the result passes through the result register back into the accumulator. The data bus lines are 8-bit lines. The lines from the

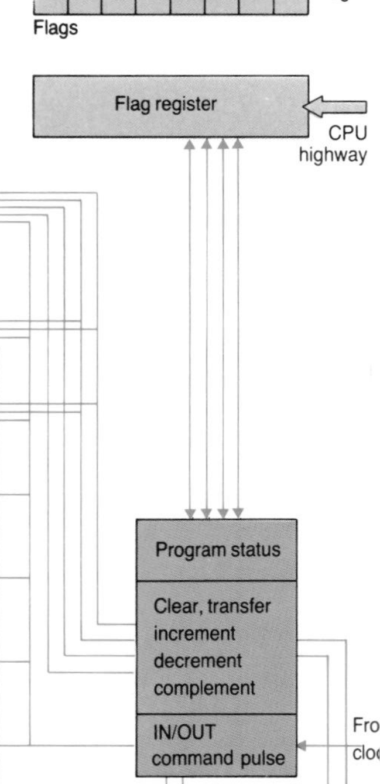

Simplified arithmetic and logic unit

command code unit are single lines. Pulses from the command code unit clear registers and transfer data, as described previously. In addition, pulses can be sent to increment any register in the register block or the accumulator; this adds one to the register. Similarly to decrement a register, that is, to subtract one, the one's complement is added. So to decrement an 8-bit register, eight ones are sent in serial transmission. There is a complement command, in addition. In and out commands are also sent by the command code unit.

All commands are timed by a pulse which originates from the CPU clock. The diagram has been simplified in that: (*a*) the result and the shift register are connected directly to the accumulator and (*b*) each clear, transfer, or other command passes along its own line to a particular register or logic gate.

The gates

The AND and OR gates have been described previously in this chapter. The CP gate, also called an EOR gate, was described on p. 108. Each logic gate in the ALU has one such gate for each bit. It is thus possible to obtain a result for 11Ø11Ø11 AND 1ØØ1ØØ11, the result being 1ØØ1ØØ11. Similarly results can be obtained for the OR and CP gates, applying the correct Boolean logic statements.

The ADD register

The most important device in the ADD register is the **half-adder**. This is composed of two AND gates, one OR and one NOT gate, as shown in the diagram. Two inputs, A and B, produce a binary number which is recorded and a binary number which is carried to the next more significant binary digit. The results from adding 1 + Ø and 1 + 1 are shown. Draw the diagrams for Ø + 1 and Ø + Ø to test

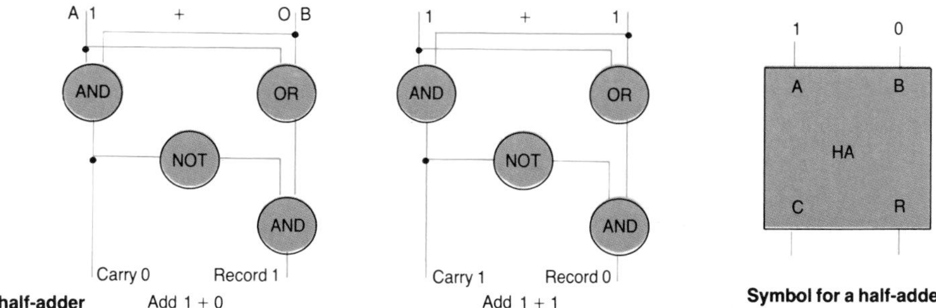

A half-adder

Add 1 + 0

Add 1 + 1

Symbol for a half-adder

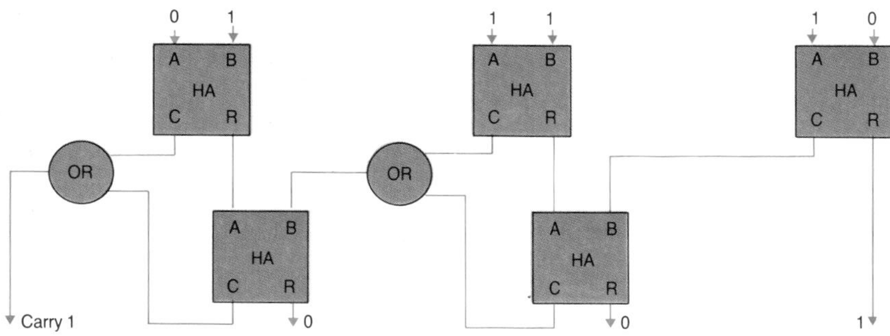

A 3-bit add register (011 + 110 = 1001)

the result. The half-adder circuit is represented by the symbol given in the diagram. An ADD register is then composed of half-adders and OR gates as shown. The ADD register adds the contents of the accumulator to the contents of another register (B, C, D, etc.); it contains eight bits or sixteen bits. Many ADD registers contain sixteen bits. All the inputs labelled A come from the accumulator (A register) and all the inputs labelled B come from another register. The output passes to the results register. The diagram illustrates the addition of 11Ø and Ø11, that is three bits. The result should be 1ØØ1, but with three bits only, the result is ØØ1 and 1 carried forward. This carried digit is put in a separate CARRY register consisting of one bit. If this carry register is set, that is shows a value of 1, then the command unit is activated to show there is a carry in the arithmetic operation.

The SUBTRACT register

This is an alternative circuit. Some microcomputers have a complementing register giving a true complement which is then added to perform the process of subtraction.

A device known as a half-subtractor is used in other forms of a SUBTRACT register. A **half-subtractor** consists of two AND, two NOT and one OR gates. The circuit is shown in the diagram. A half-subtractor can have the following inputs: Ø-Ø; 1-Ø; 1-1; Ø-1. Only the fourth subtraction necessitates borrowing from the next digit. Three results are indicated in the diagram. Draw the fourth possibility of Ø-Ø to check the working of the circuit. The output from a half-subtractor is a record and a borrow; this is shown in the symbol for a half-subtractor.

A SUBTRACT register combines half-subtractors and

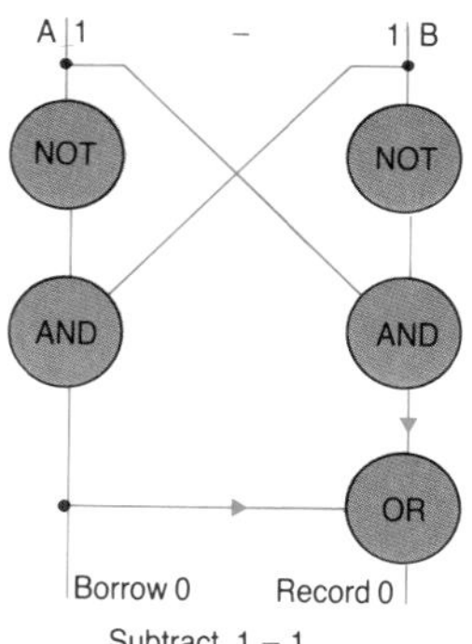

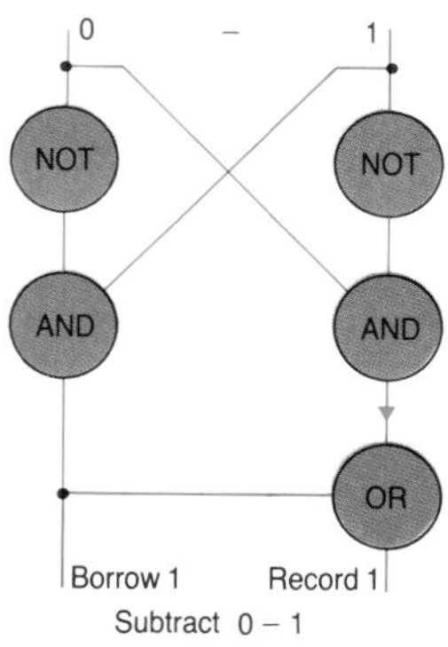

A half-subtractor

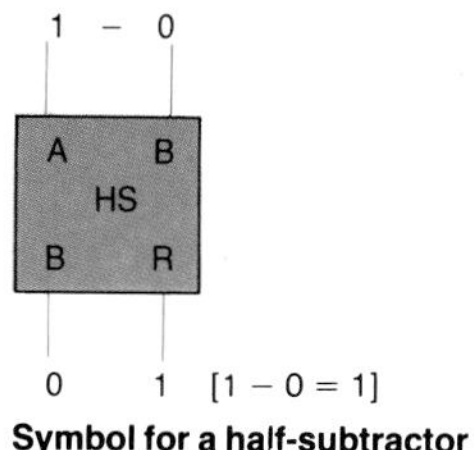

Symbol for a half-subtractor

OR gates. A 3-bit SUBTRACT register is illustrated in the diagram. Note that it is important which operand is put in the A input and which in the B. The A operand is loaded into the accumulator and the B operand into any general register (B, C, D, etc.). The result is transferred through the RESULT register to the accumulator. The overflow digit is put in a separate OVERFLOW register of one bit. If this overflow register is set, that is contains 1, then the command unit is activated to show there is an overflow in the arithmetic operation.

A 3-bit subtract register

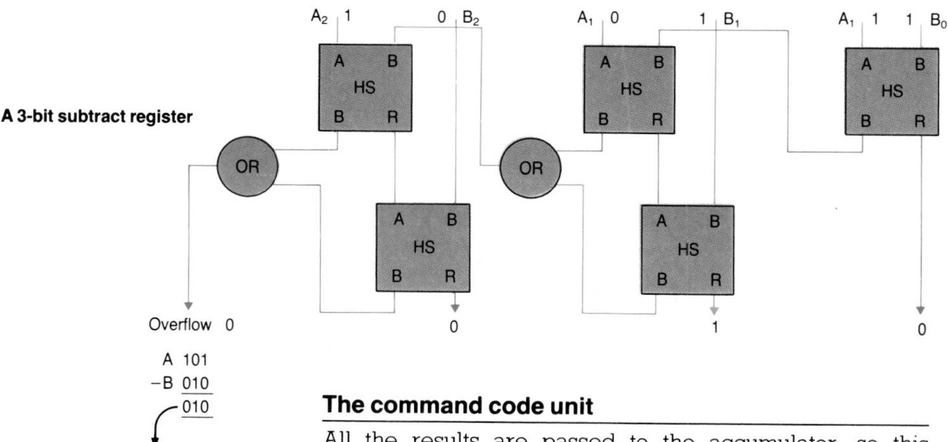

A 101
–B 010
010
Overflow 0

The command code unit

All the results are passed to the accumulator, so this register is always tested by the command code unit to determine the **status** of the answer. Eight bits are used to store the code for status. These bits are used in the following way:

Bit No.	*Value 1*	*Value 0*
0	ACC is zero	ACC is not zero
1	ACC is negative	ACC is positive
2	Carry for MSB	No carry for MSB
3	Overflow for MSB	No overflow for MSB
4	Conditional on result	Not conditional on result
5	No effect from result	Effect from result
6	Register cleared	Register not cleared
7	Bit set	Bit reset

(MSB = Most Significant Bit, i.e. extreme left-hand bit)

The value of these codes will be seen when branching programs are written in machine code, as they test for conditions. Bits 0-3 inclusive are actual conditions and bits 4-7 are the effects acting on the condition codes. The codes are known as **program status bits**.

The other functions of the unit, such as increment, decrement, complement, clear and transfer, all require a single pulse along a pulse line, together with a command to perform the actual instruction. This is seen in the clear and transfer commands for the transfer of data. The shift register also illustrates their use.

The pulse, originating from the quartz clock, ensures that the various processes keep in step.

The flag register

This register holds information on status. Status bits from the command code unit are loaded into the flag register. The use of this register differs in different CPUs. The register illustrated in the diagram of the ALU is the flag register used by a Z-80 CPU, one of the most common CPU chips. The flags represent the following statuses:

Carry flag (C). Affected by ADD and SHIFT. Set for carry, reset for no carry.
Zero flag (Z). Set if accumulator is zero, reset if not zero.
Sign flag (S). Set for negative, reset for positive.
Parity/overflow flag (P/V). Detects overflow for SUBTRACT register; also used to check parity.
Half-carry (H). Used with binary-coded decimal arithmetic.
Subtract (N). Also used with BCD arithmetic
(X). Bit not used for flag purposes.

The flag register is used for various purposes besides those dealing with purely arithmetical or logical operations. The flag data are usually stored in fixed locations in RAM in a part of the memory used for storing system variables, that is those variables concerned with the execution of a program.

The shift register

This register contains two circuits, one for shift left and one for shift right. The circuit for shift right is shown in the diagram. A transfer command supplies an input to each set terminal of a flip-flop, but there is no action until the shift pulse is sent. The pulse changes the contents of each flip-flop. A zero value is fed in at the left, and for each cycle of events, the register digit values are shifted one position to the right. The diagram demonstrates two right shifts in a 3-

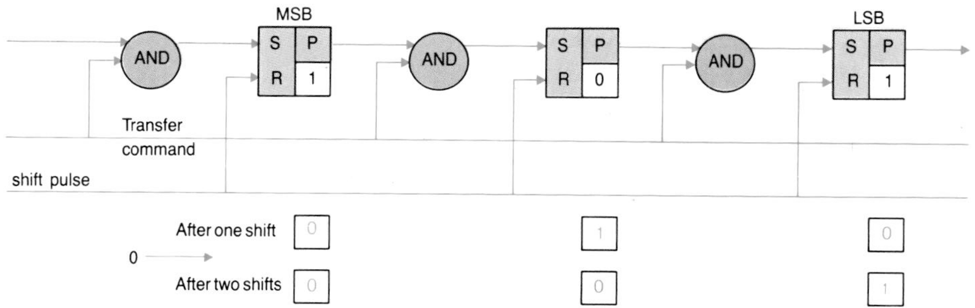

A shift register

bit register. With an 8-bit register, containing a value of 182 (decimal), the result of three shifts right will be:

Original value	1011	0110	decimal value = 182
1 shift right	0101	1011	decimal value = 91
2 shifts right	0010	1101	decimal value = 45
3 shifts right	0001	0110	decimal value = 22

Shifting right divides a number by 2, neglecting any additional half. A shift left circuit is made by reversing the patterns of the shift right circuit. The results for an 8-bit register are:

Original value	0011	0101	decimal value = 53
1 shift left	0110	1010	decimal value = 106
2 shifts left	1101	0100	decimal value = 212

Shifting left multiplies a number by 2.

Some microcomputers have an instruction to rotate the bits in the shift register. The effect of rotating to the left is shown in the diagram.

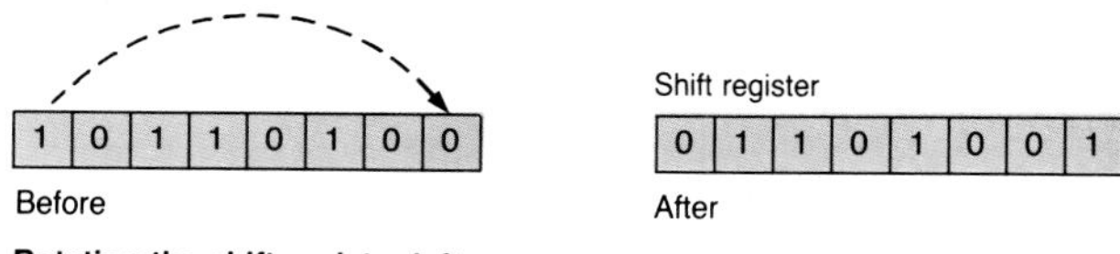

Rotating the shift register left

Using a mask

The AND gate and the CP gate are useful in extracting coded information by the use of a **mask**. The AND gate is used to test whether a bit is set, that is has a value of 1. If we wish to test whether a number is negative, the contents of the flag register are tested. A negative number has a value of 1 in bit 7. The contents of the flag register are stored in location 41ØØh (h stands for hexadecimal). A mask, of value 8Øh, is stored in location 42Ø3h. The location 41ØØh is a fixed location for a system variable; its address will be different in different computers. The location 42Ø3h is chosen for a particular program. The contents of the flag location are loaded into the accumulator. The AND gate is then used with the mask to find ACC and RAM (location), as shown in the diagram. If the condition is met, then a 1 value appears in the accumulator, that is in this case the number is negative. Notice that the values of bits 0-6 inclusive are irrelevant, that is whether a bit is Ø or 1 in the accumulator, the result is Ø. A mask can thus be used to blank out part of a byte. In the diagram the bits 0-6 inclusive are blanked out. If the RAM location held a mask of value FØh, then the bits 0-3 inclusive would be blanked out and the result 11ØØ would remain in bits 4-7 inclusive.

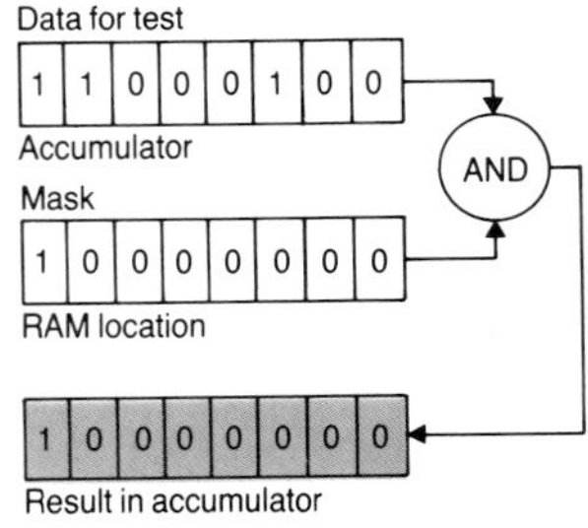

Using a mask with an AND gate

The CP gate is used with a mask if a match of information is to be tested. Suppose four characteristics are displayed by bits 0-3 inclusive in an 8-bit byte. The truth values for the four bits are as follows:

Bit	*1 value*	*0 value*
0	Male	Female
1	18 years and over	Under 18 years
2	A1 physically fit	Not A1 physically fit
3	1.7 m tall and over	Under 1.7 m tall

We want to find a person with the following characteristics: female/over 18 years/not A1 physically fit/over 1.7m tall. Such a person will have a code 1Ø1Ø, which in an 8-bit byte will be ØØØØ1Ø1Ø. This code is made a mask and the mask put in the accumulator. Each individual, with his/her characteristics coded in a RAM location, is then compared, in turn, with the mask, using the CP gate. If there is a perfect match, then each bit in the accumulator will be Ø, so zero in the accumulator indicates a person with the required characteristics. The truth table for an XOR, that is CP, gate gives a Ø for a match and a 1 for a mismatch. The result from the CP gate is transferred back into the accumulator and tested. The mask is transferred back into the accumulator for each comparison. A conditional instruction can then be made if the accumulator reads zero on being tested.

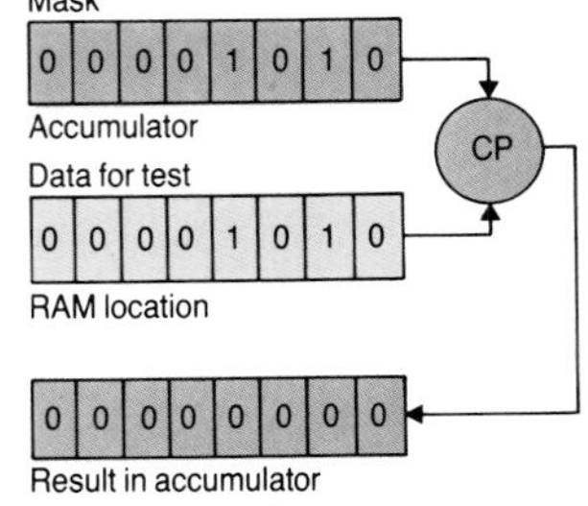

Using a mask with a CP gate

Other arithmetical processes

The processes of multiplication, division, exponentiation, are usually carried out by standard program segments using the ADD and SUBTRACT registers; these processes will be discussed later. In microprocessors able to use binary-coded decimal (BCD), numbers in this notation are processed in the accumulator, using special instructions.

Coding BCD in an accumulator

The accumulator is divided into two sections, each of four bits, called **nibbles**. Each nibble takes the value of one column of BCD. (Look up BCD on p. 56). The more significant nibble indicates the value of the ten's digit, and the less significant nibble, the value of the unit's digit. A value of 95 is represented in the diagram for the accumulator and for the normal display of BCD for paper or magnetic tape. The highest value in BCD that the accumulator can hold is 99, but by storing the results in sequential locations in RAM, larger numbers can be processed, remembering that bcd is used for integer arithmetic only.

The instruction control unit

The majority of microcomputers work on an 8-bit byte, so an instruction in machine code to the CPU will consist of an 8-bit byte. This byte is divided into three segments, indicated in the diagram. The first segment, XX, is always a command instruction, causing the CPU to execute a process. The second segment, YYY, can be either part of a command, or the address of a register. The third segment, ZZZ, is also a command or the address of a register. In the first instance, with XX as a command, then YYY is the address of a register from which information is taken, and ZZZ is the address of the register into which information is loaded. As these are 3-bit addresses, they can address

Use of a byte for instructions

X X Y Y Y Instruction command
1 1 1 Address of accumulator

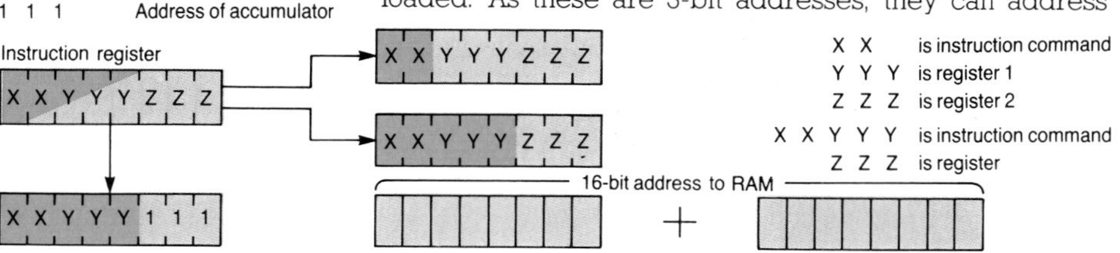

eight registers (000 to 111 in binary). In the second instance, with XXYYY as a command instruction, the last segment holds the address of one register only. This can be used with arithmetic registers and logic gates where one operand is held in the named register and the other operand is in the accumulator. In the third instance, XXYYY is an instruction command, and ZZZ holds 111, the address of the accumulator. This instruction byte must then be followed by two further 8-bit bytes to give the 16-bit address of a location in RAM. Such an instruction is then used to transfer data between the accumulator and RAM in either direction, depending on the command.

The fetch cycle

The instruction control circuit is shown by a simplified diagram. The **fetch cycle** starts with the program control (PC) holding the RAM address of the next instruction which is in machine code. This address passes through a gate when the gate is activated by a fetch impulse on the fetch line. The address enters the address decoder which,

Simplified instruction control unit

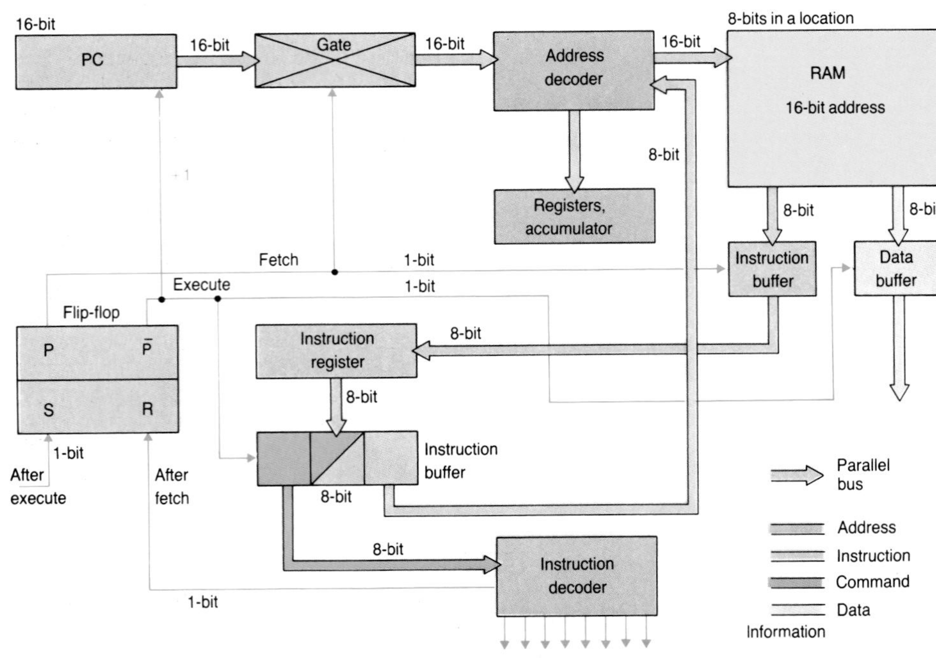

in turn, opens communication to the memory (RAM). The contents of the RAM location enter the instruction buffer, which now holds the machine code instruction for the next step in the program. The fetch pulse, suitably delayed, now activates the instruction buffer, and the instruction enters the instruction register, and then enters a gate. The gate divides the instructioin into a command and an address (no circuit shown for this). After the fetch cycle has finished, a pulse goes to the reset terminal of a flip-flop. The flip-flop has **two** outputs, the normal output at P and a second output, from the second transistor of the flip-flop at $\bar{P}$. This second output, $\bar{P}$, is the reverse of the output at P. When the flip-flop is reset, the value of P is Ø, so the value of $\bar{P}$ is 1, and the execute line is activated.

The **execute cycle** first sends an impulse to the PC which adds 1 to the contents, that is the PC now shows the next sequential address. It also activates the instruction buffer to send its contents to the instruction decoder. The instruction decoder activates those parts of the CPU needed to execute the process. At the same time, the instruction buffer sends the address of a register, or registers, to the address decoder. With longer instructions it sends the address of a location in RAM to the address decoder. The address decoder identifies and activates the RAM location and passes the data to the data buffer. After a suitable delay, the execute impulse activates the data buffer and the data are sent to the accumulator. The part of the CPU executing the process sends an impulse back when the process is completed. This impulse sets the flip-flop. The value of P is now 1, so the fetch cycle is repeated with the next sequential step of the machine code program.

The PC, address decoder and gate are 16-bit devices, connected by a 16-bit parallel bus. A location in RAM stores a byte of eight bits. The instruction register, instruction decoder and associated buffer are all 8-bit, connected by 8-bit parallel buses. If the instruction is of the third type, described previously, then two 8-bit bytes have to be sent one after the other to load the address decoder with a 16-bit RAM address. Circuits to enable this operation are not shown.

Decoders

The circuit for a decoder is given in the diagram. It is for a decoder of length two bits only. For eight or sixteen bits the circuit is more complicated, but the same type of combination of AND and NOT gates is used. The diagram

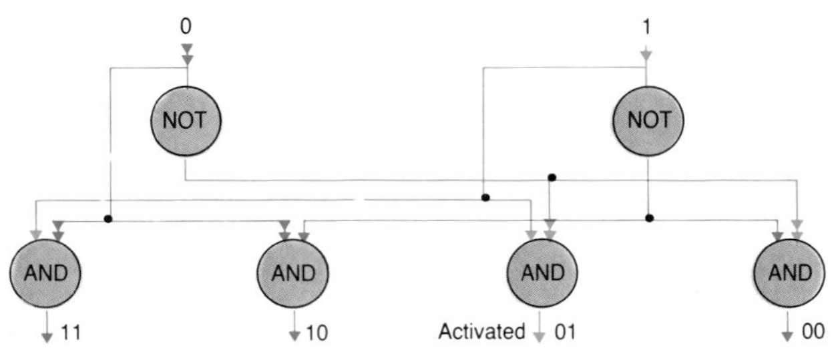

Operation of a decoder (2 bits only)

illustrates an input of value Ø1. The output activates a line to the device 01, leaving the other devices disabled. The activated device executes the command from the instruction. An instruction decoder has eight bits, although only two or five bits may be used for most commands. An address decoder has sixteen bits and thus addresses any location in a memory of 2^{16}, that 65,536 locations. This is 64 × 1024 locations, called a 64K memory.

The stack pointer

A subroutine of a machine code program is stored in RAM in a **stack**. A register pair, BC, DE or HL, is loaded with the necessary data, or an instruction. The **stack pointer** is initialised with the starting address of the stack. The process of putting data on the stack is called PUSH, and it is transferred two bytes at a time. A stack must be loaded from a register pair for this reason. The stack is formed by putting data in locations of addresses in *descending* order. The initial address in the stack pointer is therefore the highest address. The data are pushed with the most significant byte first, that is the contents of B register from a BC register pair. The least significant byte is then pushed. The stack pointer is *decreased* by 2, pointing to the next vacant location. In the diagram, register DE is then pushed

Push and pop with stack pointer, numbers and code in hexadecimal notation

Popping off a stack

Pushing into a stack

on the stack. Taking the data out is called POP, and the stack is popped from the bottom. The least significant byte comes out first, followed by the most significant byte. The stack pointer is *increased* by 2. The rule for stacked data is LIFO (**Last In First Out**). The last data byte in is the byte taken out.

Stacks are used for calculations as well as for machine code instructions. Some microcomputers reserve special areas of RAM for these stacks, so that there is no need to initialise the stack pointer, it needs only updating. A store of sixteen locations is usually sufficient for a calculation stack. The stack pointer is a 16-bit register to hold the RAM addresses. Each RAM location holds eight bits only, so two locations are needed to store data from a pair of registers.

The address and data control units

The data buffers and part of the memory control unit were included in the circuit of the instruction control unit. A further use of these devices and the memory address register (MAR) is shown in the simplified diagram of the address and data control units. The circuit is used for input by the keyboard and display on the VDU. The program counter (PC) is also used as it provides a location for each entry of a program in BASIC. Such programs usually start at a particular address in RAM, kept as a constant in the memory. The actual execution of entering a BASIC program will be discussed later. Before input starts, the

Simplified address and data control units

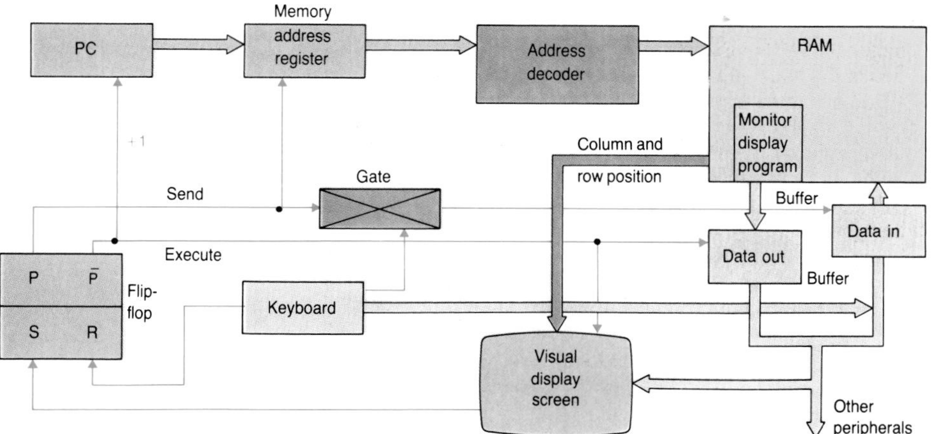

flip-flop is set, the PC stores the first program location, which is addressed to RAM. When a key is pressed to input data, the gate is opened, the data buffer is activated, and data enter the memory. At the same time the flip-flop is reset. In RAM there is a section dedicated to a monitor display program, which sends appropriate signals to the VDU. The execute signal activates the data buffer and the transfer to the VDU takes place. At the same time, there is stored in RAM a value for column and a value for row, these constituting a form of address for the monitor screen. This causes the VDU to display the input in a suitable place on the screen. When the display has been formed, an impulse sets the flip-flop, ready for the next cycle. The SEND and EXECUTE signals have to be correctly timed, so delays are built into the circuits to achieve this. The other peripherals will be discussed later, and more detail given of the circuits connecting peripherals to the computer.

Execution of programs

The program counter (PC) has been mentioned twice. The first mention was in connection with an instruction program. This program executed machine code instructions, which activated various parts of the CPU to carry out a program in a sequential order of the instructions, and could also execute branching programs. The input program for a microcomputer is written in another computer language, which, in this book, is BASIC. The BASIC program is stored in RAM, and examples of such storage are given on pages 60 to 61. The computer has a program stored in ROM (read only memory) which converts BASIC to machine code; this will be discussed in Chapter 9. The CPU thus has to operate two different types of program, each of which uses information which is stored or processed in a sequential fashion. The PC stores, in a section of RAM, the locations in other parts of RAM, the addresses of the start of these programs. The random access memory of a microcomputer is usually divided into various areas for keeping track of the different operations the CPU has to process. The division of RAM into these sections is shown by a **map**. Different computers have different ways of mapping RAM. It is useful to find out how any one particular microcomputer has its RAM mapped, particularly when peripheral devices, using programs addressed to particular areas of RAM, are added to the microcomputer.

Summary

A **central processing unit** consists of an instruction control unit, an address control unit, a data control unit, an arithmetic and logic unit and a bank of registers.

The **instruction control unit** consists of a program counter (PC), a stack pointer (SP), an instruction register and decoder, and a command control unit.

The **address control unit** consists of a memory address register (MAR) and an address decoder.

The **data control unit** consists of two data buffers, one for IN and one for OUT.

The **arithmetic and logic unit** (ALU) contains an **accumulator**, three arithmetic registers for ADD, SUBTRACT and SHIFT and three logic gates for AND, OR and COMPARE (CP).

The **register bank** contains B, C, D, E, H, L, X, Y registers which can operate singly or in pairs.

An 8-bit **highway** connects all parts of the CPU.

A **transistor** is formed from two p-type silicon pieces on either side of an n-type silicon piece. Transistors and other devices are integrated to form a circuit without connecting wires.

A **transistor** can be operated as a switch.

Logic gates are formed from combinations of transistors.

A **flip-flop** consists of two transistors; it can take either one of two possible stable states, identified as 1 or Ø and called **set** or **reset**.

Registers are usually made of flip-flops with one flip-flop for each bit held in the register. A register is cleared when it is reset to the value Ø for all bits in the register.

Transfer of data between registers is by parallel connections on a data bus.

The **ALU** has a results register which acts as a buffer.

The **accumulator** is used for complementing, incrementing, decrementing, shifting and for operations on one operand with any other gate holding the other operand in an arithmetic or logic process. The result of an operation is always put back in the accumulator.

The **logic gates** operate on all eight or sixteen bits of a byte at one and the same time.

The **ADD register** consists of half-adders and OR gates. There is a separate CARRY register of one bit.

The **SUBTRACT register** consists of half-subtractors and OR gates. Some computers use a complementing register and the ADD register for subtraction. There is a separate OVERFLOW register of one bit.

Status describes certain conditions used to determine the state of the computer generally, or the state of a particular device, for example is the accumulator holding a positive or a negative number, or is it holding zero.

A **command code** exhibits status for arithmetic or logic processes. The code is held in **program status bits**, and the **flag register** records status.

The **shift register** can shift left or shift right. The former process multiplies a number by 2 and the latter divides a number by 2, neglecting any remainder.

A **mask** is used to extract information from data; either an AND gate or an OR gate is used in conjunction with the mask.

Arithmetic processes are performed by a program using the ALU.

The **instruction control unit** has an 8-bit byte. Two bits control major instructions; a further three bits can be used to extend the instructions, or to address a register; the last three bits also either extend the instruction or address a register.

The **fetch cycle** for instructions uses the PC for a sequential list of instructions. The **fetch** cycle is: (1) activate and call instruction from RAM; (2) pass instruction to instruction buffer; (3) reset the flip-flop for execute.

The **execute cycle** for instructions is: (1) send an increment to PC; (2) send instructions to decoder; (3) send address to address decoder; (4) activate data buffer to send data to destination; (5) data destination sends impulse back to set flip-flop.

A **decoder** uses a combination of AND and NOT gates; it selects a direct connection to a device or to an address.

The **stack pointer** (SP) holds the address of the next empty location in RAM for a machine or calculator stack.

A **stack** is a series of data loaded sequentially, two bytes at a time, into RAM in descending sequential order of address; it is filled and emptied by the rule: **Last In First Out** (LIFO).

The **address amd data control units** use the PC to store a program in sequential locations in RAM. The SEND cycle takes information from the keyboard into RAM. The **execute** cycle sends data to the VDU for display. The two cycles are controlled by a flip-flop.

Execution of programs. The CPU, using the CP, operates (1) a BASIC program which is an INPUT to the computer; (2) a machine program using machine code which operates the machine.

CHAPTER 9

Machine code and machine code programs

The basic operations of a computer are controlled by a code, and as all computer operations depend on electronic circuits representing a binary system, the code has to be in binary notation. The design and architecture of a microcomputer depend on the size of a byte it will use in its operation. Most microcomputers at present use an 8-bit byte, so this will be considered as standard in the discussion of machine codes.

Machine code

Instructions for the operation of a microcomputer are coded in 8-bits, and every instruction constitutes just one operation. What does a microcomputer have to do with the information fed into it? Firstly, it must be able to move information from one part of the computer to another part. This will involve moving data from memory to the CPU (central processing unit) and back and also moving data round the CPU for processing. Secondly, it has to process arithmetical and logical operations in its ALU. Thirdly, it has to recognise elementary conditions and act upon the result. Fourthly, it has to be able to transfer data to and from peripheral devices, together with a few general commands such as stop, halt, or complement a number.

The format of a machine code

The format is the arrangement of information in a machine code. The 8-bit byte is divided into three **fields** consisting of two bits, three bits and three bits. The first two bits of an instruction are a command. The next three bits can be part of a command or part of an address to a register, and the last three bits can also be part of a command or part of an address. A command causes a microcomputer to perform a specific operation. The operations performed by a microcomputer can be classified into four groups, which would suit the four numbers available from a 2-bit code, that is ØØ, Ø1, 1Ø and 11. The groups are:

ØØ arithmetical and logical operations
Ø1 transfer of data between registers and memory
1Ø conditional operations dependent upon the results of other operations
11 unit arithmetic (e.g. increments, decrements, shift), input and output and a few general commands.

Operands

An **operand** is generally a number on which an arithmetical, mathematical or logical operation is performed. In the statement 6 add 9, 9 is an operand of the command 'add'. An operand can be any item of data stored in memory or temporarily stored in a register. Operands can be **immediate**, that is they are entered by the program, or they can be **stored**, that is located in memory.

Bytes and words

A byte is a number of consecutive binary digits treated as an entity, or single group, by the devices in a computer. Generally a byte is considered to consist of eight bits, particularly in microcomputers. In some operations, instructions are needed which consist of more than one byte. A 2-byte, 3-byte group of binary digits is generally called a **word**. A word is considered to be the largest group of bits that can be operated on by a CPU. The machine code instructions considered in this chapter will be of the following types: 1-byte instruction, 2-byte instruction, and 3-byte instruction.

Format of a machine code

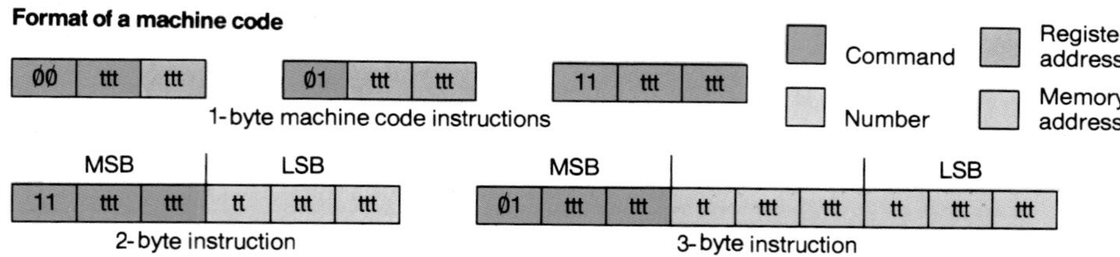

MSB = more/most significant byte LSB = less/least significant byte

The format of these instructions is illustrated in the diagram. There are four types of information displayed: (1) command instructions; (2) integer numbers which refer to program steps; (3) register addresses and (4) addresses in memory

(RAM). Refer to this diagram when considering other details of machine code which will be discussed later.

Registers

The machine code used as an example in this book is a simplified version of a machine code for an actual microcomputer. The code, and the CPU, are modelled on the Z-80 microprocessor, but the principles are applicable to other microprocessors using other machine codes. In this code, called machine code (Ex), the register address is contained in three bits, allowing for eight register addresses. These addresses are allocated as follows:

Register	*Code*	*Remarks*
B	001	8-bit register
C	010	8-bit register
D	011	8-bit register
E	100	8-bit register
BC	101	16-bit register from B and C combined
DE	110	16-bit register from D and E combined
A	111	8-bit accumulator
(DE)	000	16-bit register used for RAM addresses

Notice there is a difference between registers DE and (DE). The former is used as an ordinary 16-bit register for arithmetic or logic operations. The latter, (DE), is used to store an address (of sixteen bits) in RAM, and it refers to the data stored in the location of that address.

Addresses

The register addresses use three bits, so could be referred to by using octal notation (see p. 53). The memory addresses use sixteen bits and are best referred to in hexadecimal notation. Any integer used in the registers, programs, or data stored in memory will be recorded in eight bits, best described in hexadecimal. So the best notation to use would appear to be hexadecimal to describe all three addresses. However, the main aim of this chapter is to present the use of instruction commands, so the octal notation will be used for all addresses and data, as it is easier to handle only one notation. For 8-bit bytes, the octal system will be used with three fields for the eight bits, consisting of two, three, and three bits. A 16-bit RAM address will thus appear as RRRSSS, being octal numbers with RRR representing the **more significant byte** and SSS the **less significant byte**. The more significant byte contains the higher numbers.

Displacements

A displacement is an integer stating the number of steps in a program displaced from the step undergoing operation. For example, a program is at step 26, with an address in RAM of 000614 (octal). A displacement of +14 is made; the program jumps to step 40, which is in address 000614 + 14 = 630 (remember the notation is octal). Negative displacement can be used, causing the program to jump backwards.

Status

Status is tested as the state of the contents of the accumulator. Depending on the result, a program branches in one of two directions. The status of the accumulator can be: (1) zero; (2) non-zero; (3) positive and (4) negative. There are other tests of status employed by microprocessors, but in a simple scheme they are best omitted. The flag register (p. 130) is tested for status.

A specimen machine code

Machine code (Ex) will now be described in separate tables for each type of instruction. This code does not correspond to any one particular type of microprocessor, but is similar to the machine code for a Z-80 microprocessor. Each mircoprocessor using a Z-80 CPU chip uses machine code in a slightly different way to suit the architecture of the microcomputer. Determine the type of microprocessor used in your microcomputer and the machine code it employs, and find the correspondence between machine code (Ex) and the machine code you will have to use.

Arithmetic and logic operations

The instruction code for these operations is given in Table 1. The operation is given a three-figure **mnemonic** to

Table 1. The arithmetic and logic instructions

Operation	Code			Description
ADD	Ø	1	X	Add register X to accumulator
ADC	Ø	2	X	Add register X to ACC with carry
SUB	Ø	3	X	Subtract register X from accumulator
SBC	Ø	4	X	Subtract X from ACC with overflow
AND	Ø	5	X	Logic 'AND' for X and accumulator
OR	Ø	6	X	Logic 'OR' for X and accumulator
CP	Ø	7	X	Logic 'CP' for X and accumulator

X = address of register 1–7 for registers B to A Ø for (DE)
Result of operation put in accumulator

denote the operation. A **mnemonic** is a coded word which helps the human memory remember the meaning. For example SUB stands for subtract, easy to remember, while SBC stands for subtract with overflow, not so easy to remember, but when compared with ADC for add with carry, becomes more recognisable. All the codes have Ø for the first two bits, showing the instruction is for an arithmetic or logic operation. The next digit (in octal) describes the particular operation. The last digit describes the register used. Some typical operations will be, therefore:

Ø12 add the number stored in register C to the number in the accumulator and put the result in the accumulator.
Ø54 perform the logic operation AND on the contents of register D and the accumulator, and put the result in the accumulator.

As the accumulator is an 8-bit register, these operations can be carried out only with the registers B, C, D and E. The paired registers BC and DE compare only the less significant byte. This differs from normal practice where the accumulator can be paired with the flag register to make a 2-byte register for use with arithmetic and logic instructions. Remember that the machine code is written in octal.

Transfer of data

The general instruction code for these operations is given in Table 2, together with the mnemonic, LD, to describe

Table 2. The transfer instructions

Operation	Code			(RAM)		Description
LD Y, X	1	Y	X			Transfer data from reg. X into reg. Y
LD NN, A	1	Ø	7	N	N	Transfer data from ACC to RAM location
LD A, NN	1	7	Ø	N	N	Transfer data from RAM location to ACC
LD A, (DE)	1	Ø	Ø			Transfer data from location (DE) in RAM to ACC
LD (DE), A	1	7	7			Transfer data from ACC into RAM location (DE)

A is accumulator register
NN is a 2-byte instruction (16 bits)
X, Y are register addresses
(see Table 3)

transfer; LD stands for LOAD. The instruction mnemonic LD Y, X reads: load into register Y the contents of register X. The letters NN represent the two 8-bit bytes necessary to address a location in RAM. The instructions LDA, NN and LD NN, A are 3-byte instructions. In the instructions containing (DE), the (DE) register contains the sixteen bits for a RAM address. The symbol (DE) represents the DE paired register used for this purpose. The DE register can be loaded in the normal way, and then used as an addressing register; the different code for (DE) from that for DE alters the instruction and hence chooses a different circuit in the CPU. The register, X, Y, and (DE) instructions are single bytes.

The values that X and Y can take are given in Table 3. Examples of their use are:

Instruction	*Operation*
134	transfer the data in register E to register D
147	transfer the data in the accumulator to register D
165	transfer the data in register BC to register DE
177	transfer the data in the accumulator into the RAM location with address in (DE)
1ØØ	transfer the data in RAM location with address in (DE) into the accumulator

Remember that the data in a RAM location is contained in eight bits. The last two instructions are the general way of transferring data from RAM into the registers and vice versa.

Table 3. Register codes

Register	Octal code	Binary code
B	1	001
C	2	010
D	3	011
E	4	100
BC	5	101
DE	6	110
A	7	111
(DE)	Ø	000

Values for X and Y in transfer instructions

The conditional instructions

The status of the accumulator contents is described by the flag register. Conditions can be checked from these status flags. The conditions tested are: (1) zero; (2) non-zero; (3) positive and (4) negative. An unconditional jump can also be put in a program. These jumps specify an address in RAM where a branching program is followed. The address, NN, is given in two bytes and follows an unconditional or a conditional jump (*see Table 4*). With unconditional jumps, the address can be shown as a displacement, that is, it will give the number of RAM locations

Table 4. Condition codes

Octal code	Description	2nd or 3rd Byte
1	Unconditional	NN
2	Unconditional, displaced	d
3	Unconditional to (DE)	—
4	If zero	NN
5	If non zero	NN
6	If positive	NN
7	If negative	NN

Types of conditions
Code values of W in Table 5

above or below the location storing the jump instruction. Finally, an unconditional jump can be made to an address stored in the (DE) register.

There are two types of branching conditional programs, called **jump** and **call**. With jump, the program either goes to a new location if the condition is met, or goes to the next sequential step if not met. With call, the program does exactly the same, but can use the return instruction to return to the next sequential step after the call instruction. These instructions are illustrated below. The same instruction type must be used for call and return.

Table 5. Condition instructions

Operation	Octal code			Description
Jump	2	W	0	Jump to another step
Call	2	W	1	Jump to a subroutine
Return	2	W	2	Return from the 'call' subroutine
LD (SP), NN	2	Ø	Ø	N N Initialize SP with NN
Push BC	2	Ø	1	Put contents of BC on stack
Push DE	2	Ø	3	Put contents of DE on stack
Pop BC	2	Ø	5	Take contents of BC from stack
Pop DE	2	Ø	6	Take contents of DE from stack

The conditional instructions W code values in Table 4

The codes for conditional instructions are given in Table 5, with W codes – given in Table 4 – which specify the conditions. As the instructions are complicated, the full jump instructions are written out in Table 6. The corresponding call instructions are also given in the table, but not their codes. All codes are, of course, written in octal.

Table 6. Jump instructions

Instruction	Octal code			2nd, 3rd Byte	Description	Call instructions
JP, NN	2	1	Ø	N N	Jump to NN, unconditional	Call
JR, d	2	2	Ø	d	Jump d steps, unconditional	Call, d
JP, (DE)	2	3	Ø		Jump to address in (DE)	Call, (DE)
JPZ	2	4	Ø	N N	Jump to NN if zero	Call Z
JPNZ	2	5	Ø	N N	Jump to NN if non-zero	Call NZ
JPP	2	6	Ø	N N	Jump to NN if positive	Call P
JPM	2	7	Ø	N N	Jump to NN if minus (negative)	Call M

Jump instructions and corresponding call instructions NN is a 16-bit, address in RAM d is a displacement (−265 ∠ d ∠ +256) 15

Program RAM address	Instruction			Mnemonic	Data RAM address	Data	Comment
Ø2Ø 036	25Ø	020	152	JPNZ	—	—	Jump, if non-zero to LOC 020152
Ø2Ø 152	1 32	—	—	LD 3, 2	—	216	Transfer integer 142 d from reg. C into register D
Ø2Ø 153	Ø1 3	—	—	Add D	—	216	Add 142 d in register D to accumulator
ØØ1 255	17Ø	Ø30	156	LDA, Ø3Ø 156	Ø3Ø 156	127	Transfer 87 d in RAM to accumulator
ØØ2 346	221	Ø45	—	Call, Ø45	ØØ2 413	132	Uncond: jump to ØØ2413, obey 132

Table 7.
Data can be numbers or instructions

Using code instructions

By now there are a mass of figures to be considered, and programmers have many opportunities to be confused. To clarify the mixture of data, instructions, and numbers, a few specimen instructions are presented in Table 7. Explanations are as follows.

Instruction 25Ø. A jump instruction, with a word of three bytes. The program jumps, if the condition is met, to the instruction in location Ø2Ø152. The accumulator contains a number, either positive or negative, which is not zero.

Instruction 132. A transfer of data from register C to register D. The data in C is 216 octal which is 142 decimal. This number is now in both registers C and D.

Instruction Ø13. The contents of register D (216 octal or 142 decimal) is added to the contents of the accumulator, and the accumulator contains the result.

Instruction 17Ø. The contents of location Ø3Ø156 in RAM (127 octal or 87 decimal) is transferred to the accumulator. Both the accumulator and RAM now hold this number.

Instruction 221. The program is directed to a displaced location, found by adding Ø45 (octal) to ØØ2346. This is location ØØ2413 in RAM. This location ØØ2413 holds, as data, the number 132 (octal). This code, 132, becomes the next instruction in the branched program. After the sub-program is ended, the instruction RET, d will return the program to the instruction held in location ØØ2347, that is the next sequential instruction after ØØ2346. The number stored as data in a location can thus act as a pure number to take part in an arithmetical calculation, or it can be an instruction for the next step in a program.

Unit arithmetic, input and output, general commands

These last commands form the remainder necessary to complete the instructions to operate the CPU.

Table 8a. Unit arithmetic

Opera-tion	Code	2nd Byte	Description
INC X	31 X	—	Add 1 to register X
DEC X	32 X	—	Subtract 1 from register X
SLT, S	33 X	S	Shift register X to the left S bits
SRT, S	34 X	S	Shift register X to the right S bits
BIT, V	35 V	—	Test bit V in the accumulator. Result in FP

X = Address of register *(Table 3)*
V = Bit number *(Table 8b)*

Table 8b Bit code V

Bit number	Code
MSB 7	7
6	6
5	5
4	4
3	3
2	2
1	1
LSB ∅	∅

Unit arithmetic. These include the **increment** and **decrement** instructions, where 1 is added to, or subtracted from, a register. The register address, X, uses the same code as in previous instructions. Both 8-bit and 16-bit registers can hold the operand. The shift register (p. 130) is used for SLT and SRT instructions. The operand can be held in any register and can be shifted a given number of places, denoted by the number, 3, held in the second byte.

The bit test, mnemonic BIT, has a third octal digit to identify the bit under test. Table 8B gives the codes to identify the bit. The result of the test changes the flag register (FP) and the zero flag is either set or reset.

Input/output instructions. These instructions vary considerably from one computer to another; even those computers which use the same CPU chip can have considerably different instructions. A simple minimum code is given in Tables 9A and 9B to show the type of command. In the chapter describing input and output these commands will be clarified further.

Table 9a. Input/output instructions

Operation	Code	2nd Byte	3rd Byte	Description
In A, N	371	N	—	Store the integer, N, in the accumulator
Out A, P	372	P	Transfer contents of accumulator into peripheral device P	
In A, P	373	P	Transfer data from peripheral device P into accumulator	

P is code for peripheral device *(Table 9b)*
N is an integer number

Table 9b.

Peripheral device	Code	Description
VDU	001	Connects VDU and CPU
Status VDU	002	Tests readiness VDU
Printer	003	Connects line printer to CPU
Status printer	004	Tests readiness printer
Cassette	005	Connects cassette to CPU
Status cassette	006	Tests readiness cassette

Operation	Code	Description
JST	361	Jump to stop stops program
HLT	362	Stops microcomputer
CPL	363	Complement accumulator
NEG	364	Negative accumulator (true compl)
DAA	365	Decimal adjust accumulator changes binary to BCD use before transfer result
NOP	ØØØ	No operation
RET	366	Return returns machine code program to Basic program

Table 10. Miscellaneous instructions

General commands. The first two commands are concerned with stopping the CPU operating under different circumstances. JST is used at the end of a program. HLT is used at the end of a line of BASIC. This difference will be explained later.

The two complement commands allow both the one's complement and the true complement to be stored in the accumulator; no other register can be used for this purpose.

The DAA command changes the binary notation in an 8-bit byte into binary-coded decimal. It does this after an ADD or SUB command has been carried out. Carry and overflow commands can also be used.

NOP is a command frequently used to allow a delay in a program, a technique used when timing considerations are taken into effect. RET is a command indicating the end of a machine code program, as a CALL command has called the program.

Examples of machine code instructions

314 add 1 to register E
342, 1 shift register C one digit to the right
354 test bit 4 in accumulator; if zero, set the zero flag; if 1, reset the zero flag
371, 136 store the octal number 136 (114 decimal) in the accumulator
373, ØØ5 transfer the data from a cassette into the accumulator (this starts a transfer of more than one item. Note that commands such as 373,ØØ3 cannot exist; they can be written but not obeyed).
364 change accumulator to a true complement
Ø11 add data in register B to accumulator, answer in accumulator

These last two instructions amount to subtracting the accumulator from register B with the result in the accumulator. This is the reverse operation of SUB B. The first operation is B − A, the second is A − B.

Conversion of octal to hexadecimal

The following program converts an octal number to hexadecimal.

Program 9.1

```
5   REM    CONVERSION OCTAL TO HEXADECIMAL AND DECIMAL
10  INPUT  P$
20  LET    X = 16
30  LET    N = LEN(P$)
40  LET    Q = Ø
50  LET    R = Ø
60  LET    T = VAL SEG$ (P$, N – Q, 1)
70  LET    R = R + (T*(X/2) ↑ Q)
80  LET    Q = Q + 1
90  IF     N – Q = 0 THEN 110
100 GOTO   60
110 PRINT  R; "sp DEC."
120 LET    M = 0
130 LET    J = INT(R/X)
140 LET    K = X*J
150 LET    L = R–K
155 PRINT  AT 2,10
160 GOSUB  220
170 LET    R = J
180 IF     R = 0 THEN STOP
190 LET    M = M + 1
200 GOTO   130
210 PRINT
220 IF     L = 10 THEN PRINT TAB (10 – M); "A"
230 IF     L = 11 THEN PRINT TAB (10 – M); "B"
240 IF     L = 12 THEN PRINT TAB (10 – M); "C"
250 IF     L = 13 THEN PRINT TAB (10 – M); "D"
260 IF     L = 14 THEN PRINT TAB (10 – M); "E"
270 IF     L = 15 THEN PRINT TAB (10 – M); "F"
280 IF     L < 10 THEN PRINT TAB (10 – M); L
290 RETURN
```

Notes

(1) The use of X = 16 saves space in memory should it be needed, otherwise this step can be omitted, and the value X/2 made equal to 8.

(2) A further saving in space in memory can be made by using X – *X* instead of Ø and X/X instead of 1.

(3) Line 155 ensures the result is printed on one line; without it the digits each appear on a separate line on the VDU. If your computer does not have the statement PRINT AT, then a PRINT USING statement, if available, may be used.

Machine code programs

A simple program will be considered first using a restricted memory in a computer. The interaction between memory and program has to be considered and the stored data in the memory locations kept in view. In this program, therefore, the locations will be restricted to sixty-four in total, hence the addressing of memory will need only two digits in octal (100 is 64 in octal, and with 000 as a location, the highest address will be 77). Three digits, however, will be used to address a location. Two programs are required, one to load data and one to process data, and in that order. The data consists of five numbers, some of which will be used in arithmetical calculations.

Program 9.2 Loading data into memory

STEP	ADDRESS	INSTRUCTION		MNEMONIC	COMMENT
1	050	371,	018	IN A, N	Load 018 into Accumulator
2	052	107,	037	LD N, A	Transfer ACC to location 037
3	054	371,	021	IN A, N	Load 021 into ACC
4	056	107,	040	LD N, A	Transfer ACC to loc. 040
5	060	371,	031	IN A, N	Load 031 into ACC
6	062	107,	041	LD N, A	Transfer ACC to loc. 041
10	072				

Program 9.2, when run, loads five items of data into locations 037 to 043 inclusive. The state of the memory after the program has been loaded is shown in the diagram. The next program uses the data.

	040	050	060	070
0	0	371	371	371
1	0	018	031	012
2	0	107	107	107
3	0	037	041	043
4	0	371	371	
5	0	021	014	
4	0	107	107	
7	0	040	042	

State of RAM after loading Program 9.2

Program 9.3 is now entered in memory. The contents of locations 000 to 032 inclusive and 037 to 043 inclusive are shown in the diagram. The computer is now ready to run the machine code program. The comments describe the results of each instruction. The instructions indicate whether a code is for a command or for an address. Remember that a location in RAM stores an 8-bit byte, so instructions with an address need two locations (in use with a normal RAM, instructions will need only three bytes). The program is now followed through watching the change in contents of the registers (accumulator, B and C) and memory locations 41 and 43. The final result is a display of the number, 46, on the VDU.

Looking at the contents of the locations in RAM, it is not possible to say whether a bit pattern represents a command, an address or an item of data. If a computer does not

000	010	020	030	040
170	170	011	372	021
043	039	107	001	031
117	127	041	361	014
170	170	032		012
040	041	270		
011	117	033		
107	170	372		
043	043	002	018	

State of RAM after loading Program 9.3

Step	Accumulator	Location 041	Location 043	Register B	Register C
1	012	031	012	0	0
2	012	031	012	012	0
3	021	031	012	012	0
4	033	031	012	012	0
5	033	031	033	012	0
6	018	031	033	012	0
7	018	031	033	012	018
8	031	031	033	012	018
9	031	064	033	031	018
10	033	064	033	031	018
11	064	064	033	031	018
12	064	064	033	031	018
13	046	064	033	031	018
14	046	064	033	031	018
15	046	064	033	031	018
16	046	064	033	031	018

The contents of locations 41 and 43 and of registers A, B, C

follow instructions as given in a program, it, too, would not be able to distinguish the meanings of the numbers. It can be seen that it is relatively easy to become confused over the meaning in code, or otherwise, of any one item in a location.

rogram 9.3 An arithmetical program (machine code)

TEP	ADDRESS	INSTRUCTION		MNEMONIC	COMMENT
1	000	170	043	LD A, N	Transfer location 43 to ACC
2	002	117		LD B, A	Transfer ACC to Reg. B
3	003	170	040	LD A, N	Transfer location 40 to ACC
4	005	011		ADD B	Add Reg. B to ACC, result in ACC
5	006	107	043	LD N, A	Transfer ACC to location 43
6	010	170	037	LD A, N	Transfer location 37 to ACC
7	012	127		LD C, A	Transfer ACC to Reg. C
8	013	170	041	LD A, N	Transfer location 41 to ACC
9	015	117		LD B, A	Transfer ACC to Reg. B
10	016	170	043	LD A, N	Transfer location 43 to ACC
11	020	011		ADD B	Add Reg. B to ACC, result in ACC
12	021	107	041	LD N, A	Transfer ACC to location 41
13	023	032		SUB C	Subtract Reg. C from ACC, result in ACC
14	024	270	033	JPM	Jump if negative to location 023
15	026	372	002	OUT A, P	Test VDU ready
16	030	372	001	OUT A, P	Print on VDU: 46
17	032	361		JST	Jump to stop

Use of registers in display on VDU

Some machine codes use a specific register for display on a VDU. This, for the purposes of this book, will be taken to be the register-pair BC, and any data stored in this register pair will be displayed by the BASIC command PRINT USR on the VDU or monitor. The command, USR, will be discussed shortly. Different microprocessors in different microcomputers may use different registers for this purpose, but the pair, BC, is in common use. A program is given on p. 153 that displays on the VDU from the register-pair BC. Use the mnemonics in the program to alter the machine code to that used by your computer and then run the program to see the result.

Loading a machine code program

Before a program can be given for testing purposes, a way of loading such a program is necessary. The machine code has been given in octal notation, but a microcomputer accepts only decimal notation. The octal machine instructions have to be converted to decimal. To avoid confusion over the meaning of a number, decimal numbers will have the letter, d, after them, and octal numbers, the letter, c. The BASIC statement, ASC, prints the ASCII code for a character. e.g. PRINT ASC (A$) produces 49 for the figure 1 and 66 for the letter B when A$ = 1 and B respectively. ASC operates on strings, hence the input has to be a string variable, e.g. A$. An octal number, for example 243, is equal to $(2 \times 64) + (4 \times 8) + 3 = 163$ decimal, that is 243c ≡ 163d. Now let A$ = 243c, and represent this in ASCII code numbers before converting to decimal. The ASCII code for 2 is 50, for 4 is 52 and for 3 is 51. The converted number becomes $(50 \times 64) + (52 \times 8) + 51 = 3667$. Now $3667 - 3504 = 163$. How can the subtraction of 3504 be justified? It comes from the fact that all ASCII codes representing figures are greater than the figure by 48 (48 is the value for Ø on the ASCII code). So, we have $(48 \times 64) + (48 \times 8) + 48$ is the ASCII code value of ØØØ; it is $3072 + 384 + 48 = 3504$. So to convert a 3-digit octal number to decimal, we have:

decimal number = 64*ASC(A$) + 8*ASC(SEG$(A$,2,1)) + ASC (SEG$(A$,3,1)) − 3504

The ASC statement prints the code for only the first character in a string, so ASC(A$) produces the first number in the string.

The next question is where to put the machine code so that is does not interfere with other parts of memory. Your manual may help with this. If it does not, then try a location seventy-eight locations below the upper RAM limit. For the purposes of this chapter, the memory used with machine code (Ex) will be extended to 256 locations, that is ØØØ to 377c, and programs will be loaded into locations 3ØØc to 377c, giving 63d locations.

The next command to be considered in BASIC is POKE, which enters data into a numbered location. A program to load octal machine code can now be written; it will be called Octaload.

Program 9.4A Octaload

5	REM	LOADING MACHINE CODE IN OCTAL
10	LET	X = 3ØØc
20	INPUT	A$
30	IF	A$ = "S" THEN STOP
40	POKE	X,64*ASC(A$) + 8*ASC(SEG$(A$,2,1)) + ASC(SEG$(A$,3,1)) − 3504
50	LET	X = X + 1
60	GOTO	20

RUN this program and when in command mode, load in machine code in octal.

Notes

(1) X chosen at 3ØØc which allows 63d locations before 255 (the small memory used for the examples). The decimal equivalent of 3ØØc is 192d.

(2) Line 30 stops the input of machine code by inputting "S".

(3) Line 40 converts the octal code to decimal for use by the machine. If instructions were written in hexadecimal, then addresses and commands would have to be converted to decimal. To do this, line 40 would be changed to:

40 POKE X, 16*ASC(A$) + ASC(SEG$(A$,2,1)) − 816
and the value of X would be 4Ø.

The machine code program to be loaded into the following BASIC program subtracts one number from another and prints the result.

Program 9.4 Program for subtraction (machine code)

STEP	ADDRESS	INSTRUCTION		MNEMONIC	COMMENT
1	300 c	371	020	IN A, P	P = 16, loaded into ACC
2	302	137		LD D, A	Put P in Reg. D from ACC
3	303	371	030	IN A, Q	Q = 24, loaded into ACC
4	305	033		SUB D	Subtract Reg. D from ACC
5	306	127		LD C, A	Result in ACC transfer to Reg. C
6	307	371	000	IN A, 0	Load 0 into ACC
7	311	117		LD B, A	Transfer 0 to Reg. B
8	312	366		RET	End of machine code program
9	–	"S"			Ends BASIC program

Continuation of program

(1) The input of "S" causes a 'stop' notice on the VDU.
(2) Type: PRINT USE 192 (decimal number).
(3) RUN The VDU displays '8' the result of the subtraction.

Notes on program

(1) Note that each address is for one location and holds an 8-bit byte, so if a step has a 2-byte instruction, the next step is two locations further on.
(2) Step 8 with the command RET puts the machine program back to the BASIC program. Any input after RET is not part of the machine code program but would be part of the BASIC program.
(3) Step 9 uses an input of "S" to stop the BASIC program.
(4) The statement USR directs the microprocessor to the machine code at its starting address of 192d, which is 300c. The address after USR must be in decimal.
(5) All machine code programs must end with a RET instruction. The input of "S" for the BASIC was an arbitrary choice, useful as S is used to STOP.
(6) The machine code program ends with the result in the register-pair BC and the result is printed. If the result is in the accumulator or in the register-pair DE, no result is printed unless an OUT instruction is used with the accumulator and a peripheral address. The accumulator supplies data for the use of peripheral devices, and the register-pair for the VDU without further instruction. This type of command is used by the Z-80. Check such use in your instruction manual. If no information is given, try loading the result into different registers and use PRINT USR to see the effect. Steps 5 and 7 need alteration for this trial.

Storing machine code programs

The first method of storing machine code programs is the use of the top end of RAM, as just described in the last two programs. Another way is to use REM statements to store code. To do this the memory map of the microcomputer must be known, that is where does the microprocessor store a program. For the following examples, it will be assumed that BASIC programs are stored at a starting location of 101 decimal. The RAM uses two locations for line number, two locations for length of line and one location for the statement (see p. 61), that is five locations in all; so the first location used by the REM message will be 106 decimal, that is five locations further on from the starting location. When the starting location of program storage in RAM is known, then 5 is added to it, in decimal, and starting there, the machine code program can be stored. The REM statement must contain enough characters to allow one location for each byte of code. This is best counted by an input of: 123456789012 . . . . . to count the locations. The machine code program for the subtraction of P − Q is as follows.

Program 9.5 Continuous program for subtraction

ADDRESS		INSTRUCTION		MNEMONIC	COMMENTS
DEC.	OCTAL				
106	152	371	000	IN A, 0	Q = 0 Q IN ACCUMULATOR
108	154	147		LD E, A	Q IN REG. E
109	155	371	000	IN A, 0	P = 0 P IN ACCUMULATOR
111	157	044		SBC E	Subtract Reg. E from ACC. Result in ACC
112	160	127		LD C, A	P − Q in Reg. C
113	161	371	000	IN A, 0	Reset ACC
115	163	117		LD B, A	0 in Reg. B. (P − Q) in Reg. BC
116	164	366		RET	End of machine code program

The procedure is as follows:

(1) Type out Octaload program, putting X = 152c (= 106d).

(2) Type in REM statement; eleven locations are needed for program 9.5, so type in line 1 as follows: 1 REM 01234567890l

(3) Type in machine code program (program 9.5). The first byte is loaded in location 152c which is 106d, that is the first byte after the location storing REM. End the program with "S".

(4) Check the program by the command LIST, which will display the whole program. The REM statement will have been replaced by characters, signs, graphic signs, etc., representing the ASCII equivalents of the machine code numbers. Check that line 10 of the Octaload program still exists.

(5) Type RUN. The result should be Ø if the program has been entered correctly, as P = Q = 0, so P − Q = 0.

(6) LIST the program and delete lines 10-60 inclusive taking care to leave line 1 REM statement; this leaves the machine code program and deletes the Octaload program.

(7) Now enter the next program, 9.6.

Program 9.6

```
 5  REM     SUBTRACTING Q FROM P
 7  PRINT   "sp P"; TAB (11); "Q"; TAB (21); "P − Q"
10  INPUT   P  (Ø≤ P < 256)
20  INPUT   Q  (Ø≤ P < 256)
30  POKE    1Ø7, Q
40  POKE    11Ø, P
50  PRINT   A; TAB (10); B;
55  LET     X = USR (106)
60  PRINT   TAB (20); X
70  PRINT
80  GOTO    10
```

Results

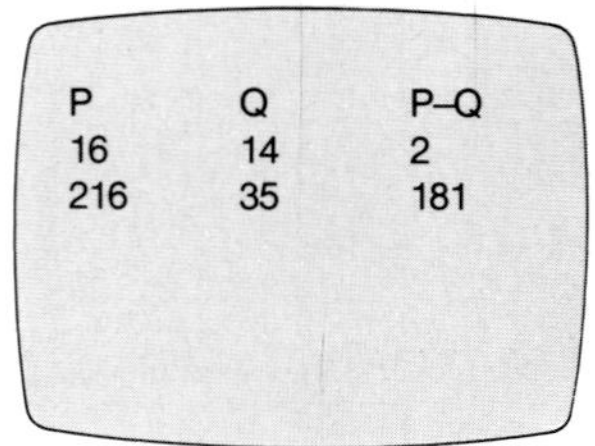

The memory now holds the machine code program and the new BASIC program.

(8) Type RUN. In the command mode, input P and then Q. Typical results are shown in the diagram.

(9) As single byte data have been used, the values of P and Q must be less than 256. Negative numbers may be used. Try a value of Q greater than P. The result should be the negative number added to 256, as there is an overflow and the machine code program has not taken an overflow into account. It will be observed in the flag register, but no action taken on it.

Other arithmetical calculations

Multiplication in a microcomputer is carried out by a subroutine program, called from ROM. The program opposite illustrates the principles on which the program works, although it is a much simpler version than an actual program.

The effect on each register of calculating 16 × 13 is shown in the diagram. The binary calculation is shown here:

1ØØØØ	(16)	(multiplicand)
× 11Ø1	(13)	(multiplier)
1ØØØØ	(16)	
1ØØØØØØ	(64)	
1ØØØØØØØ	(128)	
11Ø1ØØØØ	(208)	(product)

Inst. address	ACC	Reg B	Reg C	Reg D	Reg E	Comment	
205–210	Ø	Ø	Ø	—	—	Initialize registers B, C	Start of Program
211–216	13	Ø	Ø	13	16	Load data	
217	?13	Ø	Ø	13	16	Bit(Ø) = Ø?	NO →
222	16	Ø	Ø	13	16		
223	16	Ø	Ø	13	16	16 + Ø = 16	CYCLE
224	16	Ø	16	13	16	Sum in C	FOR
225	16	Ø	16	6	16	Divide D/2	BIT(Ø) = 1
227	16	Ø	16	6	32	Multiply 2 × E	
231	6	Ø	16	6	32		
232	?6	Ø	16	6	32	Multiplier = Ø?	NO ←
217	?6	Ø	16	6	32	Bit(Ø) = Ø?	YES →

Inst. address	ACC	Reg B	Reg C	Reg D	Reg E	Comment	
225	6	Ø	16	3	32	Divided/2	CYCLE
227	6	Ø	16	3	64	Multiply 2 × E	FOR
231	3	Ø	16	3	64		BIT(Ø) = Ø
232	?3	Ø	16	3	64	Multiplier = Ø?	NO ←
217	?3	Ø	16	3	64	Bit(Ø) = Ø?	NO →
222	64	Ø	16	3	64		
223	80	Ø	16	3	64	16 + 64 = 8Ø	
224	80	Ø	80	3	64	Sum in C	CYCLE
225	80	Ø	80	1	64	Divide D/2	FOR
227	80	Ø	80	1	128	Multiply 2 × E	BIT(Ø) = 1
231	1	Ø	80	1	128		
232	?1	Ø	80	1	128	Multiplier = Ø?	NO ←
217	?1	Ø	80	1	128	Bit(Ø) = Ø?	NO →

Multiplying 16 x 13

This calculation is performed by: (*a*) testing whether there is a 1 or Ø in the end digit of the multiplier; (*b*) if there is a 1, the value of the multiplicand in the register is added to a cumulative total. (*c*) the multiplier is shifted right, and the next end digit tested. (*d*) the multiplicand is shifted left and Ø added. The final result is obtained by adding 16 + 64 + 128 in the cumulative register.

Program 9.7

A simple multiplication program

ADDRESS		INSTRUCTION		MNEMONIC	COMMENT
OCTAL	DEC.				
205	133	371	ØØØ	IN A, N	Load Ø in ACC
207	135	117		LD B, A	Transfer Ø to Reg. B
210	136	127		LD C, A	Transfer Ø to Reg. C
211	137	17Ø	212	LD A, N	Transfer location 212 to ACC (P)
213	139	147		LD E, A	Transfer location P to Reg. E
214	140	17Ø	215	LD A, N	Transfer location 215c to ACC (Q)
216	142	137		LD D, A	Transfer location Q to Reg. D
217	143	35Ø		BIT, V	Test bit Ø in ACC
220	144	24Ø	225	JPZ, N	If bit Ø is zero, jump to loc. 225c
222	146	174		LD A, E	Transfer location P to ACC
223	147	Ø12		ADD C	Ø + P in ACC
224	148	127		LD C, A	+P in ACC
225	149	343	ØØ1	SRT D, S	Divide Reg. D by 2
227	151	334	ØØ1	SLT E, S	Multiply Reg. E by 2
231	153	173		LD A, D	Transfer Reg. D to ACC
232	154	24Ø	236	JPZ, N	If ACC is zero, jump to 236c
234	156	21Ø	217	JP, N	Jump to 217c
236	158	366		RET	Return to BASIC program

Division by a machine program

This is best demonstrated by a specific example, for example 63 ÷ 7. The dividend (63) is put in the D register and the divisor (7) in the E register. Both registers are tested, through the accumulator, to find the most significant bit, that is the bit containing 1 for the greatest digit value. For 63 this is bit 5, for 7 this is bit 2. The E register is now shifted left until the most significant bits in registers D and E occupy the same position (bit 5). Register E is now subtracted from register D. It is assumed the result is positive, that is it can be subtracted. Register C is incremented (+1). The result of the subtraction is tested. If positive, then on to the next step. If negative, then E is added back to D, and register C is decremented (−1) and on to the next step. In the next step, register D is shifted right, one digit, and register C is shifted left one digit. The process is then repeated until the divisor is reduced to zero (tested to end program). The quotient is now in register C and the remainder left in register D.

Try to write a machine code program from this description of division.

Summary

Macine code is written bytes of eight bits.

The **format** of machine code is the arrangement of a byte into three fields of two bits, three bits and three bits and with two bits as the most significant bits.

An **operand** is generally a number on which a mathematical or logical operation is performed.

A **word** consists of two or more bytes.

Each **register** has a code, consisting of three bits. A register enclosed in brackets represents an address, e.g. (DE) holds an address.

Memory addresses normally use two bytes (gives 65536 or 64K locations).

A **displacement** is a number of steps by which a program address is displaced.

Status indicates the state of the contents of the accumulator. There are four main groups of **machine code instructions**: (1) arithmetic and logic operations; (2) transfer of data; (3) conditional instructions and (4) unit arithmetic, input and output and general commands.

A machine code **program** is stored in consecutive addresses, one byte in a locatioin.

A **loading program** is needed for machine code. In practical microcomputers it is written for a hexadecimal input.

A **machine code program** can be loaded in two ways: (*a*) starting approximately eighty locations below the highest available RAM address; (*b*) in a REM statement stored at the start of the RAM section devoted to BASIC programs.

For a **continuous program** to be entered on a home computer, a BASIC program is needed to operate a machine code program. The BASIC program provides the input and the PRINT instruction; the machine code program provides the operation. Some manufacturers' programs, such as those for games and word processors, use only machine code for speed.

CHAPTER 10

Computer languages

All microcomputers, through their CPU, use machine code to carry out all operations. Machine code is suited to the operations, but requires a considerable effort on the part of the programmer to produce a program, as he has to interpret the meaning of the binary numbers. Writing the numbers in hexadecimal or octal notation makes the task slightly easier, but is not a considerable help.

Mnemonics

The use of mnemonics, described in the previous chapter, reminds the programmer of the meaning of the machine code numbers. The machine code is called an **object code**, that is, the final objective to be produced by the programmer. The mnemonics form a **machine language**, because the meaning of a word, such as ADD, is much clearer than the code, ØØ, for the word.

Machine code programs

A program in code refers to specific locations in memory and specific registers, so the programmer has to keep track of the locations used, particularly if the number of bytes in the program has to be counted for operations such as looping or branching. Once a machine code program has been written, any alteration causing a displacement of instructions, and hence locations, can lead to confusion. The early computers all had to be programmed in machine code, so programmers looked for a way out of this difficulty and the first result was a symbolic or **source language,** which, in fact, is an assembly language.

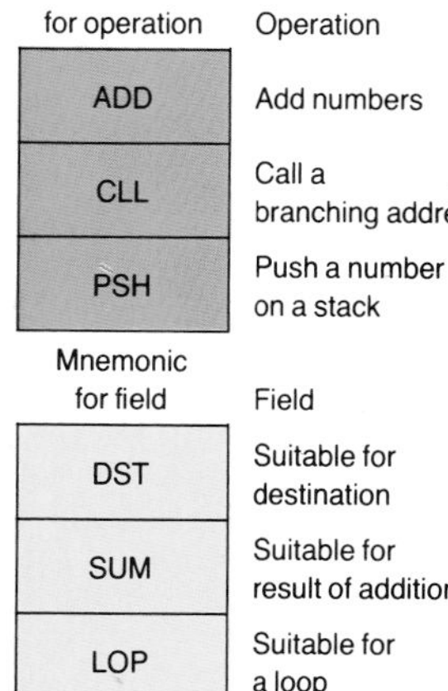

Examples of 3-letter mnemonics

Assembly languages

Different computers use different assembly languages, but all have characteristics in common. Firstly, they have letter codes which are mnemonics for an operation, that is, the operation can be recognised from the word. Examples are given in the diagram.

Each mnemonic for an operation has three letters, and only three letters. Another mnemonic describes a field. A field is a particular section of a program, for example a loop is a program section and the loop is described by a field mnemonic. Other fields indicate the aim of the program, for example DESTINATION indicates the final result required, and can be given a mnemonic such as DST.

Symbolic addressing

The computer itself determines the location of data in memory, and for this it requires a symbolic address, designated, that is described, by a three-character symbol. A common convention is that the first character must be a letter and the other two characters can be figures or letters. Other conventions allow one, two or three characters to designate an address, but the first must always be a letter. A symbolic address overcomes the difficulty of having to keep track of the locations storing particular data. There are three different ways of using symbolic addresses; they are indicated by a letter, or a blank:

- I indirect address, with the address represented by a reference mnemonic; data transferred.
- H indexed address. displacement of an address contained in an address register; data transferred.
- – the address is transferred and not the data in the addressed location.

Immediate operands

An immediate operand is a number or a letter. It is indicated by a letter, such as M. If it is a number, it is written in decimal notation and a plus or minus sign written in front. This is called a **signed** number. There are other conventions for the use of hexadecimal or other notations, but decimal notation is the easiest to use, and is generally used for numeric data in assembly languages.

Letters are enclosed in slashes, /, e.g. /B/.

The format of an assembly language instruction

Different computers use different formats, so a representative format will be used; if you have any reference to

Example of an assembly language instruction

Instruction. Add the number 43506 to the accumulator

: Add the number in address **SUM** to the accumulator

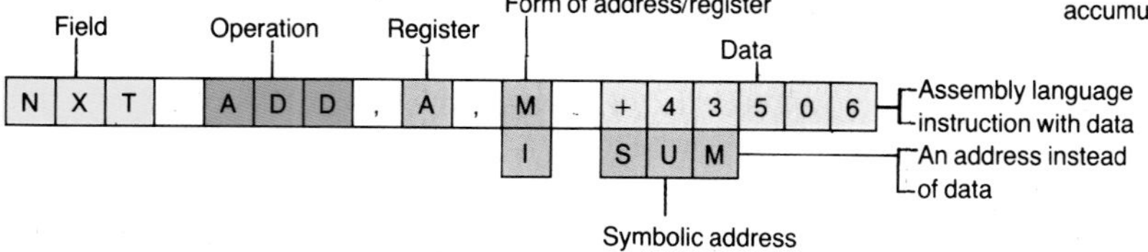

assembly language for your computer, check the format, codes, and method of use. An instruction format has a fixed length. The example of assembly language for this book uses a length of eighteen characters. The first three characters are reserved for the field label, a mnemonic of up to three characters, chosen by the programmer as a suitable reminder. A space separates the field label from the operation code, always a three-letter mnemonic. A comma separates the operation code from a letter for a register. Another comma separates this register code from a second register code or a letter showing the method of addressing (I or H; or M for an immediate operand). A space separates this second letter from the data or symbolic address. This particular format allows six places for characters in data or addresses. The format must be followed strictly, otherwise the place values will be confused by the computer.

Directives

These codes are used in connection with the addressing system; each consists of a 3-letter code. A representative selection is:

BYT	reserves one byte in RAM
WOD	reserves two bytes (one word) in RAM
DFB	defines one byte by giving it an absolute address (i.e. a numbered location)
DFW	defines one word (two bytes) by giving it an absolute address
DFS,n	defines *n* bytes needed for a program
END	the end of a program
RST	restore to main, or other, program

Directives are written before the assembly language program to allocate or to reserve space in RAM for specific variables or particular sections of the program. END and RST obviously come at the end of a program.

Examples of the use of directives

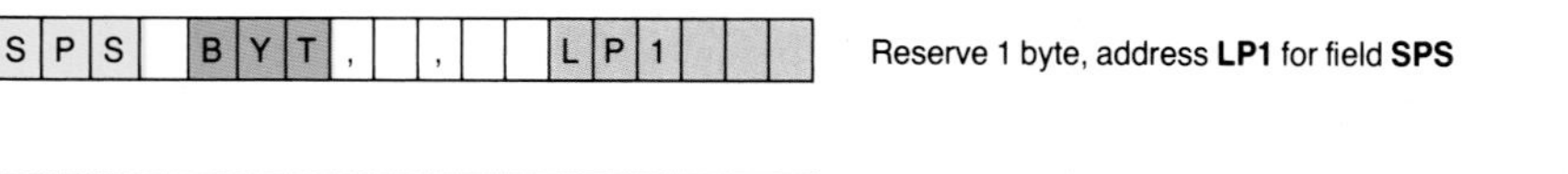

Reserve 1 byte, address **LP1** for field **SPS**

Store the constant 3685 for the field **NPT** (one word)

Reserve one word, address 2C3A (hex) for the field **SUM**

Assembly language operations

Many of the mnemonics used for machine code can be adapted without alteration to assembly language, providing they consist of three letters. Those that require alteration are given in the diagram. A label is also given for the registers and register-pairs, corresponding to their use in machine code.

Machine code	Assembly language	Description	Corresponding call and return operations	
LDNN, A	LDM	Transfer data from ACC to RAM location		
LDA, NN	LDA	Transfer data from RAM location to ACC		
LDA, (DE)	LDC	Transfer data from location (DE) to ACC		
LD (DE), A	LDR	Transfer data from ACC to LOC (DE)		
JP, NN	JPA	Unconditional jump to symbolic ADD	CLA	RTA
JR, d	JPD	Unconditional jump to indexed address, d	CLD	RTD
JP, (DE)	JPA	Unconditional jump to indexed address (DE)	CLH	RTH
JPZ	JPZ	Jump if zero	CLZ	RTZ
JPNZ	JPN	Jump if non-zero	CLN	RTN
JPP	JPP	Jump if positive	CLP	RTP
JPM	JPM	Jump if negative	CLM	RTM
OR	ORR			
CP	CPP			
LD	LOD			
PUSH	PSH			
IN	INN			
CALL	CLL			
RET	RET, Ø			

Register	Label	Register	Label
B	B	ACC	A
C	C	BC	X
D	D	DE	Y
E	E	(DE)	Z

Assembly language operations and registers

A program is written with comments, where necessary, to indicate what the program is actually doing and also to keep track of the operations. Each line of the program occupies eighteen places, but the blank spaces are left out of a written program. Specimen lines in assembly language are as follows:

```
LOP  LDC, A, Z      ; field LOP, has data in register (DE)
                      transferred to accumulator
     LOD, Y, I SCE  ; store address of location SCE in
                      register DE
DST  DFW   0400h    ; field DST, has initial address in loca-
                      tion 0400h, i.e. an absolute address
     DEC, A,          subtract 1 from accumulator
     SLA, A, N +2   ; shift accumulator two places left
     JPA,  ,  NXT   ; unconditional jump to field labelled
                    ; NXT
```

The three-letter mnemonics and single letters for registers

and address methods are printed with capital letters. The semicolon (;) shows that the comments that follow are to be ignored in the program.

Transfer of data

In machine code (Ex), all data from memory had to be transferred to the CPU through the accumulator; this allowed only one byte to be transferred at a time. With the directives, a word can be assigned and transferred, so either the accumulator has to be enlarged to sixteen bits, or other registers have to be used. In many microcomputers either the accumulator can hold sixteen bits of data, or else it is paired with another 8-bit register. For the purpose of this book, transfer of data will be allowed into the register-pairs BC (label X) and DE (label Y) with (DE) having the label Z.

Transfer of information by assembly language

Field	Operation	Register/ form of ADD				Address data	Description
	LDA	,	A	,	I	NXT	; Transfer data from RAM location labelled NXT to ACCUMULATOR
	LDM	,	A	,	I	NXT	; Transfer data from ACCUMULATOR to RAM location labelled NXT
	LDC	,	A	,	Z		; Transfer data from RAM location held in (DE) to ACCUMULATOR
	LDR	,	A	,	Z		; Transfer data from ACCUMULATOR to RAM location held in (DE)
	LDM	,	A	,	H	CHS	; Transfer data from ACCUMULATOR to location held in (CHS + H)
	INN	,	A	,	M	+206	; Load ACCUMULATOR with number immediately (+206 in ACC)
	INN	,	A	,	M	/K/	; Load ACCUMULATOR with letter immediately (K in ACC)
	INN	,	A	,	M	/9/	; Load ACCUMULATOR with character code immediately (code for 9 in ACC)
	INN	,	Y	,		NXT	; Load current address of NXT into register DE
	OUT	,	Y	,		NXT	; Load current address in register Y into word labelled NXT
	INN	,	T	,		P04	; Transfer data from peripheral device 04 into ACCUMULATOR
	OUT	,	T	,		P06	; Transfer data from ACCUMULATOR into peripheral device 06
	CLL	,		,		PRN	; Print contents of register – pair BC

The various methods by which instructions, that is data and addresses, can be moved by the use of assembly language are shown in the table. Examples of indirect and indexed addresses are given together with the transfer of immediate operands. Instructions for printing and the use of peripheral devices are included. If the method of addressing is left blank, then the address is transferred and not the data in the address. Addresses are transferred by the operations INN and OUT. The instructions INN and OUT can be used with register-pairs BC and DE to transfer

2-byte data from or to memory. Notice the difference in the instructions:

INN, Y, NXT ; load current address of NXT into register-pair DE

INN, Y, I NXT ; load data in RAM location NXT into register-pair DE. (NXT will be defined as 2-bytes with the most significant byte first).

Operations with assembly language

The operations have been described in the table in the diagram. Examples of their use are given in the diagram below. When writing the programs, the spacing observed in the diagram must be maintained, that is eighteen spaces for each instruction, as the instructions are not numbered.

Field	Operation	Register/ form of ADD				Address data	Description
	ADD	,	A	,	B		; Add data in register B to ACCUMULATOR result in ACCUMULATOR
	SUB	,	A	,	M	+18	; Subtract 16 from ACCUMULATOR result in ACCUMULATOR
	ADD	,	A	,	I	NXT	; Add data in RAM location NXT to ACCUMULATOR result in ACCUMULATOR
	CLZ	,		,		CHS	; Jump to location in RAM, labelled CHS if ACCUMULATOR is zero
	JPD	,		,	M	+16	; Unconditional jump 16 locations forward
	PSH	,	Y	,			; Push data in register-pair DE onto stack
	LOD	,	C	,	B		; Transfer data from register B to register C
	BIT	,		,	M	+0 to 7	; Test bit 0–7, as addressed, in ACCUMULATOR

Operations by assembly language

Symbolic and other addresses

The initial part of a program uses directives to reserve space in RAM for the rest of the program. Usually the reserved locations are filled with data that changes during the course of the program, so only the original bytes are needed for storage. If the location is going to change during the program, because a succession of data will be stored in sequential addresses, then this is effected by using the register (DE) and the original location retains the original data. This original location can be assigned an

Field	Operation	Register/ form of ADD				Address data	Description
CHR	BYT	,		,			; Reserve 1 byte for field **CHR**
POR	BYT	,		,		LEA	; Reserve 1 byte for field **POR**, starting address **LEA**
NPT	DFB	,		,		0604h	; Reserve location 0604h for field **NPT**
	INN	,	X	,		CHR	; Transfer address of **CHR** to register-pair BC
	INN	,	X	,	H	+14	; Add displacement of 14 forward to address of **CHR**, from previous operation
	INN	,	Z	,		POR	; Store address of **POR** in register (DE)
	INN	,	Y	,	I	POR	; Transfer data from RAM location **POR** into register - pair DE
	LDA	,	A	,	H	CHR	; Transfer data from RAM location (**CHR+14**) in ACCUMULATOR
	LDA	,	A	,	Z		; Transfer data from RAM location stored in register (DE) into ACCUMULATOR
	LDA	,	A	,	I	NPT	; Transfer data from location 0604h into ACCUMULATOR

Using symbolic and other addresses

original address, capable of symbolic reference during the program. The various aspects of symbolic addressing are illustrated in the table. Indirect addressing, using the method labelled I, is the most common form of addressing. Displacing the address by a number of bytes, represented by H, allows the original and the indexed address to be used. An indexed address uses the register-pair BC to contain the index under reference Z; this index may be constant or may change.

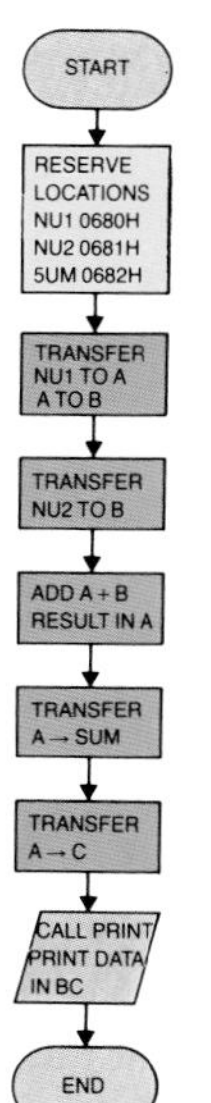

Flow chart for addition of two numbers

Assembly language programs

The first program is a simple one for the addition of two numbers. The RAM locations for this program are assigned absolute addresses. A flowchart for the process is drawn so that the program can be planned. The data in the locations must be put in the correct registers for addition, and then the answer taken from the accumulator and stored in RAM. Finally the result has to be printed on the VDU.

The program is drawn up using the information from the flowchart. The symbolic addresses, NU1 and NU2, are labels for the two numbers for addition, and are suitable reminders. SUM, similarly, is a suitable label for the answer. These symbolic addresses are used to transfer the data from memory and back to memory. A printed program would be spaced in the same way as in the diagram (without coloured backgrounds). The program differs from a machine code program in that the first three lines define the locations used for the program; in a machine code program the locations would be inserted in the program where needed.

NU1	DFB	,		,		0680h	; Reserve location 0680h for NU1
NU2	DFB	,		,		0681h	; Reserve location 0681h for NU2
SUM	DFB	,		,		0682h	; Reserve location 0682h for SUM
Start of program							
	LDA	,	A	,	I	NU1	; Transfer number in 0680h to ACCUMULATOR
	LOD	,	B	,	A		; Transfer number in ACCUMULATOR to register B
	LDA	,	A	,	I	NU2	; Transfer number in 0681h to ACCUMULATOR
	ADD	,	A	,	B		; Add two numbers result in ACCUMULATOR
	LDM	,	A	,	I	SUM	; Transfer answer to 0682h
	LOD	,	C	,	A		; Transfer answer to register C answer in register pair BC
	CLL					PRN	; Call print answer printed from register pair BC
	END						; End of program

Addition of two numbers

In the second program (Program 10.2), a loop is set up to process a sequential set of data, in this case a string of letters forming a printed sentence, or statement. The letters forming the words are loaded into sequential locations beginning with location LE1. This is given a symbolic address SPT. To start the program, register B is initialised to zero, and then the first character is loaded into the accumulator and the address of the first character is loaded into the register-pair DE. This address is then pushed on to the machine stack. In the loop, the address is popped off the stack into the register-pair (DE). Using this indexed register, the character is transferred into the accumulator. The **index register** (DE) is incremented, ready for transferring the next character, and pushed back on the stack. The accumulator is compared with a value of +15, to test whether the end of the line of characters has

Label	Op	,		,		Operand	Comment
SPT	BYT	,		,		LE1	; Characters in RAM, initial location **LE1**
Start of program							
	INN	,	A	,	M	+0	; Immediate operand, loads Ø into ACCUMULATOR
	LOD	,	B	,	A		; Transfers Ø to register B
	LDA	,	A	,	I	SPT	; Transfers data from RAM location **SPT** to ACCUMULATOR
	INN	,	Z	,		SPT	; Transfers address of **SPT** into register – pair (DE)
	PSH	,	Z	,			; Pushes **SPT** address on to stack
Start of loop							
NXT	POP	,	Z	,			; Pops **SPT** address from stack to register – pair (DE). Labels address as **NXT**
	LDA	,	A	,	Z		; Transfers data from **SPT** to ACCUMULATOR
	INC	,	Z	,			; Updates register – pair (DE) by adding 1
	PSH	,	Z	,			; Pushes **SPT** +**1** address on stack
	CPP	,	A	,	M	+15	; Compares data with +15, code for line end, so end of data
	JPZ	,		,		OUT	; If zero, end of loop, go to **OUT**
	LOD	,	C	,	A		; Transfer data to register C
	CLL	,		,		PRN	; Call and print character
	JPA	,		,		NXT	; Unconditional jump to start of loop, **NXT**
End of loop							
OUT	HLT	,		,			; Stop computer
	END	,		,			; End of program

Printing a string of characters

been reached (15 is the character code for line-end). If it has, then the result is zero, and the program jumps out of the loop to the address labelled OUT. If the result is not zero, the character is transferred to register C, and since register B is zero, the character is printed. An unconditional jump takes the program back to the start of the loop at the symbolic address NXT. A space between words in the input of characters has an ASCII value of 32d, so counts as a character. At the end of the line input, the program jumps to the symbolic address OUT which stores the instruction HLT, and then the program ends.

The third program, 10.3, is designed to move a block of data stored in consecutive locations from one position in memory to another position. This is a useful program when memory locations start to fill up. The starting address of the program, called the program source, is labelled, and so is the starting address of the destination of the program. The

BTR	DFB	,		,		0600h	;	Starting address of source program
DST	DFB	,		,		0700h	;	Starting address of destination
NUM	DFS	,		,	M	+64	;	Number of bytes to be transferred
Start of program								
	INN	,	Y	,		DST	;	Transfer address to register – pair DE
	LOD	,	X	,	Y		;	Transfer address to register – pair BC
	INN	,	Y	,		BTR	;	Transfer address to register – pair DE
Start of loop								
NXT	LDC	,	A	,	Z		;	Transfer data in source program to ACC
	INC	,	Y	,			;	Increment source program address
	PSH	,	Y	,			;	Push incremented source program, add to stack
	LOD	,	Y	,	X		;	Transfer destination address to register – pair DE
	LDR	,	A	,	Z		;	Transfer data from ACC to destination address
	INC	,	Y	,			;	Increment destination program address
	LDA	,	A	,	I	NUM	;	Transfer byte number to ACC
	DEC	,	A	,			;	Decrement ACCUMULATOR
	JPZ	,		,		OUT	;	If ACCUMULATOR is zero, jump to **OUT**
	LDM	,	A	,	I	NUM	;	Transfer decremented byte number back to RAM
	LOD	,	X	,	Y		;	Transfer incremented destination, add to BC
	POP	,	Y	,			;	Pop source program address to DE
	JPA	,		,		NXT	;	Unconditional jump to **NXT**
End of loop								
OUT	HLT	,		,				Stop computer
	END	,		,				End of program

Block transfer of data

number of bytes to be transferred must also be given. The end of the transfer is reached when the number of bytes to be transferred has been reduced to zero, this being tested in the accumulator. It is useful for this program to follow the machine operations in the registers and in RAM. This is done by compiling a table as shown on page 171:

When writing an assembly language program, after finishing a flowchart, a table, such as the one below, helps in constructing the program by ensuring that the correct registers are operated and addresses and data are not confused. The program can be written using indexed addressing. In this case 0700h − 0600h = 100h = 256d, so an H instruction with a displacement of +256 would produce the same result. The aim is always to get the neatest program. Using an indexed addressing system, the number of bytes to be transferred must still be entered, decremented and tested for zero.

INSTRUCTION	ACCUMULATOR	REGS BC	REGS DE	MEMORY SOURCE	MEMORY DESTINATION	STACK
INN, Y, DST	–	–	0700	0600(P)	0700(–)	
LOD, X, Y	–	0700	0700	0601(Q)	0701(–)	
INN, Y, BTR	–	0700	0600	0602(R)	0702(–)	
LDC, A, Z	P	0700	0600	0600(P)	0700(–)	Ø
INC, Y,	P	0700	0601			Ø
PSH, Y,	P	0700	0601			0601
LOD, Y, X	P	0700	0700			0601
LDR, A, Z	P	0700	0700		0700(P)	0601
INC, Y,	P	0700	0701			0601
LDA, A, I NUM	64	0700	0701			0601
DEC, A,	63	0700	0701			0601
JPZ,, OUT	63≠ 0	0700	0701			0601
LDM, A, I NUM	63 → Mem	0700	0701			0601
LOD, X, Y	63	0701	0701			0601
POP, Y,	63	0701	0601			0601
JPA,,NXT	63	0701	0601			Ø
LDC, A, Z	Q	0701	0601	0601(Q)		Ø
INC, Y,	Q	0701	0602			Ø
PSH, Y,	Q	0701	0602			0602
LOD, Y, X	Q	0701	0701			0602
LDR, A, Z	Q	0701	0701		0701(Q)	0602
INC, Y,	Q	0701	0702			0602

Micro and macro instructions

A **microinstruction** is a single command to a CPU that specifies an operation such as ADD, INCREMENT, CLEAR. Most assembly language instructions are microinstructions. Instructions which use indexing, immediate operands, etc., consist of two or more microinstructions. A microinstruction is completed in one **machine cycle,** which needs several timed pulses of the timing clock in the CPU. For example, if the clock in the CPU has a frequency of 4 MHz, then a **T cycle** (T for time) takes $\frac{1}{4} \times 10^{-6}$ second, that is $2{\cdot}5 \times 10^{-7}$ second, which is equal to 1T. The microinstruction LOD, using a Z80 CPU chip takes one machine cycle lasting for 4T (as an example).

A **macroinstruction** is a sequence of microinstructions forming a specific subroutine, or subprogram. Many microprocessor programs consist of a sequence of macroinstructions, each of which is given a mnemonic in assembly language. Some common macroinstructions include MLT for multiply, DIV for divide, RND for random numbers. These mnemonics are addresses, so the instruction is: xxx CLL,x,x MLT , where x represents a blank. In writing mnemonics for machine language, CALL,,MLT is used, and MLT has a specific address in ROM since it is a very common macroinstruction. Macroinstructions can be created, and a program exists in ROM for this purpose, with the instruction MCS. As an example, a program can be created to clear all registers. This is shown in the table. The operation MCS starts the program, assigns it an address, and the address has been symbolised by CLR. The operation MCF ends the macroinstruction. Any program can now have the operation: CLL, , . CLR; all registers A, B, C, D, E, will be reset to zero.

A **menu** of macroinstructions can be built up, and most microprocessors have many such macroinstructions which are useful in shortening programs. With macroinstructions such as MLT, specific registers are assigned for the operation. For multiplication, as an example, the register-pairs BC and DE could be assigned for the multiplicand and the multiplier, with the product put in DE. Macro-instructions also exist for machine language, but here the absolute address of the macroinstruction must be known; for example, it must be known that DIV is located at address ØDØ7h (for example).

	MCS	,		,		CLR	; start of micro-instruction
	INN	,	A	,	M	+0	
	LOD	,	B	,	A		
	LOD	,	C	,	A		
	LOD	,	D	,	A		
	LOD	,	E	,	A		
	MCF	,		,			; End of micro-instruction

Creating a microinstruction

Pseudo-operations

A pseudo-operation is a directive in assembly language; there is no equivalent instruction in machine language. The mnemonic for a pseudo-operation is called a **pseudo-instruction**, which is a three-letter code, as are other assembly language instructions. A pseudo-instruction does not cause an operation to be executed by a microprocessor, instead it designates, that is labels, and describes, a limited segment of an assembly language program which is intended to perform a particular task. The task is the process in the field which is described by the **field label,** a pseudo-instruction.

The characteristics of an assembly language

(1) It has three-letter codes which define operations translatable exactly into machine code instructions.

(2) The transfer of data internally in the CPU, using the register bank, is described by assembly language instructions in precisely the same operations as in machine code, that is, the programmer decides which registers will be used when and where in a program.

(3) The microcomputer will accept data written in octal, decimal or hexadecimal, but the notation must be described.
(4) Macroinstructions are accepted, reducing the length of programs.
(5) Symbolic addresses are assigned, and the CPU keeps track of the address of any location undergoing a machine operation.

Low-level languages

A computer **language** is a set of letters, numbers, and punctuation marks used to form **symbols** which define operations executed by a computer. The symbols can be groups of numbers, groups of letters, or meaningful words in English such as STOP. If a group of letters suggests a meaningful word in English, then it is a **mnemonic**. The relation between a computer language and the operation of the computer must then be defined. The computer operations are controlled by electrical impulses at two different voltages, and these impulses are equated to the values of binary notation, that is 1 and Ø. So whatever computer language is used, the final instructions to the computer must be in binary code which will control the input of the electrical impulses.

A **low-level language** uses symbols which are close in meaning to the binary code operating the CPU, which, in turn, controls the operation of the computer. Assembly languages and machine languages are examples of low-level languages, they are based on actual machine operations. The action carried out by a microcomputer when given an assembly language instruction is shown in the diagram. The **assembler** is itself a program; it takes the assembly language instruction and translates it directly into machine code. The machine code then executes the instruction.

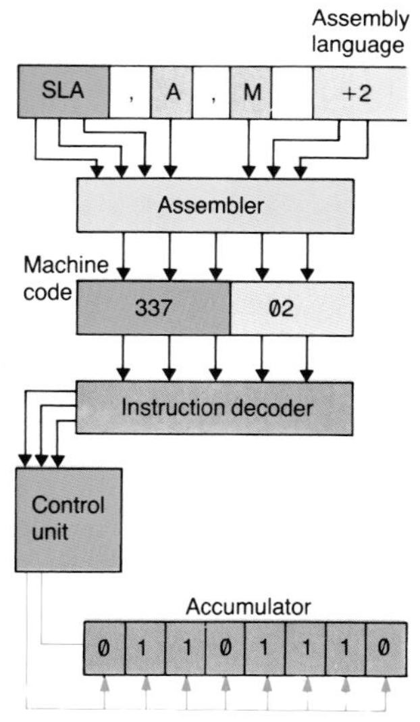

Operation of shift left two places in accumulator

Advantages of low-level languages

Firstly, the mnemonics are much easier to remember when writing a program than are machine codes. In the example illustrated above, SLA stands for shift left arithmetic, and so is easier to remember, and thus to use, than 377, which stands for shift left data in the accumulator.

Secondly, the use of symbolic addresses is a great advantage as it saves the necessity of following each item of data into memory and then making sure the item is not overwritten. Thirdly, the use of macroinstructions shortens considerably the writing of many programs. Some macro-instructions are, however, available in machine code, as has been described previously. The additional advantage of assembly language is that additional macroinstructions can be created, whereas they cannot be created in machine code.

The assembler

The **assembler** is a program stored in memory; it has the following tasks to perform:

(1) Each instruction has to be broken down into its constituent parts, namely: *the field label; the operation mnemonic code; an address; the method of address; a symbolic address/character group*. Because each assembly language instruction line is of a fixed length, this can be performed by a short decoding program.

(2) If a field is labelled, *the label* and a *machine address* must be stored in memory. Later reference to the label will produce the machine address. In most computers, the machine address is supplied during a second run through the program.

(3) *The operation mnemonic* is translated into *machine code*.

(4) *The method of addressing* and *the address* are **translated** into *machine code*.

(5) Each machine instruction is stored and the index, or other, register updated to point to the next vacant address; this involves determining how many bytes are required for each instruction.

The assembly language program is called a **source program** and the machine code program is called an **object program**. The terms source language, object code are then self-explanatory. The **origin** of a program, or a segment of a program, is the absolute memory address of its first location. An **absolute memory address** is a decimal or hexadecimal number addressing a location, for example 1023d is the top location in the first 1 K of memory, and it is an absolute address.

The assembler converts a source program into an object program, and most computers perform this task by passing through the object program twice; such devices are called **two-pass assemblers**. Modern assemblers need only one pass and are called **single-pass** assemblers. Two-pass

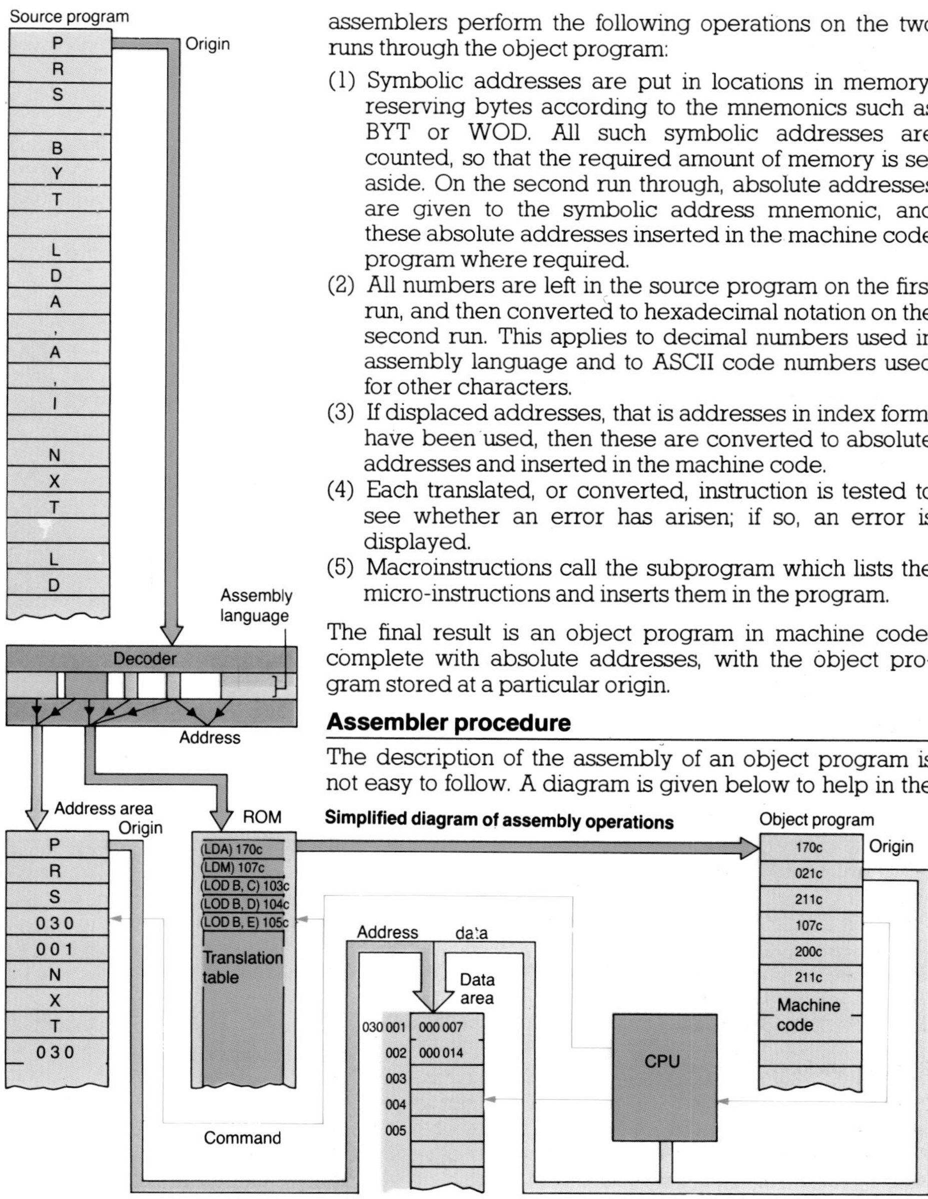

Simplified diagram of assembly operations

assemblers perform the following operations on the two runs through the object program:

(1) Symbolic addresses are put in locations in memory, reserving bytes according to the mnemonics such as BYT or WOD. All such symbolic addresses are counted, so that the required amount of memory is set aside. On the second run through, absolute addresses are given to the symbolic address mnemonic, and these absolute addresses inserted in the machine code program where required.

(2) All numbers are left in the source program on the first run, and then converted to hexadecimal notation on the second run. This applies to decimal numbers used in assembly language and to ASCII code numbers used for other characters.

(3) If displaced addresses, that is addresses in index form, have been used, then these are converted to absolute addresses and inserted in the machine code.

(4) Each translated, or converted, instruction is tested to see whether an error has arisen; if so, an error is displayed.

(5) Macroinstructions call the subprogram which lists the micro-instructions and inserts them in the program.

The final result is an object program in machine code, complete with absolute addresses, with the object program stored at a particular origin.

Assembler procedure

The description of the assembly of an object program is not easy to follow. A diagram is given below to help in the understanding of the procedure. The source program is stored in RAM. When the program is **scanned** by the assembler, each instruction line is decoded. The directives go to the address area and reserve the byte or word for the symbolic address. The operation mnemonic is matched with its code in a table of codes, stored in ROM. This produces a translation directly into machine code. This machine code instruction, which also needs, in most cases, a register, or other address, is then stored in RAM in a consecutive list which builds up the object program. Part of the source program is an input of data, and this has an area of RAM reserved for it with indirect, or indexed, addresses stored in the address area. When the object program is complete, data are loaded into RAM. The object program then gives instructions to the CPU which executes the program. This account is much simplified, to avoid all detail concerning decoding and storage of addresses and data, but it indicates the interaction between various reserved parts of RAM and the CPU.

High-level languages

Using assembly language is an advance on using machine codes to construct a program, but the programmer still has to understand the manner in which the computer executes the instructions, that is, which registers are used and how they are used. Low-level languages are called computer oriented for this reason. A **high-level language** is problem oriented, that is, it uses instructions directed towards the problem and not towards the computer. Examples of high-level languages are BASIC, FORTRAN, COBOL, PASCAL. Of these, only BASIC will be considered, but the principles which will be described are applicable to other languages.

Reserved words

Certain words are reserved for specific instructions. In BASIC such words include LET, FOR, GOTO, STOP, PRINT, etc. Some dialects of BASIC allow abbreviations of these words, as mentioned previously.

Syntax and program structure

Programs are written in lines, and in BASIC each line must be numbered. A variable, defined usually by one or more letters, must be defined by input before it can be used in later lines of the program. The order of arrangement of instructions and variables must be followed in each line, otherwise an error is reported.

Data types in high-level languages

In BASIC there are three categories of data, namely numeric, character string (which can be alphanumeric) and Boolean. Boolean data are for describing true and false values. Numeric data can be integer, real, and, in minicomputers and mainframe computers, they can include complex numbers involving imaginary quantities.

Instructions and operations

Instructions are followed in the sequential order of the program with conditions allowing for branching programs. The conditional instruction is IF . . . THEN and the operation branches if the condition is met. This instruction permits looping in a program, with a condition for looping to continue or to end. In arithmetical operations, a **priority** is created for each type of operation. The priority is given a numerical value, so that an overall precedence can be worked out for a mathematical expression. A representative table of values for priority is shown in the diagram.

Priority values and operands

Operation	Priority	Operand
( )	12	—
SIN LN EXP SQR INT	11	Unary
** or ↑	10	Binary
Unary –	9	Unary
* /	8	Binary
+ –	6	Binary
> < = >= <=	5	Binary
NOT	4	Unary
AND	3	Binary
OR	2	Binary

The priorities of mathematical operators will be in the same order in all dialects of BASIC, but the values may differ. The priority values of the logical operators may be quite different from those listed. Check on the priority values for your microcomputer. The operations have operands which are described as binary or unary. For **binary** operands, there must be two operands connected by an operator. **Unary** operands are the only operand of the operator, which is usually a mathematical function, such as COS, SIN, TAN, SQR, etc. Unary minus, priority 9 in the table, is the negative sign in -4, that is the sign which **negates** a number. Some computers have unary plus, others do not. The minus sign in $6 - 4$ is called binary minus. The statements PI and RND are called **nullary** operations as they do not need an operand.

Translation

Translation is the process of converting a source program into object code; with assembly language, an assembler performs the translation. Low-level languages, in general, use an assembler, as the translation involved is usually direct, that is straight from one language instruction to one machine code. With high-level languages, a different type of translation is needed. There are two ways of achieving translation: by using compilers and by using interpreters.

Compilers

A compiler consists of a set of programs and subroutines, located in ROM. A program is entered in BASIC and stored in RAM. The compiler scans the program and its first task is lexical analysis. In **lexical analysis**, all irrelevant detail and spaces are removed, leaving a compact program divided into statements by specific markers. Here is a specimen program in BASIC; it is not a program for any particular problem, but it shows how certain instructions in BASIC are treated by a compiler.

Program 10.4 Source program written in basic

10	INPUT	P
20	LET	Q = 20·6
30	LET	R = P + Q
40	IF	R > 0 THEN 70
50	REM	THE VALUE OF P CAN BE NEGATIVE
60	LET	P = P + 100
70	FOR	N = 1 TO 20

The next step is the production of a concise program after lexical analysis to observe errors and remove redundancies. This concise program, 10.5, is shown in the diagram. The exclamation mark (!) is used to mark the end of a line.

Program 10.5 Revised basic program

10 INPUT P!	20 LET Q = 20.6! 3Q LET R = P + Q!	40 IF R > 0 THEN 70!	60 LET P = P + 100! 70 FOR N = 1 TO 20!

The next step is **syntax analysis**, in which each BASIC line is examined for its syntax (see p. 23). The format of a line is: (line number) (instruction) (operation). This is checked for each line, and any error displayed by code on the VDU.

The variables in the program are then listed as directives in assembly language. Each variable is given a

Program 10.6 Assembly language

	LDA	,A,I	P	(line 30)
	LOD	,B,A		
	LDA	,A,I	Q	
	LOD	,C,A		
	CLL	, ,	ADD	
	LOD	,A,C		
	LDM	,A,I	R	
	LDA	,A,I	R	(line 40)
	JPZ	, ,	G	
	JPP	, ,	G70	
G	INN	,A,M	+100	(line 60)
	LOD	,B,A		
	LDA	,A,I	P	
	LOD	,C,A		
	CLL	, ,	ADD	
	LOD	,A,C		
	LDM	,A,I	P	
G70	INN	,A,M	+1	(line 70)
	LDM	,A,I	N	
H	CLL	, ,	80	
	LDA	,A,I	N (RET,,80)	
	LOD	,D,A		
	INC	,D,		
	INN	,A,M	+20	
	CPP	,D,		
	JPZ	, ,	OUT	
	LOD	,A,D		
	LDM	,A,I	N	
	JPA	, ,		

Assembly language program and associated variables

symbolic address, and the length noted. The directive **WDN** has been added to the list of directives to describe the five bytes necessary to store a number for floating-point arithmetic. The type of symbolic address is noted, as some addresses will be line numbers while others will be character codes with one, two or three characters The codes are: N for a number, C, D and E for one, two and three characters respectively. Each directive is then assigned an address in the area of RAM reserved for data, and a list compiled, and stored in RAM, of the symbolic address, type of symbol, and absolute address. This list is usually called a **dictionary**. The compiler is now ready to translate the revised BASIC program into assembly language. This program, 10.6, is shown in the diagram. It will be noticed that one instruction in BASIC generates several instructions in assembly language, also that some BASIC statements do not appear in the program, as they have been listed in the directives. The assembly language program is thus much longer than the BASIC program.

Directives area of RAM

P	WDN
Q	WDN
R	WDN
G	WOD
G70	WOD
N	BYT
H	WOD

Address area of RAM

Symbolic address	Type of symbol	RAM address (hex)	
P	C	4B	00
Q	C	4B	05
R	C	4B	0A
G	C	4B	0F
G70	E	4B	11
N	C	4B	16
H	C	4B	17

The program produced in assembly language may be unnecessarily long, as the compiler has to use standard techniques to translate the BASIC statements. Many compilers, therefore, contain additional programs to improve the efficiency of translation; this is called **optimisation**, and the result is a program which produces results more quickly. Such a program increases the size and the complexity of the compiler. The assembly language program is then translated into machine code producing the final object program. A compiler thus includes an assembler, but not necessarily so. The compiler may produce a compiler language which contains machine code, or a code which the CPU can act on; this language is known as a base language. Some compilers generate machine code from the revised BASIC program. The diagram illustrates the outline of a compiler. The purpose of a compiler, then, is the generation of machine code, with absolute addresses, which forms a **complete program** and operates the machine, having started from a BASIC program stored in RAM.

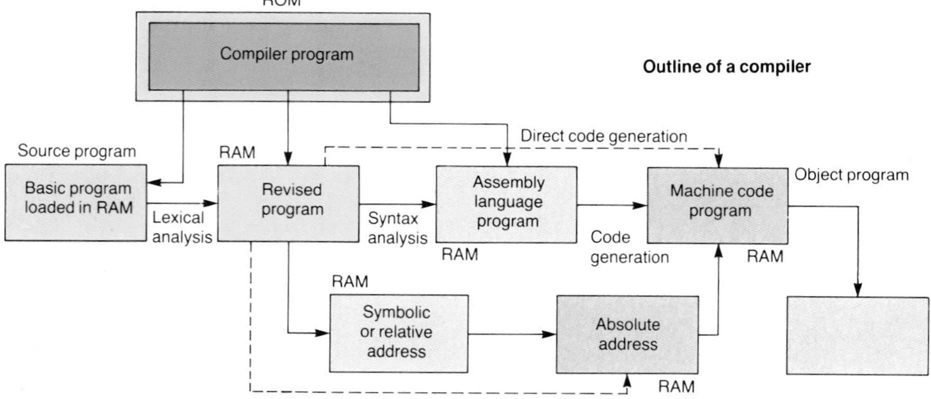

Outline of a compiler

Interpreters

Most microcomputers possess an interpreter instead of a compiler. Compilers are used on mainframe computers and some minicomputers. The remaining minicomputers and almost all microcomputers use interpreters. An interpreter generates machine code by translating one line of a BASIC program at a time. The interpreter compiles a dictionary of variables and their addresses, and inserts the absolute address in the translated BASIC line, where needed. The execution of a BASIC program is thus slower

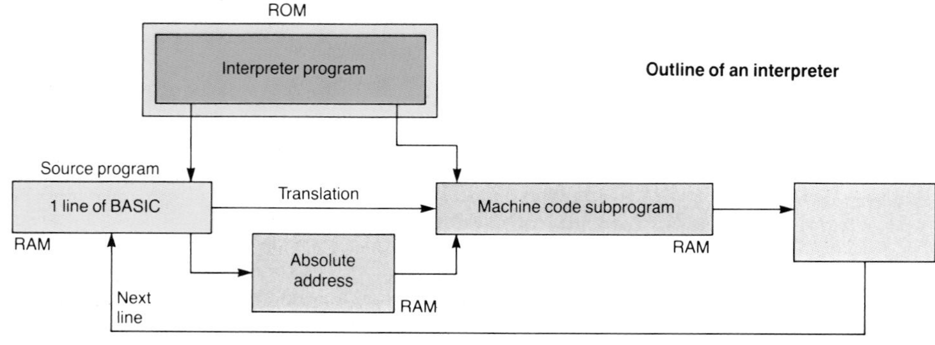

Outline of an interpreter

than its execution by means of a compiler, as there is no possibility of optimisation. However, an interpreter program is much shorter than a compiler program, and occupies much less space in memory. This is an important factor in the design of a microcomputer, where the extent of its memory is limited. Similarly, error diagnosis is less well done by an interpreter than by a compiler. The interpreter does not produce an object program, and the machine code produced during translation of one line of BASIC is deleted once the line statement has been executed.

Syntax analysis

Some simple syntax analysis of line statements in BASIC will now be attempted. We have seen that the format of a line is:

(line number) (instruction) (operation),

and this will be analysed further. Instructions can be categorised into groups of statements such as: (*a*) **defining**, (*b*) **branching**, (*c*) **conditional** and (*d*) **command**, each with its own type of format. Reserved words in these groups are:

Defining	*Branching*	*Conditional*	*Command*
INPUT	GOTO	IF . . . . THEN	PRINT
LET	GOSUB		STOP
FOR	RETURN		CLEAR
NEXT			LIST

The format of the defining statements is:

INPUT (variable)
NEXT (variable)
FOR (variable) = (number/variable) TO (number/variable)
LET (variable) = (variable/number/expression)

Rules can be made to identify the sections of the format, for example:

(1) Defining statement ≡ (WORD) (variable) (remainder)
(2) (remainder ≡ (=) (number/variable) TO (number/variable)
≡ (=) (number/variable/expression)

The variable can be numeric or string, so the rule for variable must be expanded to: (variable) ($) (=) (operand), and operand is expanded to a status table, as follows.

A status table defines the states of characters for their recognition in a logical pattern. For **string** inputs, the status table can be brief. It is:

state	"	character	"	comment
0	1	error	error	Initial state
1	error	2	3	
2	error	2	3	
3	error	error	error	OUT

A register is set to 0 before the operand is tested. The first character is that of inverted commas (") used to indicate the printing of an alphanumeric operand. The inverted commas raise the status to 1; any number other than 1 causes an error display. The next character is entered and raises the status to 2. This character can be any letter, number, punctuation sign or operator. It can be followed by any number of similar characters, leaving the status as 2. When the next set of inverted commas is entered, the status is raised to 3. If a character, status 2, is now entered, an error is displayed as status must always increase. In state 3, the line-end causes the command OUT to stop the status test.

A numeric variable is more difficult to test. The status table is:

state	±	digit	decimal point	digit	comment
0	1	2	3	4	Initial state
1	error	2	–	–	OUT
2	error	2	3	–	OUT gives error
3	error	error	error	4	
4	error	error	error	4	OUT

Starting in state 0, a positive or negative sign raises the status to 1. If the next state is also 1, then an error is displayed; it needs a digit to raise the test to state 2. Status can remain in state 2 while digits are entered. A decimal point raises status to state 3, which similarly cannot be repeated without displaying an error. The next digit raises the status to 4, and it remains at state 4 until OUT is signalled by the end of the number. OUT can be signalled at state 2, for an integer, but not after status 3. The result of testing status for the numeric variable +21·76 is shown in the table.

The next component to be analysed is (expression). The simplest analysis would be: (expression) ≡ (variable/number) (operator) (variable/number). This would analyse

Testing status for +21.76

Status	Byte tested	New status
0	+	1
1	2	2
2	1	2
2	·	3
3	7	4
4	6	4
4	(No.)	OUT

such expressions as: (*a*) 40·7 + 23·89; (*b*) B − 102; (*c*) A * 46·1; (*d*) P/Q, etc. If brackets are used, then the testing of expressions becomes complicated, and the rules for priority (p. 177) have to be used to test the validity of the expression. This test on expressions will not be attempted.

Conditional statements can be analysed as:

Stage 0	6Ø	IF	P >= Ø	THEN 12Ø
Stage 1	(line number)	IF	(conditional statement)	
Stage 2	(line number)	IF	(condition)	THEN (line number)
Stage 3	(line number)	IF	(variable) (operator) (variable/number)	THEN (line number)

Each variable or number must then itself be tested for status. In this way sets of syntax rules can be formulated to test each BASIC line by an interpreter program, and errors signalled if needed.

Use of languages in programming

The execution of a program by means of an interpreter can lead to redundancy in its operations, and thus unnecessarily lengthen the program. For that reason, machine code is sometimes used to run part of a program as this speeds up its execution. The machine code is inserted through REM statements or in other parts of memory using the USR command. Many programs recorded on cassettes and available for use by particular microcomputers are written solely in machine code for this reason. Sometimes a mixture of BASIC and machine code is used.

Other languages

A few microcomputers and many minicomputers can use a specified language. Before entering a program, a command is given to select a language such as FORTRAN, COBOL or PASCAL, etc., and the language can be selected which is most suitable for the problem in hand.

Summary

Assembly means assembly by a Z80 microprocessor.

Machine code is used for **object programs**; it is the only language a computer understands.

Mnemonics form a machine language, but must be translated into binary code.

Machine code uses absolute addresses; a record must be kept of each address used.

Assembly languages use **symbolic addresses**.

A **symbolic address** uses up to three characters, the first must be a letter. The computer converts symbolic addresses into absolute addresses.

Immediate operands are letters or numbers; a *signed number*, in decimal, is used in assembly language programs.

The **format** of an assembly language instruction is fixed for length and for the position of information.

Directives give a symbolic address to an assembly language reference. The symbol begins with a letter and can have up to three characters. Directives can also be programmed to give an absolute address.

An **absolute address** gives an exact location in RAM, using octal, decimal or hexadecimal numbers to locate the address.

Registers and the **method of addressing** are denoted by single-letter codes.

Directives reserve space in RAM for storing data.

An **assembly language program** starts with directives to reserve data storage locations; this is followed by programs and subprograms for loops.

A **microinstruction** is a single command to a CPU; most assembly language instructions are microinstructions, but some have more than one.

A **macroinstruction** is a sequence of microinstructions; a macroinstruction can be created and assigned a label for future retrieval.

A **pseudo-operation** is a directive, it has no equivalent in machine language.

In **assembly languages**, the programmer controls the use of registers, but the CPU controls the addresses of variables in RAM.

A **low-level language** uses symbols or codes to define single operations executed by a computer; it is machine oriented.

An **assembler** is a program stored in memory; its function is: (1) to break down an assembly language instruction into constituent parts; (2) create and store symbolic addresses; (3) translate assembly language code into machine code, and (4) record the machine code program with suitable RAM references for the location of data.

A **source program** is that written by a programmer; it may be in assembly language, or in a high-level language. An **object program** is that used by the computer; it is in machine code.

Two-pass assemblers scan the source program twice. **Single-pass assemblers** scan the source program once.

High-level languages are problem oriented, and use **reserved words** for specific instructions associated with data problems.

Syntax of a language describes the order of instructions and variables.

There are three **data types** in BASIC: numeric, character string, Boolean.

Programs in BASIC are either followed in sequence or by branching.

Translation is the process of converting a source program into an object program.

A **compiler** is a program stored in memory; its function is: (1) to scan the BASIC program and carry out **lexical analysis**; this results in a correct, concise program. (2) to carry out syntax analysis; each line is checked for accurcy, variables are given symbolic addresses, variables are coded for length of symbol, a dictionary of addresses is compiled. (3) the BASIC program is translated into assembly language instructions. (4) optimisation of the assembly language program is carried out, and (5) the assembly language program is translated into machine code.

An **interpreter** generates machine code for an individual line of a BASIC program; it then executes the machine program for the line. An interpreter does not produce an object program; it requires less memory than a compiler; it is slower than a compiler.

Syntax analysis involves (1) classifying statements into groups; (2) analysis of the format of a statement, and (3) checking the status of characters in variables and numbers by allocating numerical states to status.

CHAPTER 11

Input, output and storage

Both input and output of a computer use programs stored in internal memory; the organisation of internal memory is the starting point for considering input and output devices.

Internal memory

Internal memory includes all the facilities for storing information in a microcomputer; it excludes peripheral devices. Most microcomputers operate by using 8-bit bytes of commands and data, and the internal memory is organised into specific locations, each containing an 8-bit binary-coded byte of information. Each location has an address to which there is immediate access.

Transferring data

The data bus in a microcomputer (p. 122) has eight lines for transferring data in parallel. A connection is made from each line to a bit in a location, with the connection passing through an AND gate. An input command pulse, as shown in the diagram, is connected to the AND gate. The data pulses on the data bus are available for all locations, but only the required location is given an input pulse command. The input pulse command is controlled by the addressing system, to determine the correct location. Before entering the data, a location has to have all its bits reset to zero by a CLEAR command, using a CLEAR pulse.

Transferring data to and from memory.

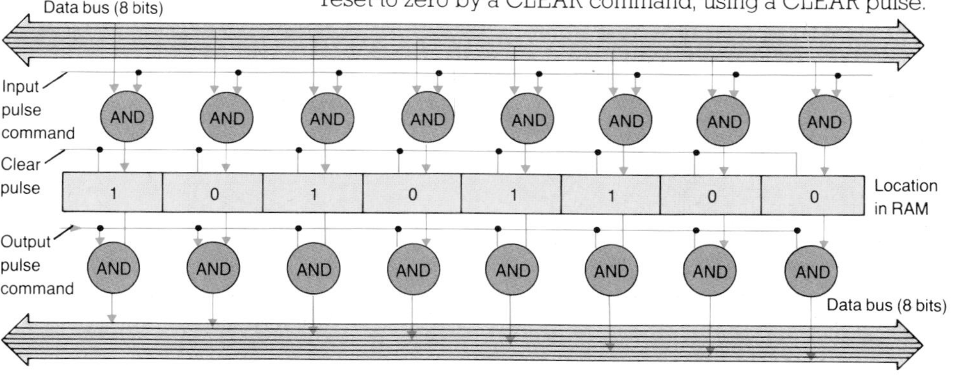

The process for the output of data is similar to that for input. The data in a location cannot be transferred to the data bus until an output pulse command is received, which is also controlled by the addressing system.

Addressing memory

Most microprocessors have a 16-bit address line, but a microcomputer does not necessarily use all the possible locations with a standard circuit. The sixteen bits permit locations to have addresses between 0000 and FFFF (hex), which is between 0 and 65535 decimal. FFFF h is 64 × 1024 decimal, and is referred to as 64K; 1024 is called 1K; contrast k in scientific units which is 1000. Memory is usually split into four sections, as shown in the diagram, each a section of 16K; the diagram shows the equivalence between the K convention, hexadecimal and decimal notation. The numbering of the address and data lines is shown in the next diagram. Address lines A15 and A14 are used to join the major sections of memory; one method is:

line A15	set to 1	32K – 64K connected
	reset to Ø	0 – 32K connected
line A14	set to 1	16K – 32K or 48K – 64K connected
	reset to Ø	0 – 16K or 32K – 48K connected

The address lines A0 – A13 inclusive, address rows and columns of memory as shown in the diagram.

Address mechanism

The circuit for selecting a location consists of AND and NOT gates, and such a circuit for three address lines, A0, A1 and A2, is shown in the diagram below.

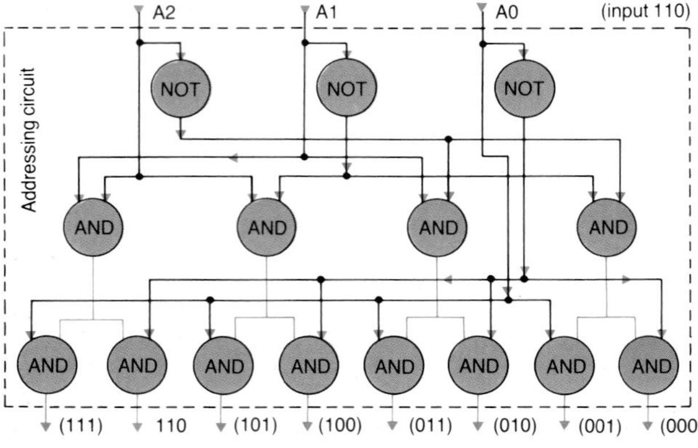

Addresses in memory

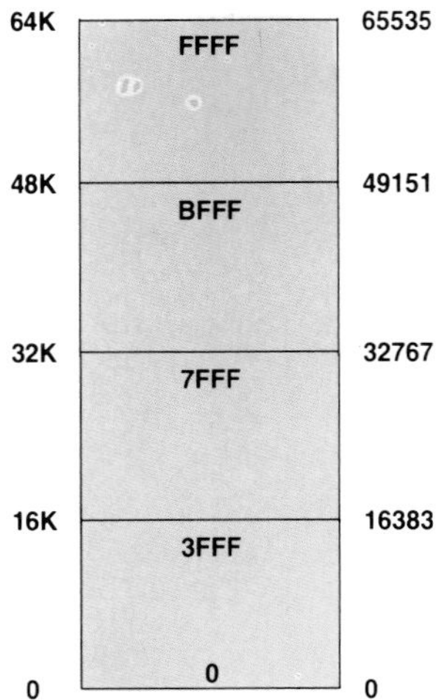

Data and address lines from CPU

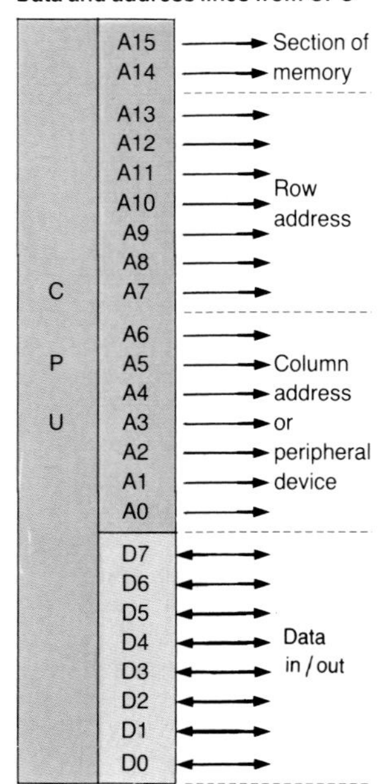

Three address lines produce eight addresses, and the circuit is followed through to address location 110. The remaining address lines form a hierarchy of circuits as shown in the next diagram. The system has been formed by using circuits for two, two and three lines, making the complete circuit of the seven lines A0 to A6. The circuit for location 7E h, that is 1111110 binary, is indicated in the diagram. This is a column location as it originates from lines A0–A6. The seven lines produce 128 column location addresses. A chip enable (CE) is used with all memories whatever their size to switch memory into the data bus. This keeps address decoding to a minimum.

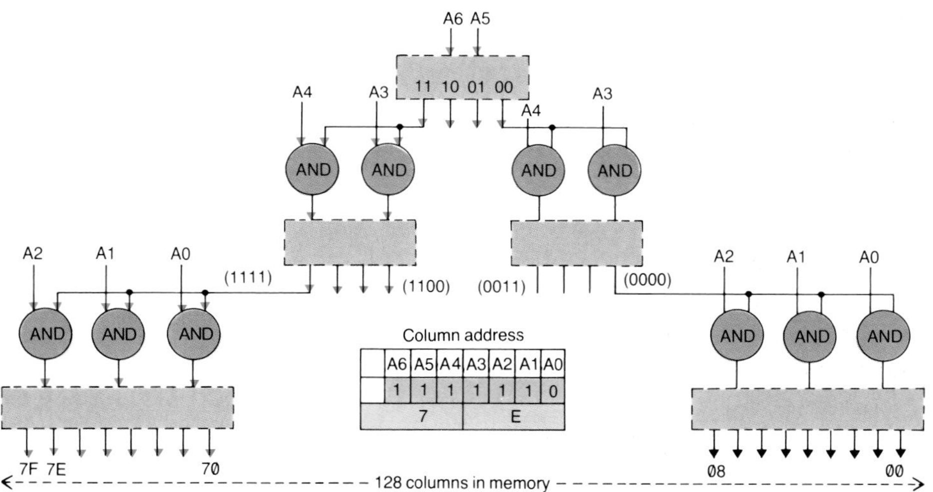

Column address

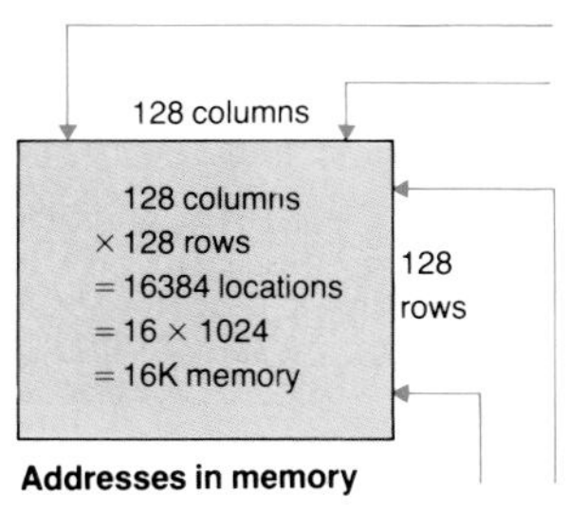

Addresses in memory

Addressing a location

The memory locations are arranged in 128 columns with 128 rows, forming 16384 addressable locations, with addresses 0-16383. This produces 16K of memory locations. With address lines A14 and A15, the full 64K of memory is available to the CPU. In each section of 16K, a location is identified from its column and row. Such an identification is illustrated in the diagram overleaf. For simplicity, only four locations are shown, with two address lines for each of the row and column addresses. All the locations in a column are activated by the same column signal; likewise all the locations in a row are activated by the same row signal. Only one location, though, is activated

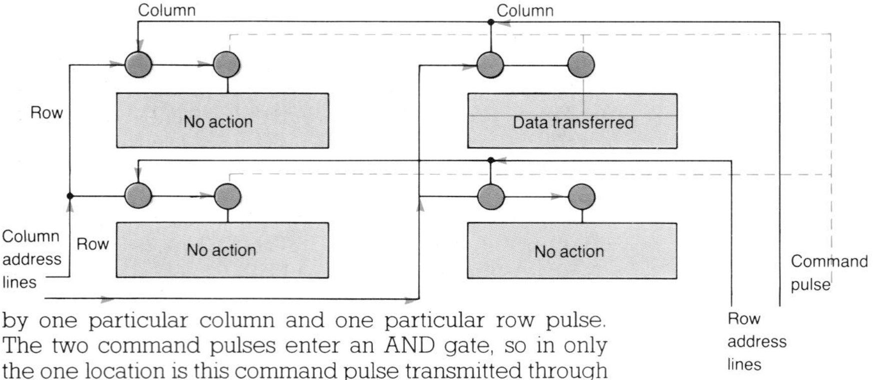

Data transfer from an addressed location

by one particular column and one particular row pulse. The two command pulses enter an AND gate, so in only the one location is this command pulse transmitted through the gate. A second AND gate combines this pulse with a command pulse, and the location is activated for an input or an output, depending on which command pulse is used. The circuit in the diagram on p. 185 has now to be reviewed in the light of the diagram above. The input and output pulses in the diagram on p. 185 have now to be modified to include an address-enabling circuit for each pulse. The diagram above indicates the general circuit for an output from memory. Other systems use lines A0-A9 to address 1K of memory. By suitably decoding lines A10-A15, the 1K of memory can be placed anywhere on the memory map (p. 189). A chip enable (CE) line when taken low connects data lines D0-D7 to the data bus; when taken high, lines D0-D7 are out of circuit.

Types of internal memory

The two common types are **static** and **dynamic** memory.

Static memory uses cells, consisting of bistable flip-flops, to form a location in the memory; each location has eight such cells in an 8-bit byte of memory. The binary data in a byte are held with a value of 1 in the set position, and a value of Ø in the reset position of the flip-flop. The flip-flops retain their setting as long as power is supplied to memory, but lose their setting when power is switched off. Such memory cells are called **volatile**; data is no longer stored after power is switched off.

Dynamic memory uses cells consisting of charge-coupled devices (CCDs). A charge-coupled device consists of a capacitor separated from a data line by a transistor switch. The capacitors store ones and zeros as high or low charges. The charges will, however, eventually leak away, so they have to be resupplied with charge, usually every two milliseconds. This action is called **refreshing**, and the microprocessor must have a **refresh** system to supply this charge on the address lines of the memory. Dynamic memory is volatile, similarly to static memory.

Pseudostatic memory uses dynamic storage cells with supporting circuits to carry out the necessary refresh. The memory thus acts as a static memory although it has some characteristics of a dynamic memory. The refresh is called **user-transparent**, that is, it is not obvious to the user that any refresh is carried out. This memory type is also volatile.

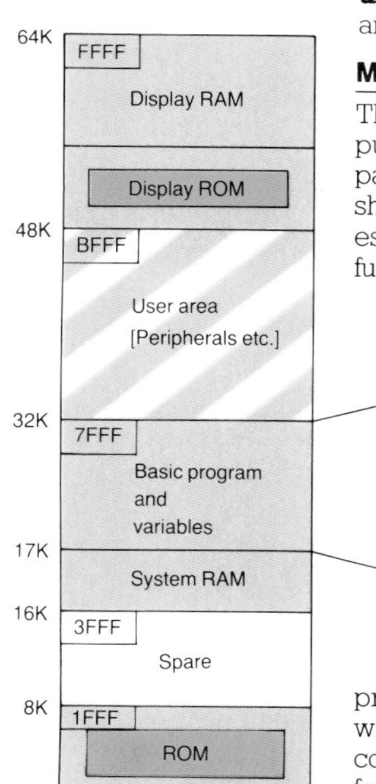

An example of a memory map

Memory maps

The memory of a microcomputer is used for various purposes, and each area is generally allocated to one particular purpose. In the diagram, a memory of 64K is shown mapped out for a variety of purposes; it has the essential information needed to allow a microcomputer to function. The memory is mapped for 64K as most micro-

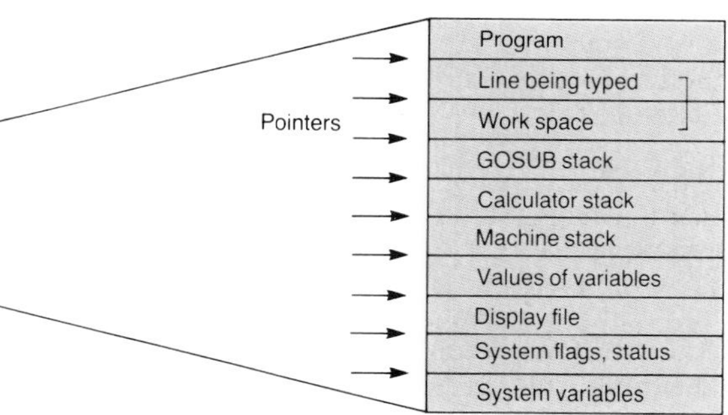

processors have 64K addressable locations, irrespective of whether the locations are used or not. The smallest microcomputers use 8K for ROM, 1K, 4K or 8K for display and 1K for RAM. This permits the simplest programs only to be processed. With 2K to 4K of RAM, larger programs can be processed, but for any reasonably large program, 16K of RAM is needed. The diagram shows 16K of RAM being used.

ROM

This is read only memory. It is a **non-volatile** memory as the data are permanently available, and not affected by switching on and off. It has **instant access**, that is, when addressed, a location is immediately connected to the data bus, and any one of all the locations can be addressed, using the address mechanism described previously. The binary-coded data are 'burnt in' during manufacture so that the microprocessor cannot alter the data. ROMs are used to store selected information and microprograms which provide the translations of high-level languages (p. 176) to machine code (p. 141). This information will be referred to when describing the functions of RAM and peripheral devices. All microprocessors need at least one ROM in order to operate, and it is part of the microprocessor's memory.

RAM

This is random access memory. Random access describes memory storage which can be addressed independently of its position, whether the position is absolute or related to a previous position. An absolute address gives the address number of the locations in memory, for example location FFFF is the last location in 64K of memory. Random access is in contrast with sequential access. Data can be 'written in' or 'read out' with fast procedures from row and column addressed locations in RAM, but all such storage is volatile, as data are lost when power is switched off.

Partial RAM

A RAM in which not all the memory locations are supplied with the original memory is called a partial RAM. This is illustrated in the diagram, with one portion of memory (8K – 16K) marked **spare**, and another portion (32K – 48K) marked **user area**. Additional memory is available in **memory-boards** to add on to the existing RAM. Such memory-boards can be used for various peripheral devices, or can supply programs for graphics, for VDU display in colour, or used as assemblers for low-level languages, etc. Data cannot be stored in those parts of RAM marked as spare, as no addressable locations are available.

Storage of programs and variables

Sections of RAM are allocated to various processes, such as machine stacks, variables, status flags, etc., as shown in the diagram. The boundaries of these sections are marked by **pointers**, location addresses stored in memory. The initial addresses are stored in ROM, transferred to system variables at specific addresses in that section, and then updated by machine programs, as described for the

program counter (p. 119). The various stacks each have a stack pointer indicating the next available location for stacking. A list of program variables is maintained and the value of each variable updated whenever the variable is used in a program.

Action on a typed line

A line in a BASIC program is as follows:

```
30 X = Y + 1·024
```

This will appear in memory in the locations reserved for 'line being typed'. When a key is pressed on the keyboard, a key code passes to the central processing unit, and from there goes to three different subroutines in ROM which convert the key code to the ASCII code for the character. More detail of this is given under the description of the keyboard. The CPU takes the ASCII code and directs the machine program to a table in ROM which provides the print pattern for the character (described later under VDU). The program also updates that part of ROM controlling the VDU so that the exact position for printing is passed to the VDU. The machine program passes this information to the VDU and the character is printed. When the ASCII code has been provided, the code number is stored in the locations in RAM used for the line being typed.

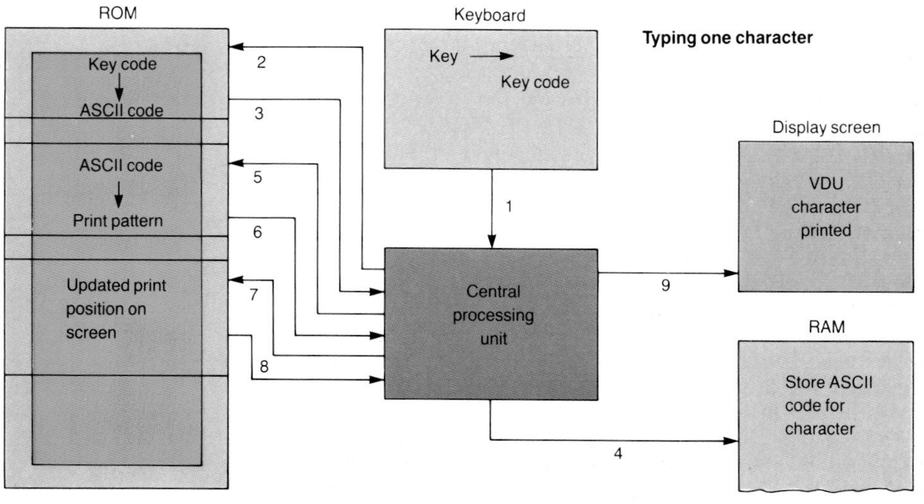

Typing one character

The BASIC line in RAM

The line, complete with line number, is stored in RAM, and the final result is shown in the diagram. The first four bytes give the line number and the number of bytes used for storing the line. The ASCII codes are written in decimal, but are stored in binary. The byte with code number 23 is stored by the ROM program, it is not an entry from the keyboard. This byte indicates the end of a number recorded in ASCII code and it is followed by five bytes of floating-point binary code for the complete number. This floating-point binary code is also generated by programs. The last byte, with code 15 for line end, is produced when the RETURN key, on the keyboard, is depressed.

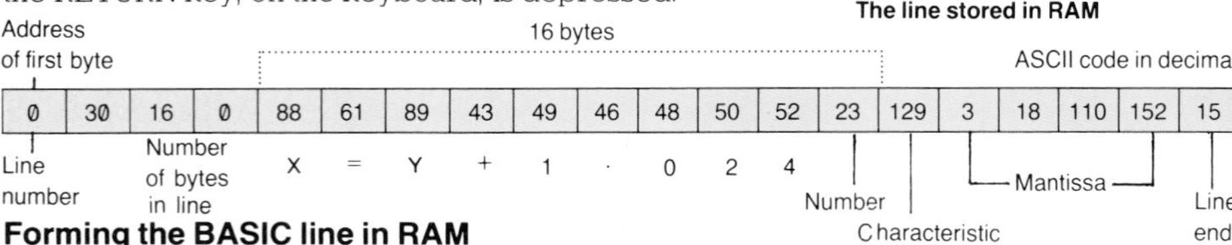

The line stored in RAM

Forming the BASIC line in RAM

Pressing a key on the keyboard activates a program in ROM which controls the CPU. The program can call several subroutines which will process the information. Firstly, the key will cause an ASCII code for the character to appear. This code will be put in a location in the area of RAM used for the line being typed. The first subroutine tests whether the code is for a printable character, that is a letter, figure, or symbol. If not, the code is for a command, such as moving a cursor, deleting a character, calling graphics, etc., and the CPU needs another subroutine to process the command. If it is a printable character, is it a figure? If it is not a figure, then the character can be stored immediately in RAM. If it is a figure then the ASCII code for 'number' (code 23 used in this book) must be entered, and shifted from one location to the next as further figures, or a decimal point, are entered. The appearance of a character, other than a figure, signals the end of the number. The code 23 then effects a subroutine to convert the decimal number to a floating-point binary number, which is stored in the next successive five bytes. During this process, the number of bytes for storing the whole line is counted. The routine program has also to record the address of the first byte of the line, and the line number; it must also update the program counter. Immediately after the program line number, a statement, or command, using

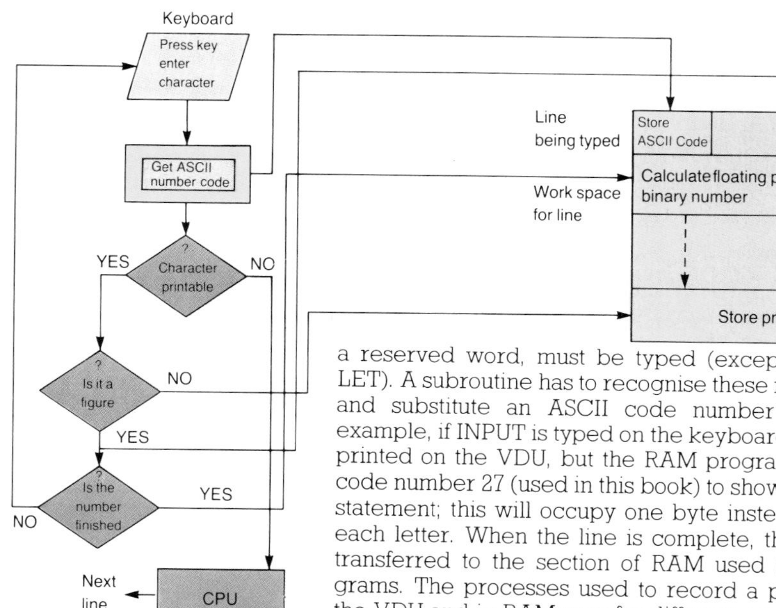

Typing a line of BASIC

a reserved word, must be typed (except for the use of LET). A subroutine has to recognise these reserved words, and substitute an ASCII code number for them. For example, if INPUT is typed on the keyboard, then INPUT is printed on the VDU, but the RAM program will store the code number 27 (used in this book) to show it is a reserved statement; this will occupy one byte instead of a byte for each letter. When the line is complete, the whole line is transferred to the section of RAM used for storing programs. The processes used to record a program line on the VDU and in RAM vary for different computers, but the important aspects of the information stored in a line follows the description given above.

The keyboard

The most frequent input is by keyboard, and any other form of input is also controlled by the keyboard. The keyboard is divided into horizontal and vertical sections, and the keys in any one particular section are connected to a common output line. Each key has a unique address

Vertical sections

1 2 3 4 5 5 4 3 2 1 6

Keyboard divided into vertical sections

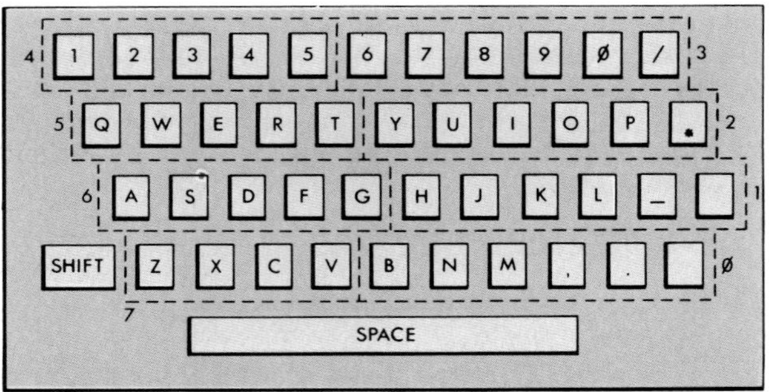

Horizontal sections

Keyboard divided into horizontal sections

by this method. The space bar is connected to vertical section 1 and horizontal section 7. The shift key is separate from all the other keys and has its own output line. The numbering and arrangement of the keyboard sections depend on the design of the keyboard, but the following description of decoding keyboard operations follows the general principles used by keyboards.

The depressing of a key sends a signal to the BC pair of registers in the CPU (with Z80 microprocessors, the HL

Keyboard code

Key pressed in: Horizontal section	(MSB)			Held in C register				(LSB)
Ø	Ø	Ø	Ø	Ø	Ø	Ø	Ø	1
1	Ø	Ø	Ø	Ø	Ø	Ø	1	Ø
2	Ø	Ø	Ø	Ø	Ø	1	Ø	Ø
3	Ø	Ø	Ø	Ø	1	Ø	Ø	Ø
4	Ø	Ø	Ø	1	Ø	Ø	Ø	Ø
5	Ø	Ø	1	Ø	Ø	Ø	Ø	Ø
6	Ø	1	Ø	Ø	Ø	Ø	Ø	Ø
7	1	Ø	Ø	Ø	Ø	Ø	Ø	Ø

Vertical section without shift	(MSB)			Held in B register				(LSB)
1	Ø	Ø	Ø	Ø	Ø	Ø	1	Ø
2	Ø	Ø	Ø	Ø	Ø	1	Ø	Ø
3	Ø	Ø	Ø	Ø	1	Ø	Ø	Ø
4	Ø	Ø	Ø	1	Ø	Ø	Ø	Ø
5	Ø	Ø	1	Ø	Ø	Ø	Ø	Ø
6	Ø	1	Ø	Ø	Ø	Ø	Ø	Ø
No key pressed	Ø	Ø	Ø	Ø	Ø	Ø	Ø	Ø

Vertical section with shift	(MSB)			Held in B register				(LSB)
1	Ø	Ø	Ø	Ø	Ø	Ø	1	1
2	Ø	Ø	Ø	Ø	Ø	1	Ø	1
3	Ø	Ø	Ø	Ø	1	Ø	Ø	1
4	Ø	Ø	Ø	1	Ø	Ø	Ø	1
5	Ø	Ø	1	Ø	Ø	Ø	Ø	1
6	Ø	1	Ø	Ø	Ø	Ø	Ø	1
No key pressed	Ø	Ø	Ø	Ø	Ø	Ø	Ø	1

registers are used). Each line is connected to a particular bit in the register. When no keys are pressed, the registers in the CPU are empty, that is each bit is reset to Ø. Pressing a key sets bits to 1 in the BC register-pair. For example, if key D is pressed, register B holds 8d and register C holds 64d.

The keyboard scan program

A subroutine in ROM is called (a macroinstruction we shall call KBS) by the CPU. This first tests the LSB (least significant bit) of the B register to determine whether it is 1 or Ø; if it is 1, it stores the number 44d in a register. The C register is then transferred to the accumulator and cleared. The accumulator is shifted right and tested for zero. Each time it is shifted right the C register is incremented. The result is a number from 1 to 8 held in the C register. This number is decremented and the result is the horizontal section number. The same procedure with the B register produces the vertical section number in the B register. The number 44d is now added to the B register if so indicated by the LSB as originally tested. The KSB instruction ends with calling another subroutine which converts the numbers in the BC register to an address.

The character address program

A second subroutine in ROM (a macroinstruction we shall call CHD) is called by KBS. This first subtracts 44d from the B register, if needed; the B register now contains the vertical section number, and another register contains 44d, if the SHIFT key has been pressed. Let the B register contain a value Y and C register a value X. Let a value Z = 8Y + X, with all values in decimal notation. Each keyboard character now has a unique value of Z. For example, the character D has Y = 3 and X = 6, so Z = 8 × 3 + 6 = 30d. If shifted characters are used, then 44d is added to Z. The character, *d*, has the value Z = 74d. The values that Z can take are 8 to 95 inclusive, from the keyboard illustrated in the diagram. The subroutine CHD calls a third subroutine.

The character code program

The third subroutine (we shall call it CTD) has an address at 161d in ROM (the address is an example only, check to find the address in the ROM of your computer). The macroinstruction CHD ends by adding 153 to the value of Z that it has calculated. It makes this an address and calls the data from that address. The data are the ASCII codes for the printable characters. The diagram shows the relevant section of ROM, commencing at address 161. This address contains the ASCII code for the symbol of a full point. The code is stored in binary, but the diagram gives the decimal equivalent for ease of reference. The action of pressing a key has now produced the ASCII code for that character, and the code can be used for printing.

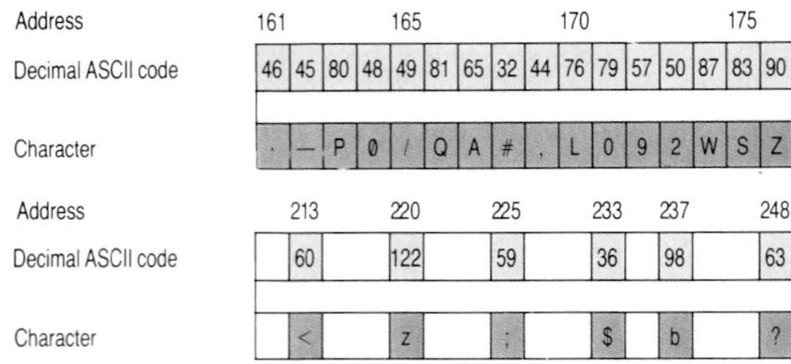

Table of character codes (ASCII)

Printing on a visual display unit

The VDU prints a pattern of dots for each printable character. The patterns for these dots are contained in a table in ROM. In microcomputers the VDU is controlled by a VDU controller chip. It is not dependent upon the microprocessor for its working, the microprocessor merely supplies update information to the VDU RAM which is shared by the VDU and the microprocessor.

The picture on the VDU is produced by an electron beam which scans the cathode-ray tube from left to right. Starting at the top left hand corner of the screen it sweeps to the right, returns to the left and starts again slightly lower down the screen, repeating this until the whole screen has been scanned. The beam returns to the top left hand corner and starts again. A single sweep across the screen is called a 'line' and a complete scan of the tube is a 'frame'. About 600 lines make a frame. The time of starting of the line and frame scans are controlled by synchronising pulses produced by counters. These counters are dependent upon a crystal oscillator, the frequency of which is typically around 9 to 16MHz. If the beam of electrons was not controlled in any way the cathode-ray tube would merely show a bright screen. By switching the beam on and off at controlled times a picture can be drawn. When the beam is on its return journey from right to left it is automatically switched off, as it also is when returning to the top of the screen after a complete frame.

A 'dot generator' operating at the crystal frequency is used to switch the electron beam on and off as it scans across the tube. In a VDU having forty characters per line about 320 dots are produced per line. By determining whether these dots should be switched on or off characters can be formed as described later.

Most microcomputers have 'memory mapped' screens. The character which appears at a particular part of the screen always displays the decoded contents of the same memory location.

After a frame and line synchronizing pulse have been generated the VDU is ready to start the first character line.

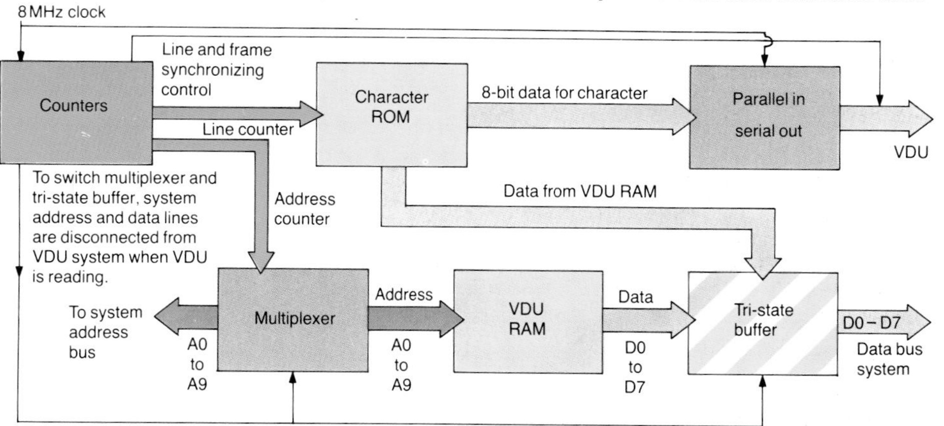

Printing characters on a VDU

Counters set the VDU RAM to its first address and the data at that address is loaded into the character ROM. The line counter into the character ROM is set at 1 and the output from the ROM is the coding of the first line of the character to be displayed. This output goes into a 'parallel in/serial out' device which is clocked by the 'dot' generator. The first line of the 8 × 8 matrix is output one bit at a time to the VDU. A 1 will switch the beam on and a 0 will switch it off. After eight dots have been output the address counter is incremented and the contents of the next memory dealt with in the same way. This continues until a complete line has been output. The line counter is then set to 2, the addresses start from the beginning again and the character generator ROM outputs the second line of the 8 × 8

Decimal code	Binary code							
0	0	0	0	0	0	0	0	0
126	0	1	1	1	1	1	1	0
4	0	0	0	0	0	1	0	0
8	0	0	0	0	1	0	0	0
16	0	0	0	1	0	0	0	0
32	0	0	1	0	0	0	0	0
126	0	1	1	1	1	1	1	0
0	0	0	0	0	0	0	0	0

Printing pattern for letter Z

Decimal code	Binary code							
0	0	0	0	0	0	0	0	0
8	0	0	0	0	1	0	0	0
62	0	0	1	1	1	1	1	0
40	0	0	1	0	1	0	0	0
62	0	0	1	1	1	1	1	0
10	0	0	0	0	1	0	1	0
62	0	0	1	1	1	1	1	0
8	0	0	0	0	1	0	0	0

Printing pattern for symbol $ [dollar sign]

Decimal code	Binary code							
0	0	0	0	0	0	0	0	0
0	0	0	0	0	0	0	0	0
20	0	0	0	1	0	1	0	0
8	0	0	0	0	1	0	0	0
62	0	0	1	1	1	1	1	0
8	0	0	0	0	1	0	0	0
20	0	0	0	1	0	1	0	0
0	0	0	0	0	0	0	0	0

Printing pattern for symbol* [asterisk]

Table of character patterns

matrix. When the line counter has caused the eighth line to be output it resets to 1 and the address counter jumps to the start of memory for the second line of characters; it carries on until the whole of memory has been output to the screen. In most microcomputers the VDU RAM can only be accessed by the microprocessor during the time of the line and frame flyback, that is, when the VDU is not writing to the screen. If this were not so there would be a form of interference on the screen as the VDU and microprocessor can not both have control of the address and data buses at the same time.

A multiplexer switches the address lines of the VDU RAM to the address counter or main address bus and a tri-state buffer is used to disconnect the main data bus from the VDU RAM. A CRT controller integrated circuit is used in nearly all microcomputers to carry out the functions of the counters, buffers and all switching.

Using the character pattern table

First, it is necessary to find where this is located in ROM; the instruction manual may help in this, or any other book describing the use of machine code or assembly language of the computer. Let the start of the character pattern table be X for ASCII code 32 (a space). Let the ASCII code for a required character be A. The following program will produce the 8-byte pattern for any printable character.

Program 11.1

```
5  REM    THE CHARACTER PATTERN CODE
10 INPUT  A
20        B = A - 32
25 CLS
30 FOR    N = 0 TO 7
40        Y = 8*B + X + N
50        Z = PEEK Y
60 PRINT  Z, Y; TAB 24; A
70 NEXT   N
80 GOTO   10
```

Result for the letter 'A'
(Assuming X = 7680)

0	7944	65
60	7945	65
66	7946	65
66	7947	65
126	7948	65
66	7949	65
66	7950	65
0	7951	65

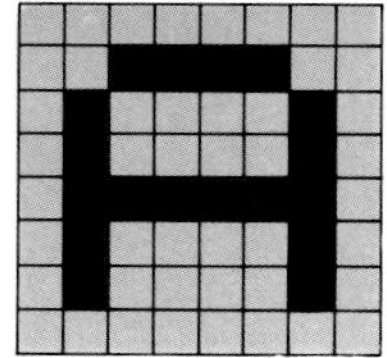

Notes
(1) A will have a value between 32 and 122 inclusive.
(2) The statement CLS will clear the screen before each table of results is printed.
(3) The program will run continuously, requesting an input, until the command STOP is entered.
(4) ASCII code number 65 is for the capital letter A, and the result shows the address of each location, and the decimal equivalent of the binary code forming the dot pattern for the letter.

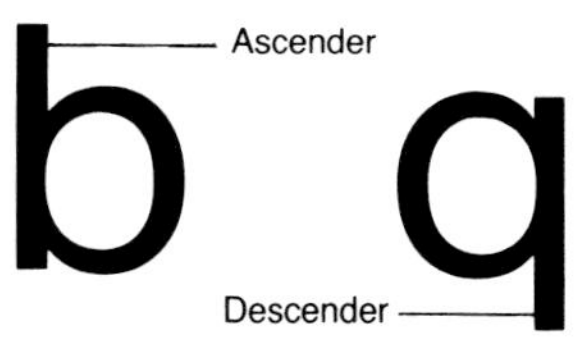

Ascenders and descenders of lower case letters

Lowercase printing

Many of the smaller microcomputers print capital letters only and use the 8 × 8 matrix code. Other machines use the same 8 × 8 matrix code to produce lowercase letters, but the letters are not particularly well formed as the 'descenders' in particular are too short. The 'ascenders' and 'descenders' of lowercase letters are indicated in the diagram. To produce a better type of lowercase letter, an 8 × 16 matrix character code is used. Each byte still consists of 8-bits, so the pattern has 8 × 16 dot positions. This permits full ascenders and descenders to be used, with capital letters occupying the middle eight bytes of the 16-byte pattern.

Peripheral devices

A **peripheral device** is a machine which is connected to a computer and is used for the transfer of data, generally with the aim of storing information. A **medium** is a material used for storing information; for example, magnetic tape, paper, magnetic disks. Most peripheral devices are **modules**, that is, they are complete in themselves, and can be interchanged, one with the other, without affecting the operation of the computer. Peripheral devices are connected to a computer through an **interface**.

Buses

Many microcomputers consist of several chips mounted on a board, with internal connections, and connections to external devices, provided by a bus. A **bus** is a set of conductors forming paths for the transfer of information among a number of locations. Buses vary from simple sets of metal wires to devices with their own silicon chips operating signals by logic gates to control the transfer of information over the whole bus. Microcomputers use either a standard bus, the S100, or a bus of their own design. The S100 bus has been adopted as an international standard; it provides facilities for the addition of extra devices, such as interface circuits, graphics software, additional memory, etc. It is less suited to more powerful micro-processors, and is not so efficient as single-board microcomputers and custom-designed boards. The S100 provides one hundred internal connecting points, but only about half are used in a typical general purpose micro-computer. The connections formed by a bus are shown in the diagram. The address lines are labelled A0 to A15 and are unidirectional, as transfer takes place out from the CPU. The lines A0 to A7 have drivers in the circuit. A **driver** is a device which amplifies the power supplied by a line. The CPU operates on, and sends out, low power signals, but the peripheral devices need higher power to operate mechanical devices, or tc get them started, so the driver amplifies the weaker CPU signal to the power required by the interface or output device. Similarly the data lines, D0 to D7, require drivers if data is sent to a

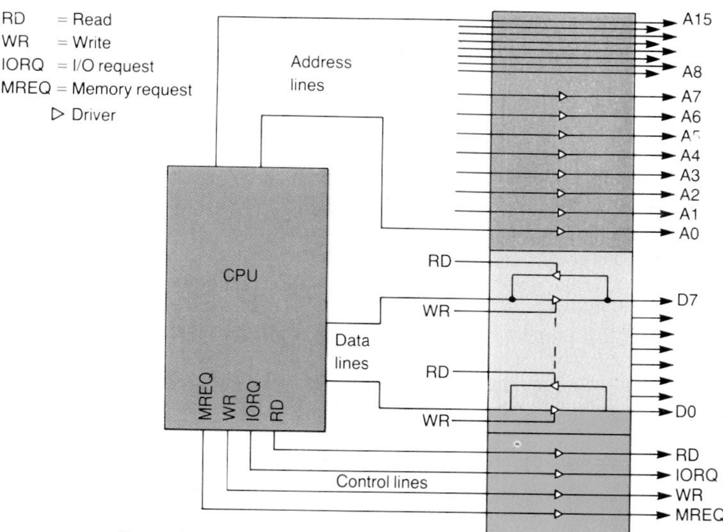

Bus and drivers

peripheral device. The data lines are bi-directional, so they require a driver for both data in and data out. Drivers are shown for lines D0 and D7 only; but all lines have driver circuits. The drivers are enabled by pulses from RD (read) or WR (write), which, in turn, are controlled by the IORQ (**in-out request**) line from the CPU. A machine instruction for transferring data to a peripheral device activates the IORQ line and a read or write line. The two lines enable the drivers for the address and data lines so the transfer can take place. The MREQ (**memory request**) disconnects the drivers so that normal transfer at low power takes place between the CPU and memory. The command lines RD, WR, IORQ, MREQ, control the operations of A0-A15 and D0-D7. A0-A7 are used to select the ports for input/output to peripheral devices. A **port** is a connector to an external device; it refers also to the associated circuits, such as control, command, status registers and drivers which operate the port.

Finally, the bus has connections for refreshing dynamic memory, testing various conditions specified by the control unit, organising intercept signals, by which some devices are switched off to allow other devices to use the CPU. These connections have been omitted from the diagram.

Universal asynchronous receiver transmitter (UART)

A CPU uses address and data buses with information transferred in parallel. Peripheral devices mainly work in serial transmission, so an integrated circuit or a silicon chip is needed to transform parallel transfer to serial transfer, and this silicon chip is called a universal asynchronous receiver transmitter. It is universal because it can process information to all types of devices, and each device necessitates a different rate of transfer, a different method of checking parity and a different method of separating one byte of information from another. It is called asynchronous because the timing of the transfer pulses is different from that used in the central processing unit. Finally, it can both receive and transmit information. The UART chip contains a **large-scale integrated** (LSI) circuit.

Interface

A circuit is needed to form connections between the CPU, the UART and an external device. This circuit is built up on a card and is an **interface**, as it is placed between the microprocessor and the external device. The UART is generally provided in the hardware of the microcomputer and of the external device; if not, it is supplied with the interface. The computer UART receives signals from the CPU and transmits suitable signals to the external device. The UART in the external device tests the signals for errors and then provides signals and power to operate the

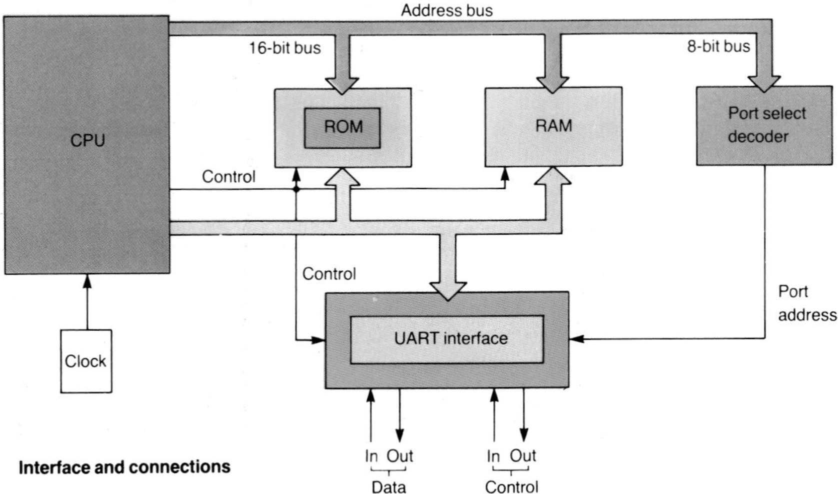

Interface and connections

external device. The general layout of the connections between the microcomputer and the interface is shown in the diagram, with the connections controlled by the bus in the microcomputer. The address bus, using a 16-bit code, addresses the ROM and RAM, as described previously. The eight bits of A0 to A7, inclusive. address a port select decoder. This is controlled by the IORQ line, activated by an INN or OUT machine-code instruction. The port select decoder identifies the peripheral device and transmits this information to the interface and UART. This action opens a path to the selected device. Data on the data highway is now passed to the interface, under control of signals from the CPU. The interface, under control of the UART, passes data by serial transmission to the peripheral device, together with control signals. The data and the signals use different transmission lines for INN and OUT. All data transfer from RAM passes through the accumulator, in the CPU, to the interface by parallel transmission. The UART converts the **parallel transmission** to serial transmission. A few microcomputers use PIO controllers (**Parallel Input Output**) instead of UARTs, and a correspondingly different interface. The circuits are more complex and the cost higher for such interfacing. The peripheral devices must also be suitable to receive parallel transmission.

The standard serial interface is a module called RS-232; it is designed to interface a microcomputer system with most asynchronous peripheral devices, and can supply serial transmission at different baud rates with different word lengths. Other silicon chips besides a UART may be used. They are a USRT (universal synchronous receiver transmitter) and a USART (universal synchronous/asynchronous receiver transmitter). These operate in a manner similar to that of a UART, the difference being in the synchronisation. The timing of all signals is under the control of the microcomputer clock (*see the diagram*); in **synchronous** transmission, the voltage pulses are in phase, in asynchronous transmission, they are **out of phase. Phase** represents alternation of peaks and troughs in a wave form; in a pulsating current produced in a microcomputer it represents the time pattern of pulse/no current, and the corresponding voltage pattern.

Transmission of information

Having seen the general connections between the various ports of the microcomputer and the interface, the next step is to look at the control of transmission. The general outline

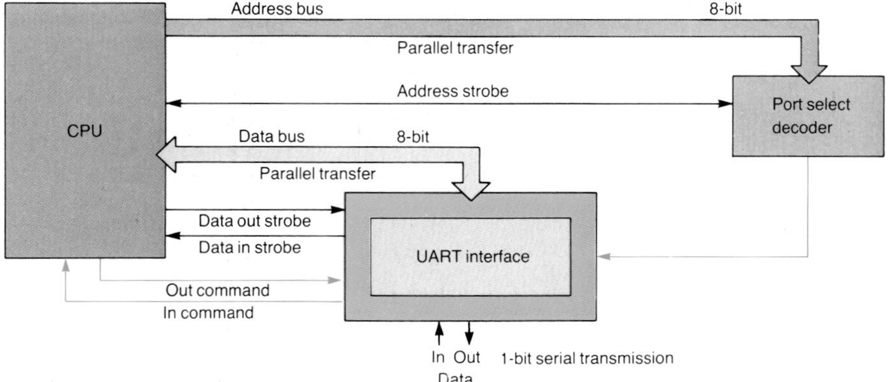

interface and UART control signals

of transmission control is shown in the diagram. The 8-bit address bus sends an address signal to the address decoder, which, in turn, is activated by a **strobe** signal (described below). This enables a port on the interface, giving direct communication with the desired peripheral device. Data are now put on the data bus. For all this to happen, the IORQ bus line is activated together with a RD or WR line. With a WR line, a data OUT strobe and a data OUT command are used. These signals cause the transfer of data from the data bus to the peripheral device.

The order of control and the method of timing is illustrated in the diagram. The sequence of events is as follows:

(1) The IORQ line is activated.
(2) The device address, using a machine-code instruction, is put on the address bus, using lines A0 to A7 and activating the drivers.
(3) After a short delay, the IORQ causes an address strobe to be sent. The signal is a single pulse and activates the decoder, which accepts the address.
(4) The decoder sends back an 'acknowledge' strobe and the address is removed from the address bus.
(5) An input/output request from IORQ is sent to the interface.
(6) Either a read or a write command is sent to the interface. Both of these signals activate the correct drivers on the computer bus, and the correct lines on the interface for onward transmission.
(7) Data from the accumulator is put on the data bus; this uses a machine-code instruction.

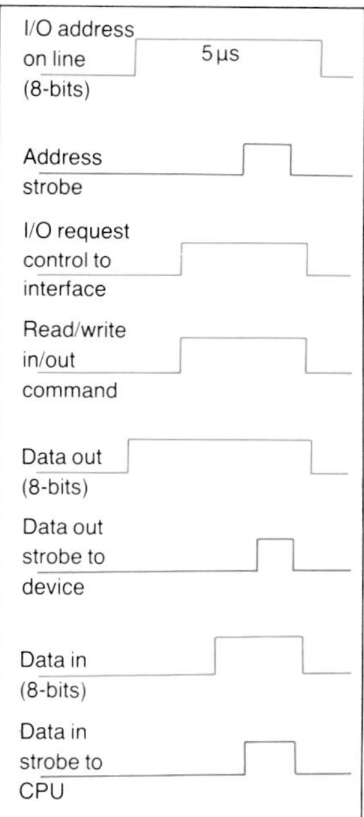

Address, data and control transmission

(8) After a short delay, a data strobe is sent. The data are **latched** into the device UART, and then the data are removed from the data bus.
(9) The device UART starts motors in printers, disks, cassettes, and causes the device to fulfil its function. This needs greater power than that supplied by the microcomputer commands; the power can either be supplied independently to the device, or through the power supply of the microcomputer.

Input. The sequence of instructions for an input are:

(1) IORQ and RD lines activated, which activate A0-A7 drivers.
(2) Address and address strobe sent.
(3) Input command, that is IORQ control and RD command sent.
(4) Peripheral device puts data on data INN line to interface.
(5) Data strobe sent to activate CPU, after a short delay.
(6) Data latched into accumulator.
(7) Data removed from data bus.

Notice that the data INN signal in the diagram is much shorter than the data OUT signal. This is discussed under output.

Output. The sequence of instructions for an output are:

(1) IORQ and INR lines activated, which activate A0-A7 drivers.
(2) Address and address strobe sent.
(3) Input commands sent, that is IORQ and RD.
(4) CPU puts data on data bus.
(5) Data strobe sent.
(6) Data loaded into a buffer store.
(7) When the buffer is full a signal stops output, while the peripheral device deals with the data in the buffer. When the contents have almost been removed, a signal restarts output. The use of a buffer allows large blocks of data to be sent without continual stopping and starting of the output. It is a more efficient method of transferring characters than continually topping up the buffer.
(8) Data removed from the data bus.

The buffer generally consists of 512 bytes of memory, and in most microcomputers is located in a reserved portion of RAM; it may, however, be located in the UART chip. The use of a buffer depends upon the relative speeds of operation of the peripheral device and the CPU. If the CPU is much quicker in supplying data than the device can receive it, then a buffer is necessary. The data on the data bus is present for a longer time during an output than it is for an input. This is caused by parallel transmission on internal buses being quicker than serial transmission on external buses. The graphs in the diagram of data input and output give a relative measure of this difference in the rate of transfer of data.

Control of transmission

A standard RS-232 cable connector is shown in the diagram. The meaning of the initials are as follows:

GND–(Pin 1) a ground connection to earth; also called a **protective ground,** as it gives the same power line voltage reference to the microcomputer and to the peripheral device.

D out the port for sending serial data to a peripheral device.

D in the port for receiving serial data from a peripheral device.

RTS the port for a control signal sent from the microcomputer to a peripheral device. It stands for **Request to Send.**

CTS stands for **Clear to Send;** a control signal from the peripheral device that it is ready to receive data.

DSR stands for **Data Set Ready;** a control signal that the peripheral device is connected and ready to receive data.

GND a ground connection to earth; also called a **signal ground,** as it gives a ground voltage reference for interface signals.

DCD stands for **Data Carrier Detect;** a control signal from a modem that indicates to a computer that a data carrier form of energy is being received from a distant modem. This can be a carrier wave on a telephone line or any similar form of energy used to carry information.

DTR stands for **Data Terminal Ready;** a control signal that the microcomputer is connected and ready to receive or transmit data.

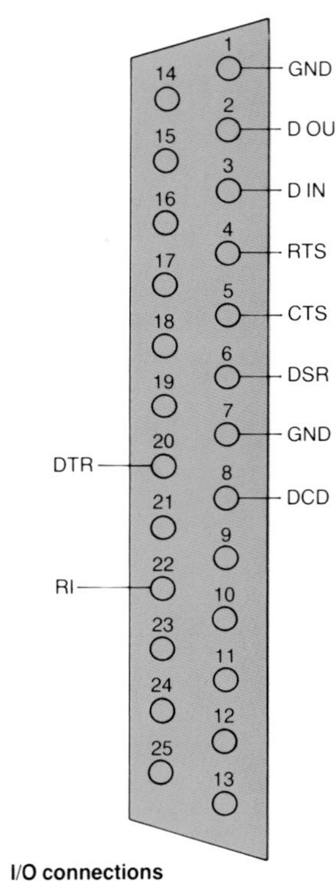

I/O connections

RI stands for **Ring In;** a control signal from a connected modem that indicates to a computer that the modem has received a ringing signal.

These are the connections that give immediate control to the microcomputer system. In addition, there are three registers which provide final detailed control to the transmission; these are described below. The signals described above permit the microcomputer and the peripheral device to communicate their readiness for each to receive or transmit data, and the signals can be paired for this purpose. The pairing of the signals is called a **handshake**.

Voltage levels of −3v to −25v are recognised as a Mark or Logic 1 and levels of +3v to +25v are recognised as Space or Logic ∅. Any voltages between +3 and −3 are ignored. This gives a large measure of noise immunity to the lines.

The handshake

The CTS/RTS lines are frequently used as a handshake pair. Let RTS(C) and CTS(C) be the signals from the microcomputer and let RTS(D) and CTS(D) be the signals from the device. The states of each of these lines for a handshake between microcomputer and peripheral device is shown in the table.

Transmission	RTS(C)	CTS(C)	RTS(D)	CTS(D)
Idle	∅	1	∅	1
Comp → Device	1	1	∅	∅
Device → Comp	∅	∅	1	1

When tramsmission is idle, both are clear to send (CTS), shown by each being set to one. When the microcomputer sends an RST, the CTS(D) is reset to zero. The microcomputer now has a request to send and a clear to send, and the peripheral device is no longer clear to send. The microcomputer now sends a control signal DTR and this is replied with DSR from the peripheral device. To clarify this table, the difference between RTS(C) and RTS(D) must be explained. RTS(C) uses the RTS port on the microcomputer with the description given previously. RTS(D) applies a similar description to the peripheral device, that is it stands for a Request to Send *from the device*. When idle, both the microcomputer and the peripheral device are clear to send (CTS). When either puts in a request to send (RTS) the other loses its CTS status. A line set to one indicates a positive status; a line reset to zero indicates loss of the status. Handshaking is necessary for the microcomputer and the peripheral device to work in harmony.

Control information

The first of the three registers is the **control register** illustrated in the diagram. This controls the baud rate, word length and number of stop bits. For each peripheral device connected to the microcomputer, these controls can vary, particularly the baud rate. So each time a particular peripheral device is operated, given values acceptable to the device must be put in this register. It is a **pseudo-register** as it is a known location in RAM, or a particular location in the circuitry of the UART chip. Stop bits are put at the end of a word sent by serial transmission (*see diagram on page 210*). The word length is usually eight bits, conforming to the standard byte of a microcomputer, but some devices operate on shorter word lengths.

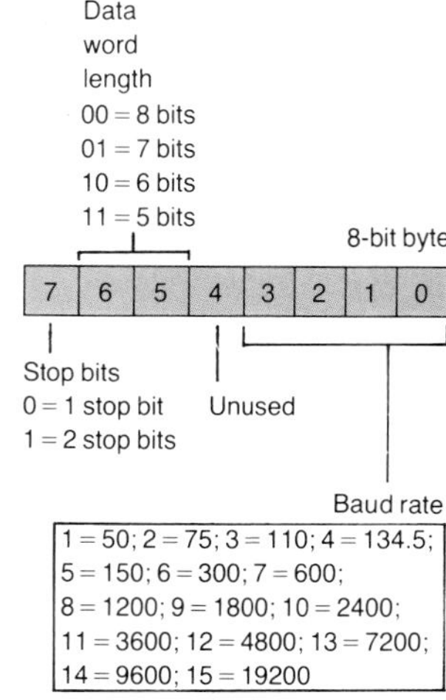

Control register

Baud rate

The baud rate is the number of binary bits sent per second. With start bits, stop bits and parity bits, eleven bits in all are needed, as a minimum, to send an 8-bit character byte. A baud rate of 1200 thus sends 1200÷11=109 characters per second (cps). Each peripheral device has its own rate of operation. A line printer prints at 40 cps, daisy-wheel and matrix-dot printers can print faster, up to 150 cps. Cassettes have a baud rate of 1200, that is 109 cps. A baud rate is fixed for each peripheral device and the information is stored in the control register. A microcomputer with a 4 MHz clock transfers two bytes in twelve time cycles, that is sixteen bits in 3×10^{-6}s, or one bit in $1{\cdot}875 \times 10^{-7}$s. This is a baud rate of $5{\cdot}3 \times 10^{6}$, very much faster than the fastest baud rate of 19200 for the interface. In using a printer, then, the buffer store is used with a handshake operation. The buffer is filled to capacity, and then the buffer overflow signal changes the DTR signal to zero, and the CPU stops sending data. When the buffer is nearly empty, the DTR signal is set again and data flow continues. This handshake operation matches the microcomputer output to the printer input.

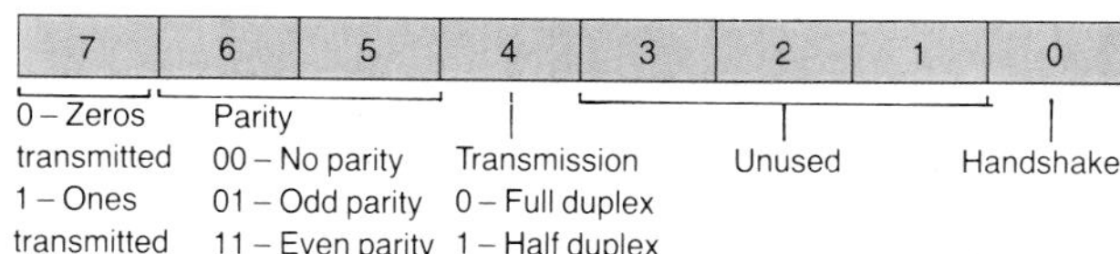

Command register

The command register

This register is illustrated in the diagram. The handshake signal in bit 0 controls the mode of transmission. The simplest mode uses three lines, one for transmit, one for receive and a common ground, that is ports 1, 2 and 3 of the I/O connections shown in the diagram on page 206. These three lines are used for signals as well as data transfer. Alternatively, all the lines of the I/O connections can be used, called a full **X-line interface.** The handshake bit is set for X-line and reset for 3-line mode. Transmission is controlled by bit 4. With **full duplex,** transmission takes place in both directions at the same time; this is used with modems. **Half duplex** transmission is used with peripheral devices. Parity is determined by bits 5 and 6. With odd parity the number of ones transmitted, including the parity bit, is an odd number. For even parity it is an even number. The parity chosen must suit the peripheral device. Finally, bit 7 determines whether ones or zeros are transmitted at a positive voltage, the zeros or ones then being at ground voltage, that is 0 volts. The serial transmission shown in the diagram on page 210 illustrates the transmission of ones at a positive voltage, usually +5 volts for peripheral devices and +12 volts for modems.

The status register

This register indicates errors in transmission. If bit 0 is set (registers a *one*) there is a parity error. A framing error is described under general errors, given below. A buffer overflow is set when the buffer becomes full, and this alters the DTR signal, as described previously. The CTS and DSR signals should function as described previously;

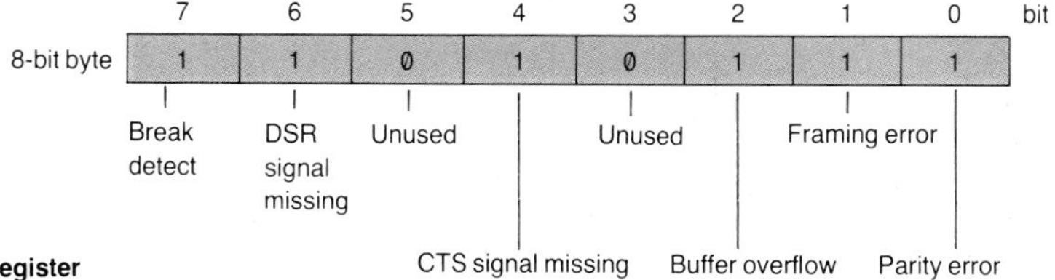

Status register

an error causes bits 4 and 6 respectively to be set. Finally, a break in transmission can be detected and an error signalled.

Serial transmission

The transmission of one byte of data is illustrated in the diagram below. The transmission begins with a START BIT, always at a positive voltage, and hence can be either 1 or Ø, depending on the type of transmission decided by

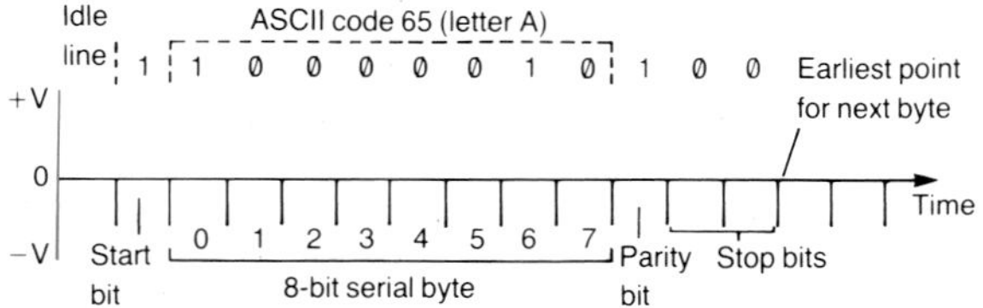

Serial transmission, odd parity, ones positive, two stop bits

the command register. Then follows eight bits of data, as the control register is programmed for an 8-bit word. The character transmitted is the letter A, with ASCII code number 65. The peripheral device needs odd parity, instructed by the command register, so the parity bit is set to 1 to give an odd number of ones. The control register indicates two STOP BITS, and these are opposite to the code of the start bit; as the start bit was 1, the stop bits are zeros. If transmission is continuous then the START BIT of the next character immediately follows the last STOP BIT.

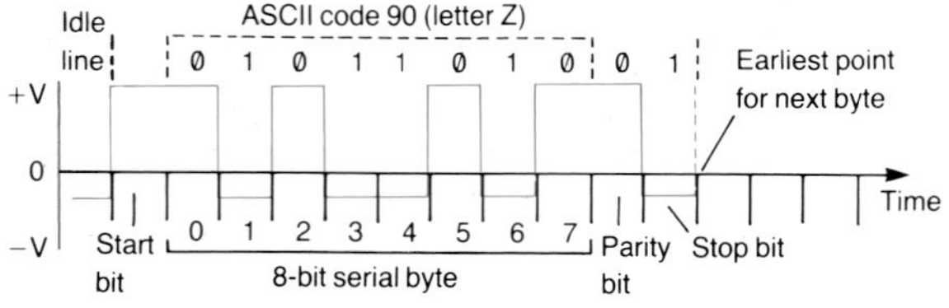

Serial transmission, even parity, zeros positive, one stop bit

The diagram above illustrates serial transmission with zeros sent at a positive voltage, and with even parity. An 8-bit word is sent for the letter Z, ASCII code number 90. The START BIT in this case is a zero, and the STOP BIT is a 1. The parity bit is zero as there is an even number of ones in the 8-bit byte. The control register instructed one STOP BIT only.

When a peripheral device is called by machine-code instruction, the UART must have a program to put the necessary information into the three registers so that transmission from the microcomputer is in harmony with the reception by the device. The normal rate of transmission to most peripheral devices and modems is 300 baud when using a program in BASIC. Machine-code instructions are used for rates above 300 baud. A VDU is assigned a baud rate of 1200, and transmission from one computer to another is at 2400 baud.

Block transmission

Data are frequently sent in blocks of a specified number of bits. When this is done the transmitting device adds a **sum check** to the data bits. The device counts the number of ones in the block and puts this in the sum check. In the diagram, the first block of data has seventeen ones, so the number 17 is added to the block. This is a correct sum. In the second block, the sum is recorded as 20, but this is incorrect, so the receiving device records an error when it counts the number of ones.

Block of data				Sum check
01101100	01110110	10101100	01101100	10001
				Correct

Block of data				Sum check
01111010	00111101	11110001	01111011	10100
				Error

Block transfer of data with sum check on ones

Errors in transmission

Errors in transmission and storage are caused by unwanted false electronic pulses called **glitches**. A glitch is the result of the power supply behaving abnormally. The most frequent cause is a 'spike' in the voltage, giving a short, sharp increase in voltage, which can distort the binary information being transmitted. Power failure, and low voltages, called 'brown-outs', similarly affect transmission. In transmission over lines between modems, interference from electrical disturbances in conductors or semiconductors causes random pulses of frequencies spread equally over all frequencies in the transmission band. This is called **white noise**, and it produces distortions in binary representation of codes. One error, on magnetic tape or paper tape, that is signalled by the status register arises in a frame. A **frame** is the array of bits across the bands of digital information on magnetic or paper tape. A frame is illustrated in the diagram for magnetic tape. Errors can arise from magnetic tape, in close contact on a spool, printing **magnetic images** from one section of tape on to the sections of tape in contact with it. Static electricity, generated by rubbing two non-

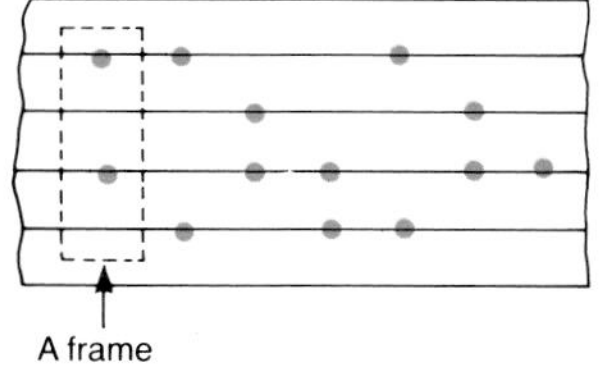

A frame on magnetic tape

conductors together, can produce erroneous data on a transmission line or in memory locations. A charge of 500 volts, with a very small current, can produce such errors. Plastic surfaces are liable to produce static electricity; walking on a vinyl floor or over a carpet made of synthetic fibres can produce static voltages of 4,000-12,000 volts, ample to discharge memory cells and produce errors. Errors caused by glitches and static can be prevented by using a unit to monitor and control the power supply and by using static-free surfaces in the vicinity of the computer and peripherals.

Errors in stored programs produce a **corrupt** program, which, if run, results in useless data being produced. Programs are available to check and mark errors, which then have to be corrected manually. Some simple errors, such as parity, may be corrected by a suitable program.

LED displays

Light Emitting Diodes (LED) are used to signal errors and to display the contents of registers. A LED has gallium arsenide and gallium phosphide as the semi-conductor material. The diode emits light when a voltage is applied to it. The colour depends on the proportions of the two semi-conductor materials. Red, yellow, green displays are available. The diode emits light without heat. The semi-conductor material is usually about 1mm square and the emitted light is spread into the desired area by a plastic lens. An arrangement of tubes is made as shown in the diagram, so that any figure from 0 to 9 inclusive can be generated by lighting up the correct tubes. The light display is controlled by one byte of data, as indicated in the diagram and an example is given for producing the figure 5. The figures can be used to indicate the type of error or display any other type of numerical information.

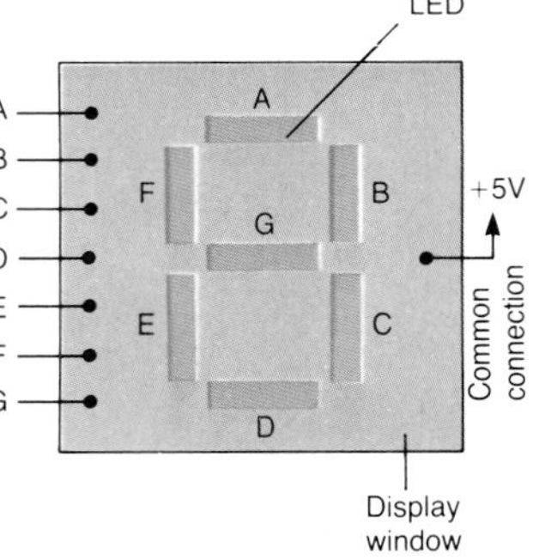

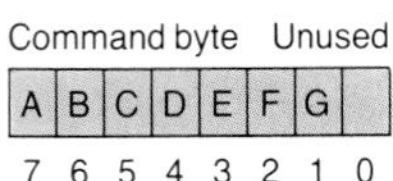

Light emitting diode (LED) figure display

Printers

Printers are either **line printers** which print a whole line in one action, or **character printers** which print successive characters along a line. All line printers and most character printers are **impact printers**, that is, the appropriate character is hit on to typewriter ribbon to print a character on paper. The remaining character printers use **heat-sensitive** paper; these are small printers, usually with forty characters or less per line, using a hot spot to create a blue dot on the paper.

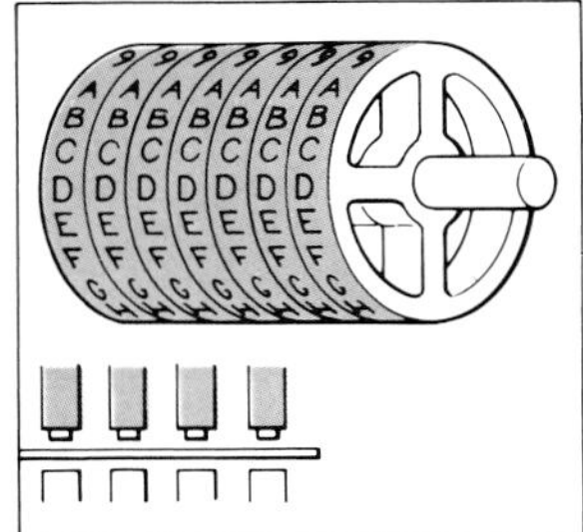
Print wheel on a line printer

Line printers

A line printer has a set of wheels with characters on the rim of each wheel. A wheel is shown in the diagram. There is one wheel for every character that can be printed on one line of print; this can be between 80 and 120 characters. The wheels are kept spinning and stopped at the required character for printing. The carriage on which the wheels are mounted moves forward and all 120 characters are printed at the same time as the wheels hit a typewriter ribbon. Using a line printer, from 300 to 1200 lines per minute can be printed. The wheels are controlled by electromechanical devices which operate by using the ASCII code for characters. The quickest printing rate is achieved by line printers.

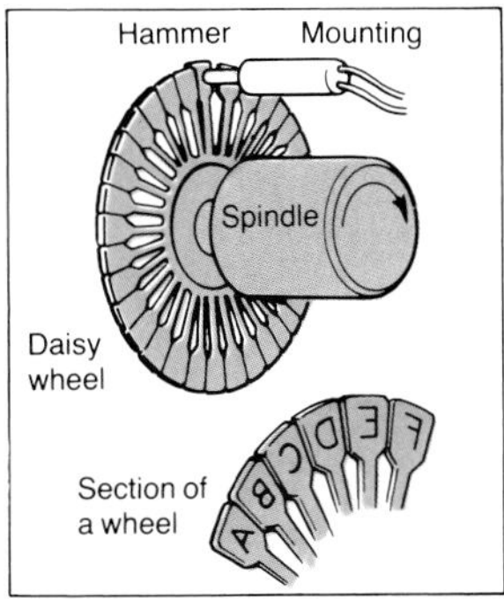

Daisy wheel printer

Daisy-wheel printers

The characters of a daisy-wheel printer are set round the circumference of the wheel, as shown in the diagram. The wheel rotates on an axle, and is arrested at the correct character. A hammer hits the wheel and the character is printed by using a typewriter ribbon. The daisy-wheel is mounted on the machine frame and the paper moves on a carriage as on a conventional typewriter. An interface card is used to convert the ASCII character code to daisy-wheel positions; transmission can be either serial or parallel. Daisy-wheel printers have a speed of thirty to fifty-five characters per second. The daisy-wheel is made of plastic and most printers offer an assortment of wheels so that different printing fonts can be used.

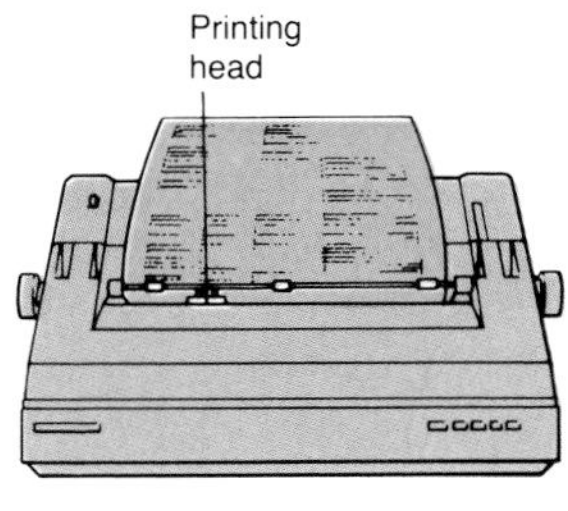

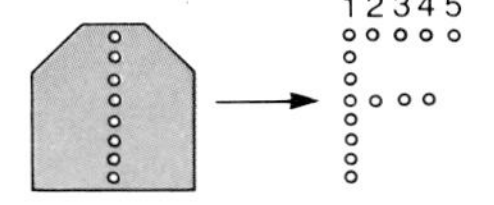

Matrix printer

Dot-matrix printers

The majority of matrix printers use a 7 × 5 pattern of dots. A printing head contains seven needles mounted one above the other. These needles are controlled by electromagnets which push them against typewriter ribbon to form a dot on paper. The printing head moves along the line of print and is supported by a carriage. For each character, the printing head operates in five positions. In the diagram, the movable printing head is shown, together with the position of the seven needles. The formation of a letter F by the pattern of dots in the 7 × 5 matrix is also shown. The printing head moves on to the next character, leaving an appropriate space. The ASCII code number, sent by the CPU, needs a table in memory to convert the code number to a set of five bytes containing the print code for the matrix needles. This table is similar to that of the VDU converter. Printing rates for matrix printers are between one hundred and two hundred characters per second.

Matrix printers can reproduce graphics, by means of dots. The dots can also reproduce a black and white picture by a pattern of dots; this is the same technique as employed in newspapers to reproduce photographs. Examination of a newspaper photograph under a magnifying glass will show the pattern of dots. The **resolution** of a dot pattern is a measure of the smallest possible distance between any two dots. Very small distances produce a high resolution; greater distances a low resolution. The higher the resolution, the better the picture from a dot pattern. Some matrix printers use a 9 × 9 matrix, which allows true lowercase ascenders and descenders (*see page 199*) to be printed; this matrix also produces high resolution graphics, that is a line of dots which looks like a continuous line.

The three types of printers, discussed above, are all impact printers, using typewriter ribbons and ordinary paper. Matrix printers can be used with heat-sensitive paper, but not the other two types.

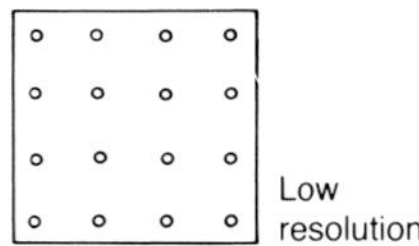

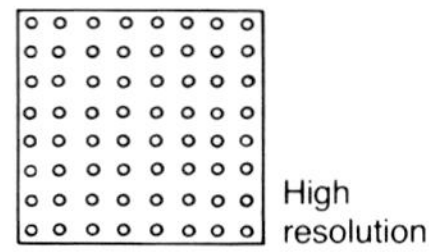

Resolution of a dot pattern

Comparison of printers

Line printers produce good quality printing, are extremely expensive and basically designed for mainframe computers and the larger minicomputers with a big output of paperwork. Daisy-wheel printers produce good quality printing, are much less expensive than line printers, but are very much slower in action. Matrix printers, particularly the 7 × 5 matrix type, are relatively cheap, reasonably quick in action, but produce poor quality printing. They are, however, the only type of printer to produce good graphics. The cheapest type of printer is a matrix printer using heat-sensitive paper. The paper itself is expensive and usually available in 5 cm or 7·5 cm widths only. A suitable choice of printer thus depends entirely on the circumstances under which it is purchased and used.

Spooling

Spool is an acronym for Simultaneous Peripheral Operations On Line. It is a technique used with low-speed devices such as printers. The rate of supply of data by a microcomputer is many times faster than the rate of printing the data, so the computer is held up while printing is taking place. Even the use of buffers does not help considerably. In **spooling**, the procedure is to store data temporarily on a disk, and later to print from the disk while the computer carries on with other work. Printing from a spooled disk is called **despooling**. Despooling requires greater flexibility by a CPU than is normally available in a microcomputer. The CPU has to be capable of conducting two operations at the same time. The latest advanced microcomputers are being provided with spooling and despooling facilities.

Bounce and debounce

Printers, disks and cassettes use mechanical switches operated by electromagnets. A mechanical switch may not be fully and finally closed for a few milliseconds, and during this time several separate impulses may be generated by the contact. These impulses are called **contact bounce**. Such current impulses may cause glitches, and so have to be eliminated by a **debouncing circuit**. A debounced switch ensures a single sharp switching action completed within a few nanoseconds. There is usually a test in the circuitry to determine the **debounce status** of a peripheral device, and hence of the computer connected to the device.

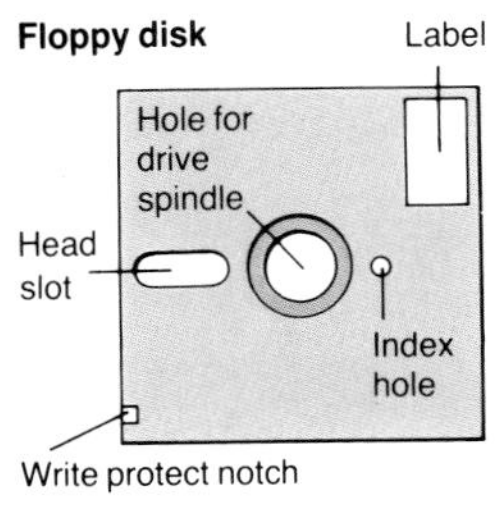

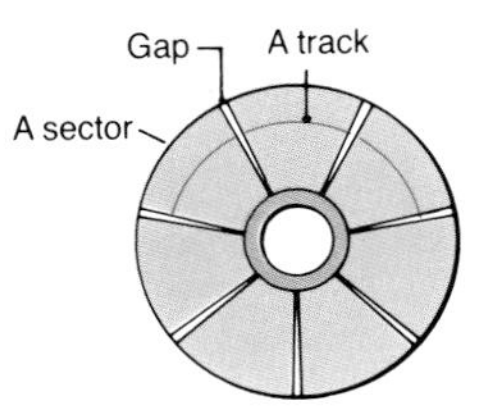

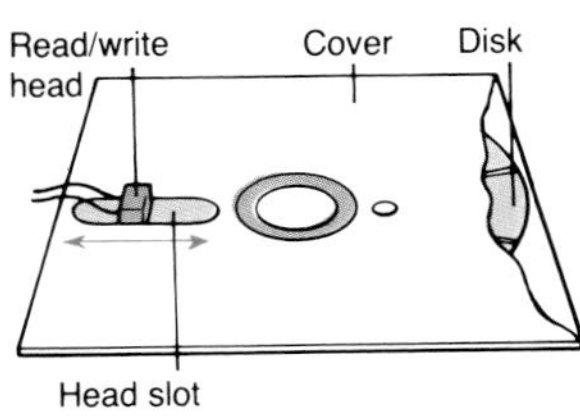

Disks

Floppy and hard disks are described on page 12. A disk is divided into sectors and the **sectors** are separated by gaps, as shown in the diagram. Each sector contains a number of **tracks**. A read/write head moves up and down the head slot, scanning all the tracks on the disk. Information is addressed to locations on the disk by sector and track. Access is rapid, but not as quick as with RAM, as the head must wait for the appropriate sector to appear under the head slot. Disks must be kept free from dust and scratches; magnetic objects such as tools and telephones must not be put close to a disk, otherwise the disk may be damaged and the data corrupted. Hard disks are permanently enclosed and kept in a dust-free atmosphere. The read/write head is in intimate contact with the disk, kept at a distance of 3μm above it by a pressure pad. The head planes on a viscous film of air. A sector on the normal 8-inch disk stores 128 bytes of data; in some systems this is called a **record**. There are usually thirty-two sectors on a disk and eight sectors store 1024 or 1K bytes. Files on a disk are usually assigned 16K bytes for storing data. The gaps on the disk allow for movement of the read/write head to switch from one track to another when changing sectors. The data stored on a track in a particular sector thus tends to be stored serially, and read in serial fashion. The disks generally store data on both surfaces.

The memory of a disk has to be mapped for the various functions it can perform, and a record kept of the locations used. A disk with a permanent data system is shown in the diagram. The system would be a proprietary one for organising data files. The system has a control program, a system control for dealing with various categories of information and a control for various input/output devices that can be operated through the computer. The first program is a **bootstrap loader**. A bootstrap loader activates itself when the computer is switched on and the disk input connected. It consists of a short routine which loads the sytem program into RAM, allowing the computer to control the use of the disk according to the system. This is necessary otherwise the program may be overwritten and lost. With special systems purchased for a computer it is a good precaution to copy the system's disk and operate with the copied disk in case the system does get erased. Most disks are equipped with a **write-protect** notch. A standard floppy disk has this notch covered with aluminiumised paper; if this paper is removed, the disk head is no longer able to write on the disk. This preserves any useful data or programs stored on the disk. The system maintains a **directory** of files, and the organisation of an individual entry is shown. A **file** is given a name and can be addressed by name. The computer searches through the directory for the file name, and then acts on the instructions using the data from the file address in file positions. A file need not necessarily be stored in consecutive sectors or tracks, but can be scattered throughout the disk. File positions have sufficient space to record up to 16K bytes of addressed data with a *record* as the minimum address. The transient data storage area is used for activities such as spooling, file sorts and file rearrangements.

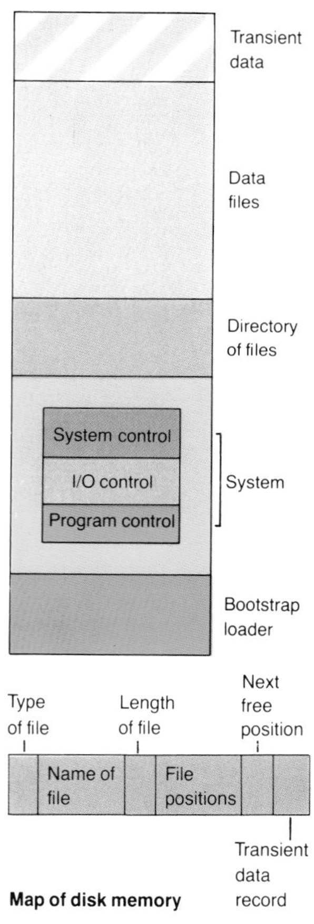

Map of disk memory

Magnetic tape

Magnetic tape is used with **tape decks** (page 13) and with cassettes. A tape deck has a read/write head which provides nine tracks on the tape. The organisation of the tracks is shown in the diagram. The tracks store the ASCII equivalents of a hexadecimal notation with numbers 0 to F, as indicated. A byte in the accumulator is divided into two

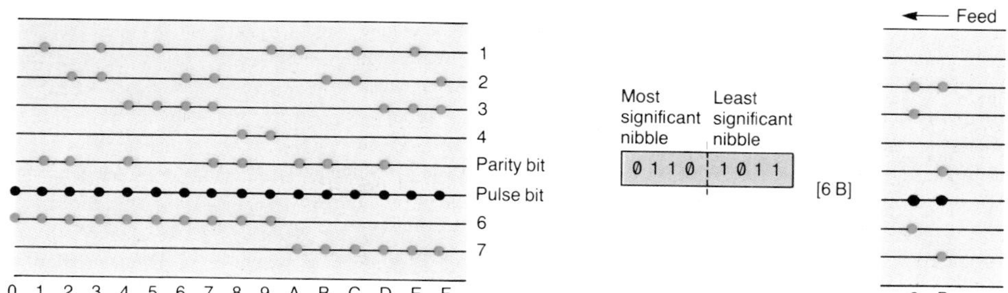

Recording on magnetic tape

nibbles: the most and least significant nibbles. Each nibble is then given its hexadecimal value; in the diagram this is a value of 6Bh. The computer then changes the one byte into two ASCII bytes and records them on the tape. The data is transmitted in blocks, first being stored as a block in RAM,

Block transmission of serial data

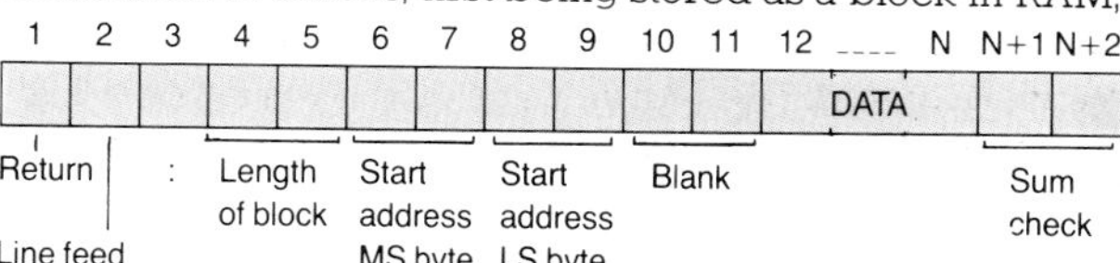

so that the number of bytes can be counted. The organisation of a block is shown in the diagram. Bytes 1 and 2 are commands used when the information is loaded back on to the computer. The start address is used to store the program in the required locations in RAM. All data are recorded with two ASCII code bytes for one byte in memory. The sum check at the end of block transfer has been described previously. All transmission to magnetic tape is by block transfer. The usual rate of transfer is 600 baud, but different baud rates can be specified by the control register (p. 208). An **interblock gap** is left between blocks of data on magnetic tape; the gap lengths in common use are 19 mm and 14·2 mm. In these gaps the tape may be accelerated to full speed or stopped. Reading/writing takes place only at full speed.

The tape cassettes used with microcomputers have a different recording system. Such tapes are designed to record sounds within the ordinary sound frequencies for speech and music. The binary code in a byte has to be changed to two frequencies, one representing ones and

Recording binary code on a cassette tape

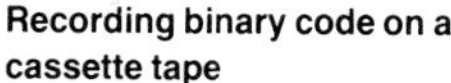

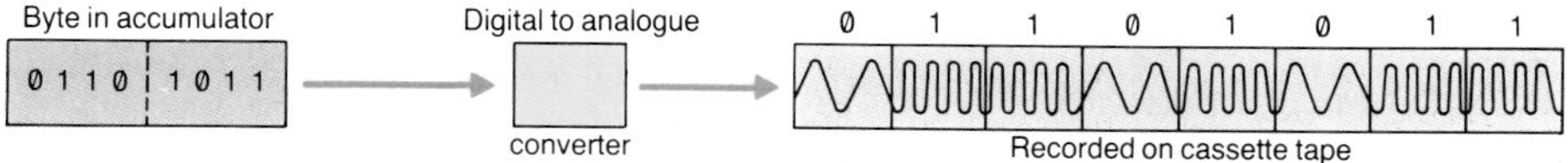

the other zeros. The frequency is recorded as a wave pattern, as shown in the diagram; a high frequency has been selected to record a 1 and a low frequency to record a Ø. A digital to analogue converter is required for this purpose and the converter is provided in the microcomputer. Different microcomputers can use different frequencies, so a tape recorded by one microcomputer cannot be used by another microcomputer. The information is sent in blocks to the cassette recorder, and each program or file of data has to be given a name. The program, or file, can then be retrieved when the name is supplied.

SAVE

A program can be recorded on tape by the command SAVE. The program is first typed on the VDU. The cassette recorder is then connected to the microcomputer. Let the name of the program be 'FILE TWO'. Carry out the following sequence of operations:

(1) Type: SAVE "FILE TWO".
(2) Start the cassette recorder recording; note reading on tape counter.
(3) Press RETURN key.
(4) Watch the VDU screen; it will stop flickering and show a visual prompt that the program has been completed.

Alternatives to SAVE are CSAVE, STORE.

LOAD

A program can be loaded from a cassette tape into a microcomputer by the command LOAD. The recorder is adjusted by fast forward or reverse until the counter indicates the correct position of the program. Let the program to be loaded be 'FILE TWO'. Carry out the following sequence of operations:

(1) Type: LOAD "FILE TWO".
(2) Start the cassette recorder playing.
(3) Press RETURN key.
(4) Watch the VDU screen; it will stop flickering and show a visual prompt that the program has been completed.

An unnamed program can be loaded. The tape recorder is positioned at a given reading and the following command typed:

(1) Type: LOAD "   "
(2) Start the recorder.
(3) Press RETURN key.

The microcomputer now loads the first program available on the tape. Alternatives to LOAD are CLOAD, RECALL.

Hierarchy of memory

There are four major ways of storing information and two minor ways. The major ways are: disk, magnetic tape, printed paper, random access memory. The two minor ways are punched paper tape and punched cards; these are used to a lesser extent and will not be described here. The storage of information forms a hierarchy based on time of access:

RAM access is almost instantaneous, and the information can be addressed at random. Cost is high, and the memory is volatile.

Disk access is very fast, but slower than for RAM. The information can be addressed at random. Cost is fairly high, and memory is non-volatile, but may be corrupted.

Magnetic tape access is slow as it is sequential (it can take up to fifteen minutes to find a required program). Cost is low and memory is non-volatile but may be corrupted.

Printed paper there is no access by the computer, it is for the user only. Cost varies from high for line printers to fairly low for matrix printers. The memory is non-volatile and cannot be corrupted.

Disk and magnetic tape can be used for both input and output; printing and a VDU are for output only. The choice of memory type depends upon the use to which it will be put, balanced by the cost, and the significance of accuracy.

Symbols for planning operations

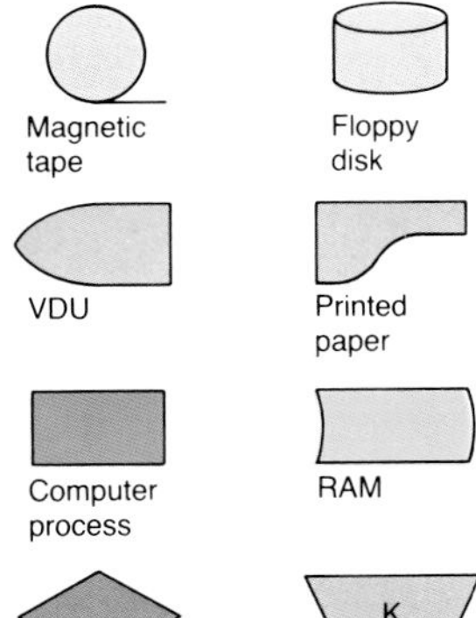

Recording a program on a cassette

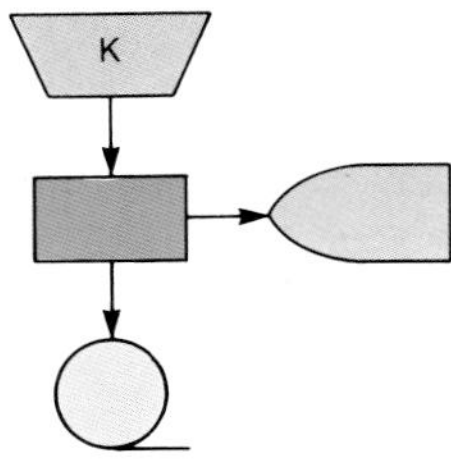

Planning operations

Different types of memory are used in different stages of an operation, and it is useful to prepare a plan, using symbols, to determine how a problem will be tackled in order to operate a program in the minimum time. The symbols used in planning are shown in the diagram. A disk will usually be a floppy disk for a microcomputer, a hard disk for a mainframe computer and a choice for a minicomputer. Magnetic tape will be on a tape deck for a mainframe, but on a cassette for a microcomputer.

The simplest operation is recording a program on cassette; this is shown in the diagram. The program is entered through the keyboard and checked on the VDU monitor. It is then loaded, by command process, on to the cassette tape.

A more advanced operation is the updating of a file. The original data file and the operation program is stored on a disk. The program and data are transferred to RAM. New data, entered through the keyboard, and the original data are processed by the program. The VDU monitors new data and checks the update. The updated file is returned via RAM to the disk. A copy of the data is taken on magnetic tape. This guards against corruption of the file as the two files can be compared and any differences printed out for the operator to check and later correct the errors.

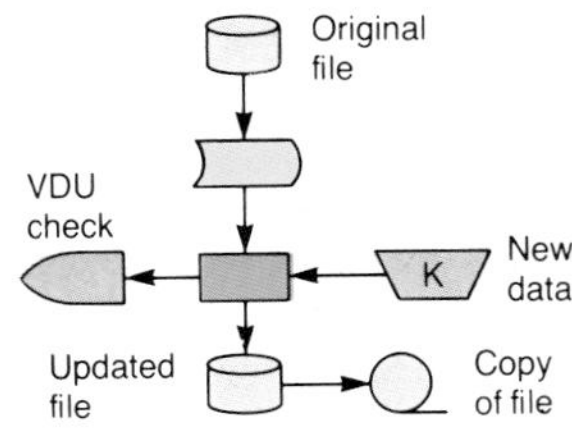

Updating a file

Database

A database is a continuously updated collection of data used by all the file systems operated by a computer; the database is not designed to satisfy any one particular application. A simple example is that of a firm supplying agricultural products. The products can be grouped by *type* of product and an *item* is given a code number. One code number will satisfy both these requirements. An account of stock is needed, for which entries are required for both stock purchases and stock sales. The names and addresses of customers and suppliers are also needed. Finally the date of each transaction will supply the first entry for that transaction. The diagram illustrates a plan of operation. The database file contains a **menu** of programs from which the required program can be selected. The programs and data are loaded into RAM. The new information is entered by keyboard; a check of the data can be made by VDU, if required. The chosen program then presents the computer with decisions concerning the selection and presentation of data to be displayed or recorded. First of all, the customer file is updated for sales and cash receipts. As this is an important file, a copy is made on magnetic tape. This is a cheaper alternative than making a copy on another disk, although this, too, could be done. An item check list is then displayed on the VDU for immediate action, and a list printed to check that action has been completed by a predetermined date, using visual inspection. The updated customer file is examined for unpaid debts and a list printed, or standard reminders, depending on the length of time overdue, can be printed, ready to be mailed.

From these few examples, it can be seen that the data in the database can be organised in different ways. Files can be maintained for important areas of data control and printed records prepared for use by the office staff.

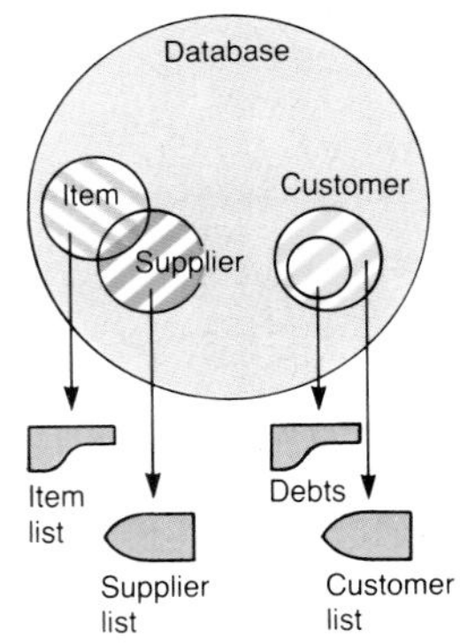

Using a database

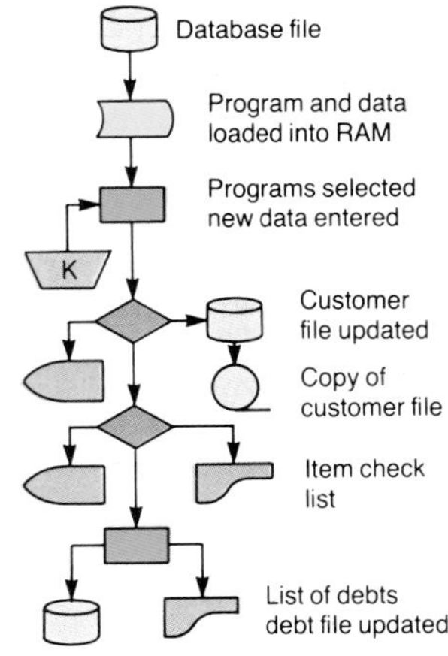

Using a data model

Summary

Transfer of data is along a data bus; memory locations are cleared before transfer takes place; an AND gate controls the input command.

Address mechanism: address lines A15, A14 for major areas of memory, lines A0 to A6 address columns and A7 to A13 address rows.

Static memory consists of bistable flip-flops. It is volatile

Dynamic memory consists of capacitors with a transistor switch; it needs refreshing every 2 ms. It is volatile.

Memory maps divide RAM into areas used for specific purposes.

ROM (read only memory) is non-volatile with data 'burned in'. It is used to store instructions, code tables, and other selected information necessary to operate the computer.

RAM (random access memory) is volatile. Data can be written in or read out, with random, instantaneous access to any location. Locations are addressable and each stores one byte, generally of eight bits.

A **pointer** marks a boundary between the different mapped portions of RAM. The address can be amended by program and the pointer updated.

A **program line** in BASIC is entered in an area of memory designated 'line being typed'. When complete, and checked, the RETURN key adds it to the existing program.

ASCII codes are written in decimal, but stored in RAM in binary. The codes are translated by ROM into characters, numbers and symbols for the VDU.

The **keyboard** is divided into horizontal and vertical sections; pressing a key sends a keyboard code to the CPU. This activates the subroutines in ROM to produce the ASCII code.

Printing on a VDU is carried out by reference to a subroutine table in ROM. The table supplies a list of eight bytes. A figure 1 in the table produces a black dot, and the figure Ø a blank on the VDU. The dots build a picture which forms a printable character.

Lowercase printing needs a 16-byte pattern of dots to obtain full ascenders and descenders. This facility is not available on many computers.

A **peripheral device** is connected to a computer; generally it stores information.

A **medium** is the material used for storing information.

An **interface** connects peripheral devices with a computer.

A **bus** is a set of conductors forming paths for information transfer.

A **driver** is a device that amplifies a current or a voltage.

A **UART** (universal asynchronous receiver/transmitter) is an integrated circuit on a silicon chip, which controls the transfer of information between the computer and peripheral devices; it works through the interface which provides the necessary connections.

USART and **USRT** are similar devices to a UART.

A **port** is an outlet from a computer to external devices; it comprises the connection and a supporting circuit.

The lines controlling **input/output** are marked IORQ, MREQ, RD and WR on the interface. These are used in combinations for internal memory, and external devices and information in or out.

A **handshake** is necessary between a computer and a peripheral device; it is a signal sent in one direction and acknowledged by a signal in the other direction.

The **interface** has special lines to conduct signals signifying readiness, or otherwise, of devices, or the computer, to engage in data transfer; these are controlled by registers.

The **control register** selects the baud rate, word length, and number of stop bits required to send one byte of information to a particular peripheral device. All three quantities depend on the nature of the individual device.

The **command register** controls handshake procedure, transmission method (duplex or half duplex), parity checks, voltage transmission for ones and zeros.

The **status register** indicates the following errors in transmission: parity, buffer overflow, framing error, DSR and CTS handshake signals, break in transmission.

Serial transmission of one byte of data involves sending: one START BIT, data BITS, PARITY BIT, STOP BITS.

Block transmission is used by a computer to send data in serial mode; a **sum check** at the end of the block checks the number of ones sent; the device checks the number of ones received.

A **glitch** is a momentary abnormal power supply causing errors in recorded data or in the operation of programs. **White noise** is a series of electrical disturbances spread equally over a waveband of energy.

LED (light emitting diodes) displays are controlled by one byte of data; used to signal errors or display the contents of registers.

Printers are line or character machines; most are impact printers, others use heat-sensitive paper.

Character printers are either daisy-wheel or matrix machines.

Matrix printers form letters from a pattern of dots on a 7 × 5 matrix.

Resolution is a measure of the smallest distance between any two dots.

Spooling is a technique used with low-speed devices; data are stored on disk and printed later.

Debounce is the status of a computer or device when all contact bounce has been eliminated; **contact bounce** forms varying electrical impulses from the closing of mechanical switches.

Disks are divided into **sectors** separated by gaps. Circular tracks on each sector form addressable locations. Disks are equipped with a write-protect notch; they can store programs as well as data.

Magnetic tape has data recorded on tracks using ASCII code with parity bits; cassette tapes have binary codes recorded as wave patterns of audible frequencies; different frequencies are used to record 1 and Ø.

SAVE is the command to store on tape.

LOAD is the command to transfer a program on tape to a computer.

A **hierarchy** of memory is based on access time; RAM has almost instantaneous access, disk is slower although access is random, magnetic tape is slow and access is sequential.

Operations are planned, using symbols for storage devices, so that minimum time is used in executing a program.

CHAPTER 12

Using BASIC as a language

The restricted vocabularies of BASIC can be grouped under four headings:

commands, e.g. CLEAR, CONT, LIST, LOAD, RUN
statements, e.g. DIM, FOR, LET, GOSUB, IF, NEXT, REM, READ, CLEAR, LIST, PRINT
functions, e.g. ABS, COS, EXP, INT, LOG, ATN, SQR, TAB
operators, e.g. *, +, ", =, <, > =, ( ), AND, E,

A **command** is used by itself, for example CLEAR or CONT tells the computer what direct action to take. A **statement** can be **narrative**, in which assignments are made, or **directive**, which controls the operation of the computer through its program, that is indirect control. A **function** operates on an argument to produce a result, in most cases mathematical, or concerned with code numbers. An **operator** is mathematical, logical, or syntactical (concerned with the syntax of an instruction). Some words can be used as either commands or directive statements, for example PRINT can be used as either.

Commands

These fall into four groups: (*a*) starting an operation; (*b*) stopping an operation; (*c*) intermediate commands during an operation; (*d*) operating a peripheral device.

Starting an operation on a computer

RUN
GOTO

Both these commands have been described in Chapter 2. The command GOTO must always have a line number, whereas RUN does not need a line number. The important difference in most computers is that RUN removes the value of all variables, whereas GOTO does not. GOTO is thus used in statements as well as in commands, but RUN is not used in statements.

Stopping a program

The instructions STOP and END are directive statements about a program and not commands to the computer. The command NEW erases* a BASIC program stored in RAM; it also erases a machine-code program stored in the RAM program area. DELETE removes specified program lines, for example DELETE 20 erases line 20. Most computers have the facility to delete one line by typing the line number and pressing the return key. Alternative spellings are NE or N for NEW and DEL for DELETE.

NEW

DELETE

Intermediate commands

The command CLS clears the screen on the VDU, but leaves the program undisturbed, so variables remain unaltered. This command is useful; if a program is likely to overflow the screen, the screen can be cleared for new material. The command CLEAR, with alternative spelling CLR, varies in operation with different computers. It can perform the operation commanded by CLS, which it replaces. It may perform the operation commanded by NEW†. In some computers it performs an intermediate operation by clearing the screen and removing the value of all variables. There are thus three possible stages of stopping a program or an operation:

(*a*) CLS clears screen, no effect on variables or program
(*b*) CLEAR clears screen, clears variables, no effect on program
(*c*) NEW clears screen, deletes variables and possibly the program

Check the commands on your computer to ascertain the possibilities for programming at your disposal.

CLS

CLEAR

The CONT command is used to continue a program after a STOP statement. The program is continued at the line following the STOP statement. The command is also used if the screen on a VDU has been filled, but the program is not completed. The screen on the VDU is cleared by CONT and the computer continues with the execution of the program. CONT is never used as a program statement because it is used only when an operation has stopped.

CONT

Peripheral device commands

LOAD and SAVE are used with cassette recording (*see Chapter 11*). LPRINT is frequently used to operate a printer; it causes the result from a program to be printed instead of displayed on a screen. LLIST commands the current program in RAM to be printed. Most computers have few command words in common, so the computer manual should be checked for command words to operate peripheral devices.

*NEW does not erase the program in all computers; it may be recalled by a command, OLD. If another program is entered it overwrites the previous program.

†This procedure is found in only a few computers; CLR is generally used to set all variables, numeric and string, to zero.

Statements

READAND
DATA

The most common statements have been described in Chapter 2. The supplying of data for a program has been limited, so far, to the statement, INPUT. The alternative method of supply uses the statements READ and DATA.

The READ statement reads data from a DATA line. The format of the READ statement must correspond to the format of the DATA statement. In the following program, the data consist of an alpha string and a number:

Program 12.1

```
5  REM    USE OF READ AND DATA
10 READ   A$, M
20 PRINT  A$, M
30 STOP
40 DATA   "B.JONES", 7800
50 END
```

Result

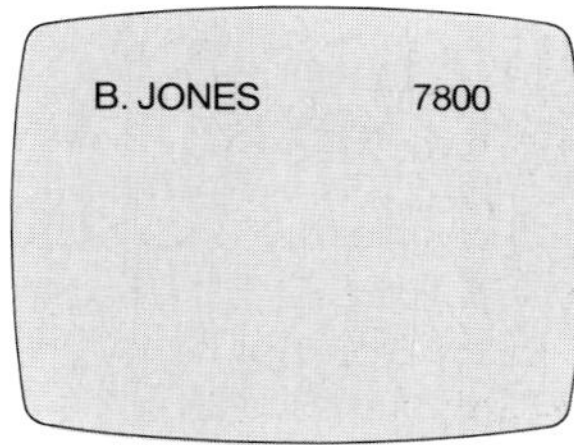

Notes

(1) A$ reads the alpha data, while M reads the number.
(2) The **data** items and the corresponding **read** items are separated by a comma.
(3) The number of **read** items must not exceed the number of **data** items.

In the next program, the number of data items is increased:

Program 12.2

```
5  REM    USING SEVERAL DATA ITEMS
10 READ   A$, A, B$, B, C$, C
20 PRINT  A$, A
30 PRINT  B$, B
40 PRINT  C$, C
50 STOP
60 DATA   "BROWN", 32
70 DATA   "R.SINGH", 43
80 DATA   "BEAUFORT", 35
90 END
```

Result

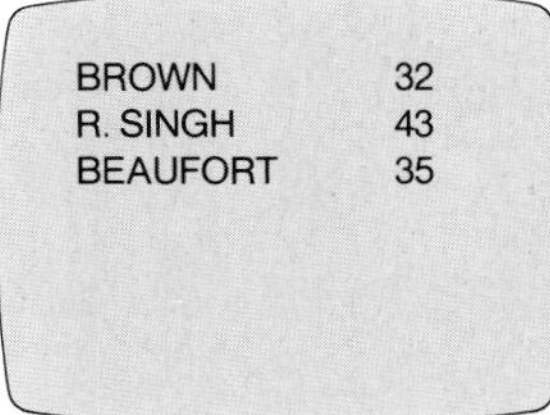

Notes

(1) One READ statement obtains data from three DATA statements, but observe the correspondence of alpha strings and numeric strings.
(2) The program stops after the PRINT statements. The last line contains END. Some computers allow END to be placed other than on the last line.

The result from program 12.2 can be achieved by a looping program, as in program 12.3.

Notes
(1) The result is the same as for the previous program.
(2) This program is preferable particularly if there are many items of data.
(3) Notice the position of the STOP and END statements.

The two methods of supplying data, that is INPUT and READ . . . DATA, each have their advantages and disadvantages. With READ . . . DATA, the list of data can be checked from the program, but the content of data supplied is fixed by the program. With INPUT, it is more difficult to check the accuracy of the list of data, but the amount of data supplied can be variable.

The data on a DATA line can be read once only by a READ statement. If the data lines are required more than once, then a RESTORE statement must be used. The RESTORE statement resets the DATA pointer to the first line of data. Alternative spellings are REST. and RES and RESTORE$ for string data. Program 12.4 shows the use of RESTORE:

Program 12.3

```
5   REM    USING READ IN A LOOP
10  FOR    N = 1 TO 3
20  READ   A$, A
30  PRINT  A$, A
40  NEXT   N
50  STOP
60  DATA   "BROWN", 32
70  DATA   "R.SINGH", 43
80  DATA   "BEAUFORT",
90  END
```

Program 12.4

```
5   REM     USING DATA MORE THAN ONCE
10  PRINT   "SALESMAN"; TAB 10; "JAN"; TAB 16; "FEB"; TAB
            22; "MAR"; TAB 28; "TOTAL"
15  PRINT
20  FOR     N = 1 TO 3
30  READ    S$, J, F, M
40  LET     T = J + F + M
50  PRINT   S$; TAB 10; J; TAB 16; F; TAB 22; M; TAB 28; T
55  PRINT
60  NEXT    N
70  RESTORE
80  LET     A = 0
90  LET     B = 0
100 LET     C = 0
110 FOR     P = 1 TO 3
120 READ    S$, J, F, M
130 LET     A = A + J
140 LET     B = B + F
150 LET     C = C + M
160 NEXT    P
170 LET     D = A + B + C
```

Result

SALESMAN	JAN	FEB	MAR	TOTAL
SMITH	210	230	140	580
WANG	260	120	330	710
KUMAR	220	100	290	610
TOTAL	690	450	760	1900

Printout from program using restore

175	PRINT	
177	PRINT	
180	PRINT	"TOTAL"; TAB 10; A; TAB 16; B; TAB 22; C; TAB 28; D
190	STOP	
200	DATA	"SMITH", 210, 230, 140
210	DATA	"WANG", 260, 120, 330
220	DATA	"KUMAR", 220, 100, 290
230	END	

Notes

(1) The program is in two parts, separated by RESTORE; each part reads through the data once, so there are two READ statements.

(2) The first part prints the salesmen's names and their commissions for the months of January, February and March, together with calculating the total commission for each salesman. The second part produces the totals for each month and the grand total for all salesmen for the three months. RESTORE allows the data to be used a second time to calculate these totals.

(3) The two READ statements are identical, as they must follow the DATA statements. The second READ statement does not use the salesmen's names, although it has to read them to conform with the DATA format.

(4) The STOP and END statements occur in the second part and conform to their normal place in a program.

Printing

PRINT USING

Printing real numbers is best done using the PRINT USING statement. It reserves a place for a specified number of digits to the right and left of a decimal point, and then prints the decimal points of a set of numbers one exactly below the other. The statement uses the number sign (#) as an operator to control the number of digits in a number.

Program 12.5

5	REM	DISPLAYING NUMBERS WITH A PRINT USING STATEMENT
10	FOR	N = 1 TO 6
20	READ	X
30	PRINT USING	"# # # # # # #. # # #"; X
40	NEXT	N
50	STOP	
60	DATA	3.6, 250, 4 100200, 723·45, 368·179, −0·75
70	END	

Notes

(1) Seven digits to the left of the decimal point, and three digits to the right of the decimal point are specified in line 30. Input X, from READ X, is specified to be printed in this format.

(2) Only relevant digits are printed to the left of the decimal point, but all three digits are printed to the left, zeros being supplied if there is no input of a digit.

The capabilities of PRINT USING vary from one computer to another, so check the facilities offered by your computer in your computer manual. Useful capabilities are (*a*) printing an asterisk (*) in all unused places to the left of the decimal point; (*b*) putting a dollar ($) or yen (¥) or pound (£) sign in front of the printed number; (*c*) putting commas between every third number to the left of the decimal point, for example 4,100,200·00 (*d*) expressing a number in standard form, for example 60000 is printed as 6E+Ø4.

Result

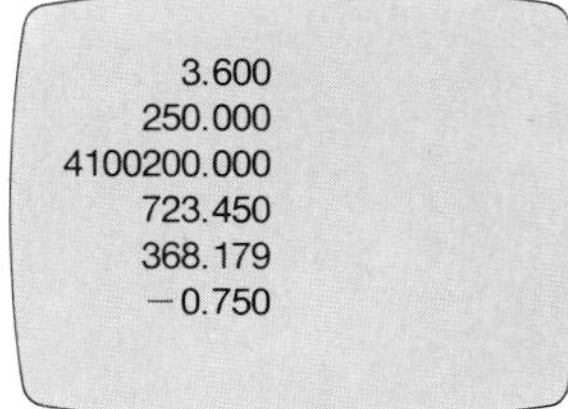

The print using statement

Conditional statements

IF . . . THEN

IF . . . GOTO

The word IF states a condition determined by an operator such as =, >, < and combinations of these operators. This is followed by the word THEN which gives a directive statement for a branching program. The statement IF . . . GOTO has the same effect. Some computers use IF . . . THEN GOTO. If the condition is not met, the program passes to the next line. Instead of supplying a branching directive, THEN can be followed by a command or a directive statement, for example:

```
IF X > 15 THEN STOP
IF Y < = 50 THEN END
IF Z < > X THEN PRINT "Z = 25"
```

IF . . . LET

A condition can be followed by an assignment, using the statement IF . . . LET. The statement varies from one computer to another. Some computers leave out the LET, others use IF . . . THEN and a few use IF . . . THEN LET. The following program can be used to test your computer:

Program 12.6

5	REM	TESTING THE IF . . . LET STATEMENT
10	INPUT	A
20	IF	A > 20 LET A = 10
30	PRINT	"A = ";A
40	GOTO	10

Notes

(1) Input A = 21. If the computer allows the statement, then it will print A = 10; if it does not it will print A = 21. Test also with A = 19, when it should print A = 19.

(2) Replace line 20 by:

(*a*) IF A > 20 A = 10
(*b*) IF A > 20 THEN A = 10
(*c*) IF A > 20 THEN LET A = 10

Try all three choices to see which is accepted.

If a computer accepts an assignment statement, then it will usually accept other directive or assignment statements in place of LET. Repeat the program above, replacing line 20 with the following alternatives in turn:

IF A > 20 PRINT "B = 5"
IF A > 20 INPUT B
IF A > 20 READ A (A DATA line needed for this directive)

If the computer needed either THEN or THEN LET, try the three alternatives again inserting THEN before the directive, for example IF A > 20 THEN PRINT "B = 5".

More than one condition

Some computers using IF . . . LET allow a second condition to be used, that is an IF statement in place of the LET statement. For example line 20 can be replaced by IF A > 20 IF A < 30 A = 10. Try this combination on your computer, and the alternatives suggested above.

A more usual way of imposing more than one condition is to use a logical operator such as AND, OR, NOT, for example:

IF A > 20 AND A < 30 THEN A = 10

An endless variety of conditions can be imposed by the use of logical operators.

More than one branching instruction

ON . . . GOTO

The ON . . . GOTO directs a program to more than one branch, depending on the value of a variable. Program 12.7 shows its use:

Program 12.7

5	REM	THE USE OF ON . . . GOTO
10	INPUT	A
20	ON	A GOTO 6Ø, 1ØØ, 14Ø
30	PRINT	"A > = 4"
40	GOTO	1Ø
60	PRINT	"A = 1"
70	GOTO	1Ø
100	PRINT	"A > 1 AND A < = 2"
110	GOTO	1Ø
140	PRINT	"2 < A < = 3"
150	GOTO	1Ø

Notes

(1) Make the input successively 1, 2, 3, 4. If A = 1, the program branches to line 60; if A = 2, it branches to line 100; if A = 3, it branches to line 140. If A = 4 or more, it continues to line 30.

(2) Make the inputs real numbers, not integers; for example A = 3·98, A = 1·5, A = 0·6. The integer value of the number is found and then values of 1, 2, 3 used to direct the branching.

(3) Change line 20 to: ON A − 20 GOTO 6Ø, 1ØØ, 14Ø and make the input 21, 22, 23, or 24.

(4) Change line 20 to: ON A/10 GOTO 6Ø, 1ØØ, 14Ø and make the input 10, 20, 30, 40.

By using different arithmetical operators, the options on the conditions can be varied widely.

ON . . . GOSUB

A variation of ON . . . GOTO is the statement ON . . . GOSUB. The subroutine program includes the statement RETURN, so whatever subroutine is chosen, the program returns to the next line after the ON . . . GOSUB statement. The next program illustrates the use of the ON . . . GOSUB statement.

Program 12.8

```
5   REM    THE USE OF ON . . . GOSUB STATEMENTS
10  INPUT  A
20  ON     A GOSUB 5Ø, 8Ø, 15Ø
30  GOTO   10
50  PRINT  "SUBROUTINE 1"
60  RETURN
80  REM    SUBROUTINE NO. 2
90  LET    B = A*30
100 PRINT  "B =  "; B
110 RETURN
150 IF     A < 3 THEN PRINT "3 < A < 4"
160 PRINT  "A =  "; A
170 RETURN
```

Notes

(1) Make the input successively 1, 2, 3, 4. Branching is the same as for the previous program (Program 12.7).

(2) If 4, or a greater number, is entered, then another input is requested, as line 20 fails and the program proceeds to line 30, from which it is directed to line 10.

ELSE

If your computer does not use the ON statements, they can be replaced by: (*a*) GOTO A*5Ø; (*b*) GOSUB A*1ØØ. The value of A can be multiplied by any number which is suitable. This use of GOTO and GOSUB places a restriction on the numbering of the relevant lines. A suitable replacement for line 20 in the last program would be: 20 GOSUB A * 50, and line 80 would have to be renumbered line 100.

The statement ELSE instructs the computer to branch to another line if a condition is not met. All possibilities are thus included in the one line.

Program 12.9

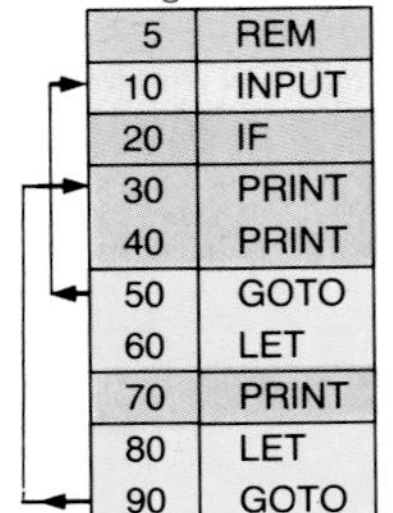

```
5   REM    THE USE OF ELSE
10  INPUT  A
20  IF     A < 10 THEN 4Ø ELSE GOTO 6Ø
30  PRINT
40  PRINT  "A =  "; A
50  GOTO   1Ø
60  LET    A = 1001
70  PRINT  "A =  "; A
80  LET    A = A/1000
90  GOTO   30
```

Notes

(1) If the computer uses the ELSE statement, then there is no possibility of the program going from line 20 to line 30 with the present statements.

(2) If ELSE is followed by STOP or by GOSUB 6Ø, then the command CONT would direct the program to line 30 if STOP had been executed and RETURN in the subroutine would direct the program to line 30.

The direct use of RAM

PEEK

The statement, PEEK, examines the contents of a location in RAM or ROM, for example PEEK (16509) examines the numeric value stored in location 16509. In order to use PEEK, it is necessary to know how the locations in RAM and ROM are used. For this, the computer's memory map must be known. The contents of any location can be examined, but giving a meaning to the numbers is more difficult, as the numbers can be (*a*) ASCII code, (*b*) part of a number in binary standard form or in binary coded decimal, (*c*) a number in binary, for example a line number, or (*d*) part of a two-byte word for an address in memory location. Unless the starting point is known for a particular process the meaning of the numbers cannot be readily determined. PEEK is also used to look at numbers entered by the statement, POKE.

The memory map of your computer should tell you which locations are used to store a program. Let the starting location be 1201. (Check for the correct value on your computer). The following program will display the type of information given in the diagram on page 70:

Program 12.10

```
5   REM    THE USE OF PEEK
300        A = 321·56
400 FOR    N = 1 TO 20
410        X = PEEK (1200 + N)
420 PRINT  X, 1200 + N
430 NEXT   N
```

Result

```
1     12Ø1
44    12Ø2
15    12Ø3
Ø     12Ø4
65    12Ø5
61    12Ø6
51    12Ø7
50    12Ø8
49    12Ø9
46    121Ø
53    1211
54    1212
```

Printout from PEEK

Notes

(1) Do not forget to change 1200 in line 410 to the correct location for the memory map of your computer.

(2) The results, in the diagram, show the numeric values in the first twelve locations. Check the values of the ASCII code and check the locations against the appearance of the diagram on page 70.

(3) In lines 300 and 410, use LET as a statement if your computer allows it.

It will be noticed that the line number is stored in two locations, recorded as 1 and 44 to make 300 from (1 × 256 + 44). The number of bytes in the line is stored in the next two locations as 16 (with LET) or 15 (without LET) and Ø. If there were three hundred bytes in the recorded line, the two locations would store 44 and 1, that is the reverse of the method of storing the line number as the least significant byte is placed first. The following program shows how the line number and the number of bytes can be obtained from the RAM locations. This method is useful to determine the address of a location which has been stored in RAM, that is a number between 0 and 65535.

Program 12.11

```
5    REM    USING PEEK FOR A 2-BYTE WORD
300         A = 321·56
400  PRINT  256 * PEEK (1201) + PEEK (1202), "= LINE NUMBER"
410  REM    LINE 400 IS USED IF THE MOST SIGNIFICANT
            BYTE IS STORED FIRST
420  PRINT  PEEK (1203) + 256 * PEEK (1204)
430  REM    LINE 420 IS USED IF THE MOST SIGNIFICANT
            BYTE IS STORED LAST
440  END
```

Note
Do not forget to change 1201 . . . 1204 in lines 400 and 420 to the correct location for the memory map of your computer.

POKE

Using the statement POKE, an integer, from 0 to 255, can be stored in a specified location. The statement used is POKE 16514, 29 by which the number 29 is stored in the location 16514. Before using POKE, you must be sure that the location can be used for that purpose, for example it is not possible to POKE a location in ROM, or wise in part of RAM dedicated to another use. For the next program, program 12.12, it is assumed that a program is stored in locations starting at location 1201. A REM statement is entered, as such a statement can be POKE d without disturbing the rest of the program.

Notes
(1) If you have the correct starting point, the result should be: computer, that is capital letters changed to lower-case letters.
(2) X is the fifth location after the start of locations used to store a program. Two locations are used for line number, two for the number of bytes in the statement and one location for REM.

Program 12.12

```
5    REM    COMPUTER
10   LET    X = 1205
20   FOR    N = 1 TO 8
30   LET    X = X + 1
40   LET    Y = PEEK (X)
            + 32
50   POKE   X, Y
60   LET    Z = PEEK X
70   PRINT  CHR$ (Z)
80   NEXT   N
```

(3) Y gives the number corresponding to the ASCII code for C (capital letter); 32 is added giving the ASCII code for c (lowercase).
(4) In location 1206, C is changed to c.
(5) The character for the ASCII code is printed.
(6) List the program again; notice that the REM statement has been replaced.

It is unwise to use POKE unless you are sure of the program locations, and have a knowledge of the memory map. Try changing X to another number, run the program and see if it crashes (see below). Programs designed for different BASIC dialects can usually be altered to suit a particular computer, but if PEEK and POKE are included in the program, then a suitable alteration will always be difficult.

Crash

A program crashes when the screen goes blank, and no key can be pressed to restore the program. Alternatively, the screen may be filled with strange patterns, usually black and white, and the restoration of the program is not possible. The definite cure for a crashed program is to switch the computer off and start again*. Crashes are most common with POKE and USR statements.

List

LIST

LIST can be either a command or a statement, although it does not effect or affect the running of a program. LIST can be typed in at any point and will produce a list of the program lines. By itself, it starts with the first line. Many computers allow a number after LIST, in which case it begins with the line at that number, or the next numbered line, for example LIST 26 will start line 30 if there are no lines 26, 27, 28 or 29. The command is useful in the middle of a long program as it can be typed and run and the first part of the program displayed, while still retaining the whole program, so far, in memory. Different computers use LIST in different ways, for example a few allow LIST only; many allow LIST *n*, where *n* is a number, and then display all lines from line *n* onwards; some display one line only. Try the command on your computer, following the instruction manual. Alternative spellings are LIS, LI and L.

*For computers with suitable facilities, the instruction: RESET, BREAK, ESCAPE, may be used.

Functions

STR$

A function is a reserved word which calls a microprogram, or a macroinstruction in machine code, to perform a particular process. There are two types of function, general and mathematical. General functions are concerned with computer codes, and numbers.

The function STR$ converts a number into a string. The string can then be manipulated by the functions LEN, LEFT$, RIGHT$, MID$ and SEG$ as described before. This function is useful in dealing with numbers that represent codes, for example the code for a date, or a truth table. Consider the following code:

CODE	1	MALE	BROWN HAIR	BROWN EYES	TALL	THIN	RIGHT HANDED
CODE	0	FEMALE	BLOND HAIR	BLUE EYES	SHORT	FAT	LEFT HANDED

A person coded 101010 is a left-handed, thin, short, brown-eyed male with blond hair. Here is a list of four people with their coded description:

FATIMAH	011101	SMITH	010101
RAJAH	111011	TAN	111000

We wish to sort from this list a blue-eyed female with brown hair. The code for such a person is 010XXX where X indicates a code value which is not required. The coded description can be entered as a number. There is one difficulty, a number cannot start with a zero, as the computer suppresses it, so all the code numbers must start with a dummy number, which will be chosen as 2.

Program 12.13

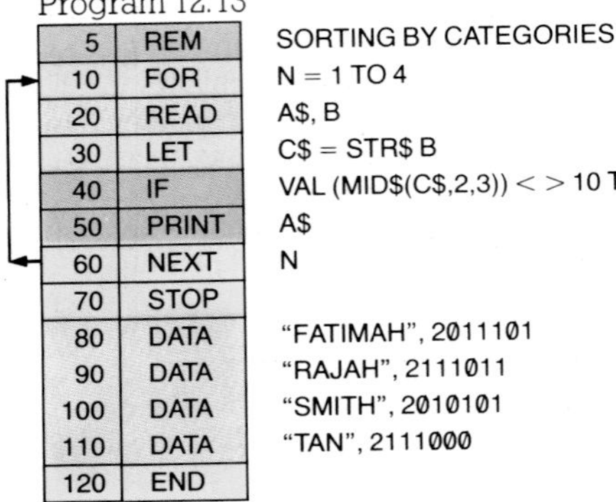

```
5   REM   SORTING BY CATEGORIES
10  FOR   N = 1 TO 4
20  READ  A$, B
30  LET   C$ = STR$ B
40  IF    VAL (MID$(C$,2,3)) < > 10 THEN 60
50  PRINT A$
60  NEXT  N
70  STOP
80  DATA  "FATIMAH", 2011101
90  DATA  "RAJAH", 2111011
100 DATA  "SMITH", 2010101
110 DATA  "TAN", 2111000
120 END
```

Notes

(1) The condition in line 40 is that the code is not equal to 10. If that condition is not met, then the code *is* equal to 10, and the description fits, so line 50 prints the name of the person satisfying the condition of a blue-eyed female with brown hair.

(2) The required code of Ø1Ø is found in the digits 2 to 4 hence the value of MID$ in line 40. Ø1Ø is recorded in decimal notation in RAM, hence its value is 10.

(3) The answer is SMITH.

(4) Write down the code for a tall, fat, right-handed person. How would such a person be found by altering the program?

STRING$

The STRING$ function, when joined to PRINT, prints the same character for a specified number of times. The ASCII code number is used to specify the character. For example, the ASCII code for a hyphen (-) is 45. The command PRINT STRING$ (2Ø, 45) prints twenty hyphens along a line. Some computers allow characters enclosed in quotes (inverted commas), or a string variable to be used in place of the ASCII code number, for example PRINT STRING$ (2Ø, "Z") prints twenty letters Z; PRINT STRING$ (2Ø, "A$") prints the variable of A$, twenty times. Try these on your computer to see which produces a result. Alternative spellings of STRING$ are STRING and STR.

Code related functions

ASC

CHR$

The binary code using an 8-bit byte permits a description of 256 items with code values from 0 to 255. These items are figures, letters and operators, each consisting of a single symbol, or a **token**. A token is one of the reserved words of BASIC, for example RETURN, DATA, RUN, SAVE, etc. The function ASC converts characters, operators or tokens to code numbers while the function CHR$ performs the reverse operation of converting code numbers to characters, operators or tokens. If your computer manual does not list the code numbers and their printed equivalents, then it is best to start by printing the whole list, using the following program:

Program 12.14

```
5   REM    THE CHARACTER CODE SET (1)
10  FOR    N = 0 TO 255 (see footnote*)
20  PRINT  N, CHR$ (N)
30  NEXT   N
```

*If this program does not work, then use N = 32 to 255; values of N less than 32 have probably stopped the microcomputer.

Notes

(1) All characters and most tokens will be displayed. Tokens such as DELETE, EDIT, NEWLINE, etc., have a question mark.
(2) All unused codes are represented by question marks.
(3) Keep a printed record of the result if your manual does not contain a list of the code numbers.

The reverse process is carried out using the function ASC applied to a string:

Notes

(1) Make the input ABCD. The function ASC prints the code for the first letter only.
(2) Some computers allow one character only as an input for A$.

Program 12.15

```
5  REM    THE CHARACTER CODE SET (2)
10 INPUT  A$
20 PRINT  ASC(A$), A$
30 GOTO   10
```

An alternative spelling for ASC is ASCII; the Sinclair computers use CODE instead of ASC and they do not use the standard ASCII code.

The use of ASC and CHR$ can be demonstrated in the encoding and decoding of a message:

Notes

(1) Enter for M$: READING A CODED MESSAGE.
(2) RUN the program and record the result.
(3) Change line 60 to: LET P = X − 4.
(4) Enter for M$ the printed result from the first program.
(5) RUN the program and the original message should be returned.
(6) Line 60 can be changed to provide different codes, all simple in execution.
(7) Line 40 isolates each character in turn and then follows the encoding or decoding process.

Program 12.16

```
5  REM    ENCODING A MESSAGE
10 INPUT  M$
20 LET    L = LEN (M$)
30 FOR    N = 1 TO L
40 LET    A$ = LEFT$ ((M$), N, 1)
50 LET    X = ASC (A$)
60 LET    P = X + 4
70 PRINT  CHR$ P
80 NEXT   N
90 STOP
```

INKEY$

The function, INKEY$, has no argument and reads the keyboard. Unlike INPUT, it does not wait for a key to be pressed, but passes on to the next line, unless it is kept circling round the keyboard by a loop. A specific key can be assigned to INKEY$ which then sets a condition for the program to proceed. Only the specified key will cause the program to continue.

Program 12.17

```
5  REM    THE OPERATION OF INKEY$
10 IF     INKEY$ = "X" THEN 50
20 GOTO   10
30 PRINT  "NO"
40 STOP
50 PRINT  "*"; (an asterisk)
60 GOTO   10
```

Notes

(1) If any key other than X is pressed, the screen remains blank; no cursor or request for input is seen.
(2) If X is pressed, the screen is filled with row after row of asterisks, as long as the key is kept pressed.
(3) If there is no semicolon at the end of line 50, then one column of asterisks is printed.
(4) If line 20 is deleted, then 'NO' is printed immediately after RUN is operated, that is the program does not wait for INKEY$ to be pressed.
(5) If line 60 is deleted, only one asterisk is printed.

A time period can be used with INKEY$. The function is placed in the middle of a long loop, which is used to keep the computer occupied. To do this, delete line 20 and add the following lines to the program:

```
 7 FOR N = 1 TO 500
20 NEXT N
```

This should give a delay of five or ten seconds, depending on the computer's cycle time. RUN the program and time the appearance of 'NO'. The number, 500, can be altered to give any desired period of time. A program module of this nature is useful in timed games where a player has to give a response within a short period of time. The number, 500, can be replaced by a variable, which can then be changed by a subroutine, etc., to alter the timed period.

More than one INKEY$ condition can be assigned. This is done by assigning a string to INKEY$:

Program 12.18

```
5  REM    MULTIPLE
          CONDITIONS
          WITH INKEY$
7  PRINT  "READY"
10 LET    A$ = INKEY$
20 IF     A$ = "B" THEN GOTO 60
30 IF     A$ = "C" THEN GOTO 70
40 IF     A$ = "D" THEN GOTO 80
50 GOTO   20
60 PRINT  "*"
65 GOTO   20
70 PRINT  "+";
75 GOTO   20
80 PRINT  "Ø";
85 GOTO   20
```

Notes

(1) Line 50 keeps the computer circling until a key is pressed.
(2) Only keys B, C, D produce a response; other keys have no effect.
(3) A line of asterisks, pluses, or zeros, is printed if the relevant key is pressed.
(4) Lines 65, 75 and 85 are needed to prevent the print instructions being followed consecutively. Try deleting 65 or 75 and see the result. Try deleting line 50 and see the result.

Use of logical and arithmetic operators

Logical and arithmetic operators are used in conjunction with conditions to form multiple conditions. A simple case is illustrated by examination conditions. For example, an examination consists of three papers, and, in order to pass, a candidate must obtain 36 per cent in paper 1, 31 per cent in paper 2, 41 per cent in paper 3 and a total of 130, or more, in all three papers. Failure is thus represented by: $P1 \leqslant 35$; $P2 \leqslant 30$; $P3 \leqslant 40$; $T < 130$. Any one of these conditions will cause failure, hence:

$$P1 \leqslant 35 \text{ OR } P2 \leqslant 30 \text{ OR } P3 \leqslant 40 \text{ OR } T < 130$$

gives the logical condition for failure. This condition is then written into a program, which can be designed for any number of candidates (let K = number of candidates):

Program 12.19

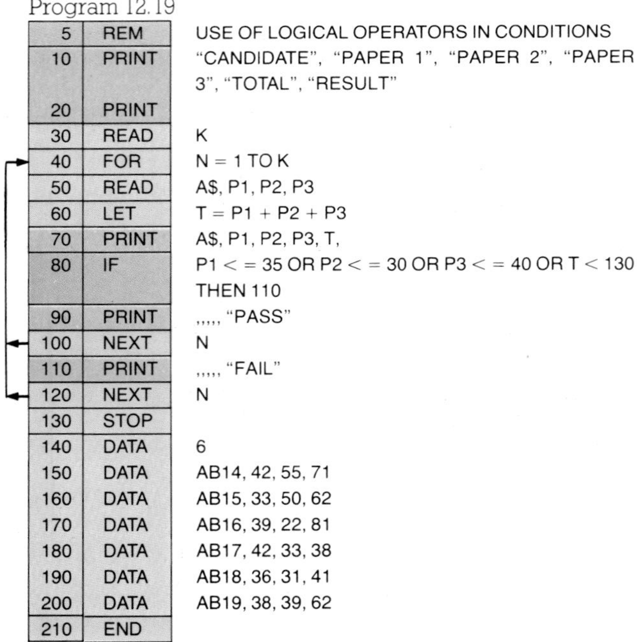

```
5   REM   USE OF LOGICAL OPERATORS IN CONDITIONS
10  PRINT "CANDIDATE", "PAPER 1", "PAPER 2", "PAPER 3", "TOTAL", "RESULT"
20  PRINT
30  READ  K
40  FOR   N = 1 TO K
50  READ  A$, P1, P2, P3
60  LET   T = P1 + P2 + P3
70  PRINT A$, P1, P2, P3, T,
80  IF    P1 < = 35 OR P2 < = 30 OR P3 < = 40 OR T < 130 THEN 110
90  PRINT ,,,,, "PASS"
100 NEXT  N
110 PRINT ,,,,, "FAIL"
120 NEXT  N
130 STOP
140 DATA  6
150 DATA  AB14, 42, 55, 71
160 DATA  AB15, 33, 50, 62
170 DATA  AB16, 39, 22, 81
180 DATA  AB17, 42, 33, 38
190 DATA  AB18, 36, 31, 41
200 DATA  AB19, 38, 39, 62
210 END
```

Notes

(1) Lines 30 and 140 are READ and DATA for six candidates. K can be altered to suit the number of candidates supplied by DATA.

(2) Line 50 reads each candidate's number and marks for one value of N as N follows the loop K (=6) times.
(3) Line 80 provides the conditions for PASS or FAIL. Two candidates pass and four candidates fail. Each failure exhibits one feature of a condition for failure.
(4) Line 80 can be rewritten with the conditions for passing, that is P1 > 35 AND P2 > 30 AND P37 > 40 AND T > = 130. Lines 90 and 110 are then interchanged.
(5) If your computer does not accommodate eighty characters per line, calculate how many characters per column are available and use TAB instructions for each column.

Linear programming

This is a method of solving problems with two variables when the variables are subject to certain restrictions. It is called 'linear' because linear inequalities are involved. Here is a problem solvable by linear programming.

A manufacturer makes two types of radio sets, medium wave and short wave. The following conditions and restrictions apply:

(1) Each medium-wave set costs $20 and each short-wave set costs $70 to make.
(2) Only $1750 is available for manufacture of the sets.
(3) Materials are in short supply so only fifty sets can be manufactured.
(4) Medium-wave sets sell better than short-wave sets, so the number of short-wave sets produced must not exceed the number of medium-wave sets.
(5) The profit on a medium-wave set is $8 and on a short-wave set is $16.

The problem is to find the number of each type of set which will produce the maximum profit.

First set up variables for the problem; all calculations will be in dollars.

Let M = no. of medium-wave sets	let X = maximum profit
let S = no. of short-wave sets	let Y = no. of M for X
let P = profit	let Z = no. of S for X

If all the sets were medium wave, then there would be $1750/$20 = 87 sets. The number of short-wave sets = $\frac{\$1750 - \$20 \times M}{\$70}$, but this must be an integer, so

$$S = INT((1750 - (20{*}M))/70).$$

The profit, P, is given by P = 8*M + 16*S. The conditions (3) and (4) are that S + M < = 50 and S < = M.

All the conditions are now stated. A loop is formed using M=1 TO 87, giving all the possibilities for M. The resulting profit is calculated and a routine used to find the maximum profit. This maximum profit and the number of each type of set is then printed.

Program 12.20

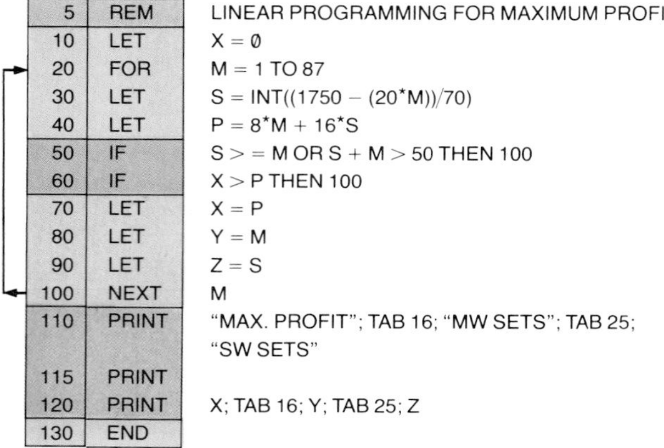

```
5   REM   LINEAR PROGRAMMING FOR MAXIMUM PROFIT
10  LET   X = Ø
20  FOR   M = 1 TO 87
30  LET   S = INT((1750 – (20*M))/70)
40  LET   P = 8*M + 16*S
50  IF    S > = M OR S + M > 50 THEN 100
60  IF    X > P THEN 100
70  LET   X = P
80  LET   Y = M
90  LET   Z = S
100 NEXT  M
110 PRINT "MAX. PROFIT"; TAB 16; "MW SETS"; TAB 25;
          "SW SETS"
115 PRINT
120 PRINT X; TAB 16; Y; TAB 25; Z
130 END
```

Result

MAX. PROFIT	MW SETS	SW SETS
520	35	15

Linear programming, maximum profit

Notes

(1) Line 50 states conditions which must not be exceeded, that is if realised the next value of M must be used.
(2) Lines 60 and 70 determine the maximum profit.
(3) Lines 80 and 90 give the number of radio sets manufactured to produce the maximum profit.

With a program which is complicated, it is useful to test the program at intervals before it is completed. To do this, select a value of M halfway between 1 and 87, that is M = 30 to 48, and then print out the following program, after typing lines 5–40:

Program 12.21

```
20 FOR   M = 30 TO 48
32 IF    S + M > 50 THEN 38
35 GOTO  40
38 LET   S = 50 – M
90 PRINT P, M; TAB 25; S
```

Check the print out, then delete lines 20, 32, 35, 38, 90 and continue with the program. The results of the test are shown in the diagram.

496	30	16
504	31	16
496	32	15
504	33	15
512	34	15
520	35	15
512	36	14
504	37	13

Linear programming, test result

With some problems it may not be possible to find a minimum solution, in which case a result must be printed to represent this fact. A very large number is chosen which could not possibly represent the conditions met in the problem. The following problem provides an example.

A haulage firm can hire two types of vehicles – trucks and vans, but it cannot hire more than seven vehicles altogether as it has insufficient drivers for more vehicles. It carries two types of load, crates and boxes. The conditions for a particular delivery are:

(1) Total vehicles cannot exceed seven.
(2) A truck carries nine crates and three boxes, a van carries four crates and ten boxes.
(3) The hire of a van is £40 and of a truck is £60.
(4) An order is received for thirty-six crates and thirty boxes.

The problem is to find the minimum cost of delivering the order. First we must allocate variables:

F = no. of crates to be carried
G = no. of boxes to be carried
V = no. of vans used
T = no. of trucks used
P = cost of haulage
C = no. of crates that can be carried
B = no. of boxes that can be carried
X = minimum cost of haulage
Y = no. of vans for minimum cost
Z = no. of trucks for minimum cost

The conditions

V + T < = 7	number of vehicles less than, or equal to, seven
C = 4*V + 9*T B = 10*V + 3*T	haulage capacity of vehicles
P = 40*V + 60*T	cost of haulage
F = 36, G = 30	haulage order

The order need not necessarily involve seven vehicles, so two loops are needed, one loop for 0 to 7 vans, and for each cycle of the van loop, we need 0 to (7 − V) trucks in order to cover all possibilities. In addition to the variables above, M and N are needed to provide the two loops. The haulage capacity must be equal to or greater than the haulage order, but must also produce the minimum cost.

Program 12.22

```
5   REM    A MINIMUM COST LINEAR PROGRAM
10  LET    X = 1 E 16
15  REM    THE VALUE OF X IS SO LARGE IT CANNOT BE
           PRODUCED BY THE PROGRAM
20  INPUT  F
25  INPUT  G
30  FOR    N = 0 TO 7
35  FOR    M = 0 TO 7 – N
40  LET    V = N
50  LET    T = M
60  IF     V + T > 7 THEN 160
70  LET    C = 4*V + 9*T
80  LET    B = 10*V + 3*T
90  IF     C < F OR B < G THEN 150
100 LET    P = 40*V + 60*T
110 IF     X < P THEN 150
120 LET    X = P
130 LET    Y = V
140 LET    Z = T
150 NEXT   M
160 NEXT   N
170 PRINT  "MIN. COST", "VANS"; TAB 24; "TRUCKS"
180 PRINT
190 PRINT  X, Y; TAB 26, Z
200 PRINT
210 PRINT  "CRATES =  "; F, "BOXES =  "; G
220 STOP
```

Result

```
MIN. COST      VANS TRUCKS
300            3      3
CRATES = 36  BOXES = 30
```

Linear programming, minimum cost

Notes

(1) If line 35 is: FOR M = 0 TO 7 – N, then line 60 is not needed; if line 35 is: FOR M = 0 TO 7, then line 60 is needed and the program takes longer.

(2) The first INPUT is F = 36, G = 30. Thereafter either RUN or GOTO can be used to try other INPUTS. The first result is shown in the diagram.

(3) The program tries all combinations of vans and trucks successively; in line 90, it rejects combinations with insufficient capacity.

(4) Line 100 calculates the cost of haulage; lines 120 to 140 inclusive record the minimum cost and the number of vans and trucks for that cost.

(5) In order to see how the program tries the combinations of vans and trucks, try the following program. Type lines 30, 35, 40, 50, 150 and 160; add:

Program 12.23

```
5   PRINT  "VANS", "TRUCK
55  PRINT  V, T
```

After running this test program, delete lines 5 and 55 and type in the remainder of the program.

(6) Some typical results from inputs are:

No. of crates	29	38	42	15	48
No. of boxes	42	52	88	69	24
No. of vans	5	5		7	1
No. of trucks	1	2		0	5
Minimum cost	260	320	1E16	280	340

The minimum cost of 1E16 is produced when the haulage requirement cannot be met, that is 42 crates and 88 boxes.

Specifying significant figures

The value of SIN(A) is required to three significant figures. The computer produces a value with eight digits. The value is multiplied by 1000, 0·5 added to the value, the value for INT is produced, and this is divided by 1000, yielding the required result. For example:

SIN(A)	= 0·64421769	(eight digits print-out)
1000 × SIN(A)	= 644·21769	(multiply by 1000)
INT(1000 × SIN(A) + 0·5)	= 644	(rounding to nearest integer)
to three significant figures	= 0·644	(dividing by 1000)
SIN(A)	= 0·99166481	
(× 1000)	= 991·66481	
(rounding up)	= 992	
(to three significant figures)	= 0·992	

In calculations involving money, a result correct to two decimal places, that is dollars and cents, is usually required, particularly when calculating rates of exchange.

A program for monetary conversion is given below.

Program 12.24

```
5   REM    RATES OF EXCHANGE
10  INPUT  X
20  INPUT  Y
25  REM    X IS STARTING CURRENCY, Y IS RATE OF
           EXCHANGE
30  LET    A = X/Y
40  PRINT  A
50  LET    B = A*100
60  PRINT  B
70  LET    C = INT(B + Ø·5)
80  PRINT  C
90  LET    D = C/100
100 PRINT  D
110 GOTO   100
```

Note: The program allows a calculation to be followed in full.

Random numbers

RND

Almost all computers have a function RND to produce random numbers, but the use of the function varies with many machines. Determine exactly what type of random number is produced by the function on your machine.

A common practice is for the function RND to generate a number between 0 and 1; it can have the value 0, but not the value 1.

The use of random numbers

One of the major uses of random numbers is in computer games, where random information, such as the throws of dice, a set of cards, a hand of dominoes, is required. Graphic games where objects appear at random positions, or move in a random way, are also controlled by the RND function.

Practical applications are often concerned with queueing problems. People, or objects, arrive in a random manner, to obtain a service, and the length of the queue varies with the random arrival.

A queue problem

A road has a set of traffic signals which change from red to green every minute, that is one minute red, followed by one minute green. Traffic along the road averages 180 vehicles per hour. When the light is green, a vehicle goes through every ten seconds. What is the longest queue of vehicles that can be expected?

In ten seconds the probability of a vehicle arriving is 180/60 × 6, that is 0·5. If a set of random numbers (N) is used, then if N > 0·5, a vehicle will not arrive, if N < = 0·5, a vehicle will arrive. By finding the probability every ten seconds, a random selection of arrivals can be forecast by using the RND function. When the traffic lights are red, the queue builds up; when the lights are green, one vehicle passes through every ten seconds, while, at the same time, vehicles continue to arrive. This state of affairs is shown in the diagram, and it would appear, on average, that the

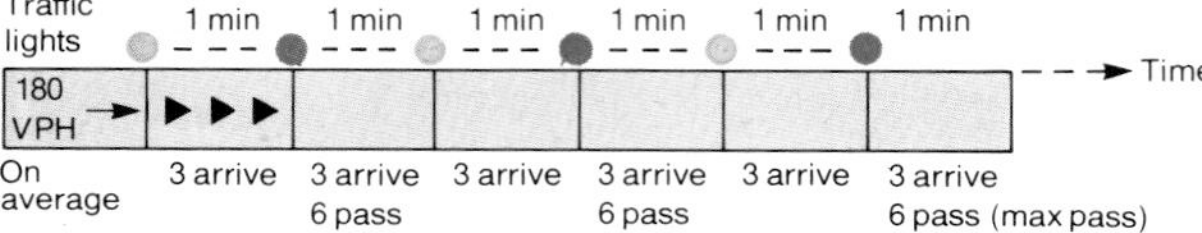

longest queue is three vehicles. A program will now be run to simulate the vehicle queue for a period of one hour. The probability of arrival is determined for ten-second intervals, and the queue calculated for two separate periods of one minute each, that is one minute for red and one minute for green.

Program 12.25

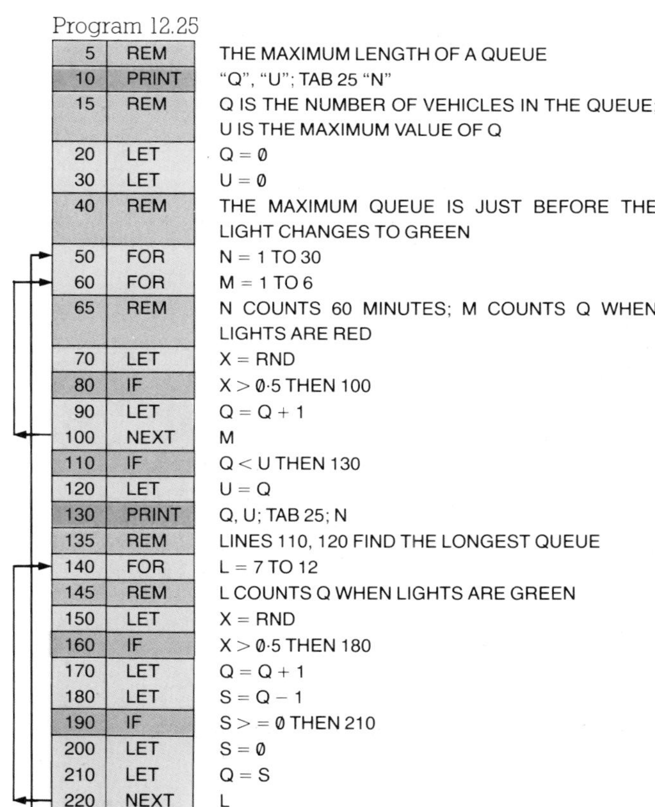

```
5    REM    THE MAXIMUM LENGTH OF A QUEUE
10   PRINT  "Q", "U"; TAB 25 "N"
15   REM    Q IS THE NUMBER OF VEHICLES IN THE QUEUE;
            U IS THE MAXIMUM VALUE OF Q
20   LET    Q = Ø
30   LET    U = Ø
40   REM    THE MAXIMUM QUEUE IS JUST BEFORE THE
            LIGHT CHANGES TO GREEN
50   FOR    N = 1 TO 30
60   FOR    M = 1 TO 6
65   REM    N COUNTS 60 MINUTES; M COUNTS Q WHEN
            LIGHTS ARE RED
70   LET    X = RND
80   IF     X > Ø·5 THEN 100
90   LET    Q = Q + 1
100  NEXT   M
110  IF     Q < U THEN 130
120  LET    U = Q
130  PRINT  Q, U; TAB 25; N
135  REM    LINES 110, 120 FIND THE LONGEST QUEUE
140  FOR    L = 7 TO 12
145  REM    L COUNTS Q WHEN LIGHTS ARE GREEN
150  LET    X = RND
160  IF     X > Ø·5 THEN 180
170  LET    Q = Q + 1
180  LET    S = Q − 1
190  IF     S > = Ø THEN 210
200  LET    S = Ø
210  LET    Q = S
220  NEXT   L
230  NEXT   N
```

Notes

(1) The program determines the longest queue at the traffic lights in a period of one hour.

(2) Line 180 determines the length of the queue, S, in each period of ten seconds.

(3) If S > Ø, then all the vehicles did not pass during the period of the green light. Hence Q must start with this number for calculating line 90 for the red light; this is done in line 210.

(4) If more vehicles could pass than are in the queue, then S would be negative. S can only be Ø or a positive number, so line 200 makes S = Ø instead of a negative number.

A result from the program shows that a maximum queue of seven was reached over a period of fourteen minutes.

Q	U	N
4	4	1
5	5	2
7	7	3
3	7	4
Ø	7	5
4	7	6
3	7	7

Result

Conversions between numerical notations

The following programs are useful for the conversion of a number in any notation to a decimal number and vice versa. Information on microcomputer programs may be given in hexadecimal, octal or even binary notation, but all data inputs have to be in decimal notation for a microcomputer.

Program 12.26

```
5    REM    CONVERSION FROM ANY RADIX (< 36) TO
            DECIMAL NOTATION
10   INPUT  P$
20   INPUT  X
25   REM    P$ IS THE NUMBER WITH RADIX X
30   LET    N = LEN P$
40   LET    M = Ø
50   LET    R = Ø
60   LET    S$ = SEG$(P$, N – M, 1)
65   REM    S$ ISOLATES EACH DIGIT, FROM RIGHT TO LEFT,
            IN TURN
70   LET    T = ASC(S$)
80   IF     T < 65 THEN 110
85   REM    T < 65 SORTS FIGURES FROM LETTERS
90   LET    U = T – 55
100  GOTO   120
110  LET    U = VAL S$
120  LET    R = R + (X**M*U)
125  REM    IF M = Ø THEN X**M = 1
130  LET    M = M + 1
140  IF     N – M = Ø THEN 160
150  GOTO   60
160  PRINT  P$; "RADIX";X; " = ";R; "DECIMAL"
170  GOTO   10
```

Notes

(1) T gives the ASCII code number for each character. T – 55 converts the code number to a figure, for example ASC(A) = 65. 65 – 55 = 10, that is A = 10.

Input

P$	X
210	8
FAB	16
8000	16
11001100	2
AFG	24
2088	20

```
210       RADIX  8 = 136   DECIMAL
FAB       RADIX 16 = 4011  DECIMAL
8000      RADIX 16 = 32768 DECIMAL
11001100  RADIX  2 = 204   DECIMAL
AFG       RADIX 24 = 6136  DECIMAL
2088      RADIX 20 = 16168 DECIMAL
```

Result

(2) To convert each digit to a decimal value, it must be multiplied by the place value of the radix, for example for radix 16 the place values are 16^4; 16^3; 16^2; 16; 1. This is achieved by X**M with successive values of M from 0 to the length of the string of digits.

(3) Almost all computers, except the Sinclair, use the ASCII code, and can use this program. The Sinclair code has no gap between its figures and its letters and the above program can be simplified as follows:

line 60 replace by S$ = P$(N − M)
line 70 replace by T = CODE S$
line 90 replace by U = T − 28
lines 80, 100, 110, delete

In addition to the listed inputs, try ZZZZ, radix 35. Radix 35 uses all ten figures and twenty-six letters of the alphabet. The main use of the program is for the conversion of hexadecimal numbers to decimal numbers.

The next program converts decimal numbers to hexadecimal numbers.

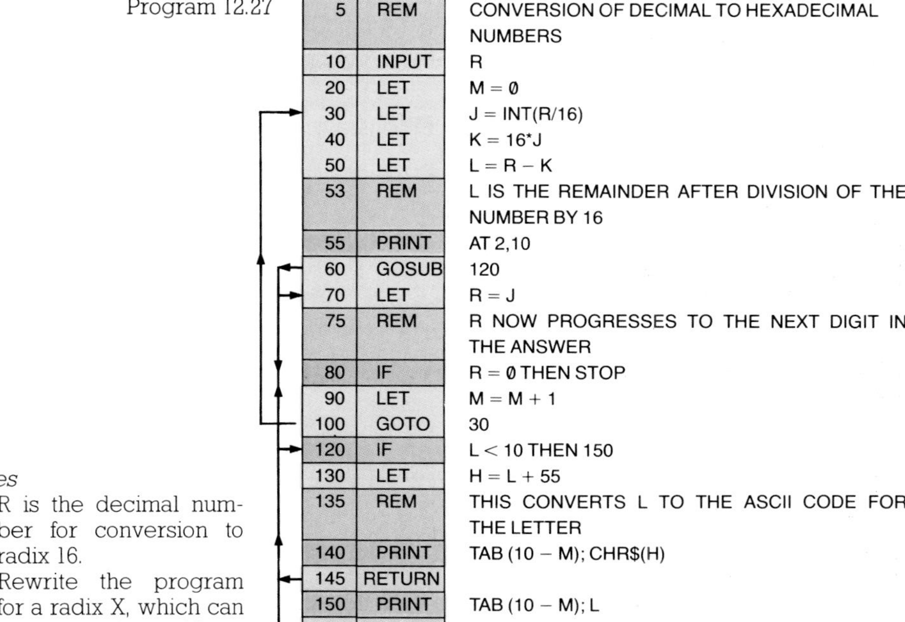

Program 12.27

```
5    REM     CONVERSION OF DECIMAL TO HEXADECIMAL NUMBERS
10   INPUT   R
20   LET     M = Ø
30   LET     J = INT(R/16)
40   LET     K = 16*J
50   LET     L = R − K
53   REM     L IS THE REMAINDER AFTER DIVISION OF THE NUMBER BY 16
55   PRINT   AT 2,10
60   GOSUB   120
70   LET     R = J
75   REM     R NOW PROGRESSES TO THE NEXT DIGIT IN THE ANSWER
80   IF      R = Ø THEN STOP
90   LET     M = M + 1
100  GOTO    30
120  IF      L < 10 THEN 150
130  LET     H = L + 55
135  REM     THIS CONVERTS L TO THE ASCII CODE FOR THE LETTER
140  PRINT   TAB (10 − M); CHR$(H)
145  RETURN
150  PRINT   TAB (10 − M); L
160  RETURN
```

Notes

(1) R is the decimal number for conversion to radix 16.

(2) Rewrite the program for a radix X, which can have any value < 36.

Program modules

The following modules, all used in previous programs, are useful when compiling a program:

	Program number
(1) Using a loop of variable length	12.16
(2) Calculating a total from a set of entries	2.11
(3) Supplying an answer correct to a given number of significant figures	12.24
(4) Printing a two-dimensional array	7.2
(5) Slicing subscripted strings	7.6
(6) Finding the smallest, or greatest, number in a set of numbers	6.17
(7) Arranging a list in alphabetical order	6.16
(8) Sorting by coded categories, using truth tables	7.14; 12.13
(9) Providing multiple conditions by keyboard selection	12.18
(10) Using logical operators for multiple conditions	12.19
(11) Linear programming	12.20; 12.22

Summary

Reserved words in BASIC are commands, statements, functions or operators.

GOTO and **RUN** start a program; GOTO always has a line number.

NEW may erase a program; **DELETE** erases a line.

CLS and **CLEAR** may both clear the screen; CLEAR may erase variables.

CONT continues a program after STOP, starting at the next line; it also continues a PRINT instruction after the VDU screen has been filled.

READ and **DATA** are used for input; **RESTORE** allows **DATA** to be used again.

PRINT USING reserves a place for a specified number of digits and lines up decimal points in a column of numbers.

IF . . . THEN is used for conditional statements (also IF . . . GOTO) to cause a program to branch.

IF . . . LET is used for assigning a value after a conditional statement.

ON . . . GOTO directs a program to more than one branch.

ON . . . GOSUB directs a program to more than one subroutine.

ELSE directs a program to a particular line if a condition is not met. It is part of IF . . . THEN . . . ELSE statement.

PEEK examines the contents of a location in RAM or ROM.

POKE stores an integer in a specified location. PEEK and POKE are used only if the map of the computer's memory is known.

LIST produces a list of the current program on a VDU screen; it can be instructed to start at a specified line.

STR$ converts a number into a numeric string.

STRING$ prints a given character a specified number of times.

ASC converts a character to its ASCII code number.

CHR$ converts an ASCII code number to a character.

INKEY$ has no argument; it reads the keyboard, but does not wait for an input. It is used to set a condition for an operation.

Logical and arithmetical operators are used to form multiple conditions.

Linear programming solves problems with two variables, when the variables are subject to limiting conditions.

The vocabulary of BASIC

BASIC words have four categories:

(1) **Commands**: direct instructions for a computer operation; as part of a program some of these words act as directive statements.
(2) **Statements**: the detailed instructions in a program; they are either narrative statements or directive statements.
(3) **Functions**: instructions, usually mathematical, which act on a number to produce a result.
(4) **Operators**: instructions which modify or compare program items.

a5The BASIC words and symbols operate on the following items which are represented as under:

Q represents a single letter
G represents a string of characters (letters or figures)
a,b,c represent real numbers
n represents an integer
v represents a variable
f represents a mathematical expression
s represents a statement; statements have narrative syntax (S) or are directives (D)
d represents an address in RAM

The following information is also given:

* indicates a standard ANSI word, e.g. END*
() indicates an optional use, e.g. LIST (n), the integer is optional
; indicates an alternative use, e.g. READ G; v (strings or variables can be read)

A function has an **argument** (A); a command may have a **directive statement** (D); a statement has a narrative syntax (S); an operator has a narrative syntax (S); brackets, (), show limits, or arguments of words; a token is a reserved word with an ASCII code number.

word	category	syntax or argument		result	page
ABS*	function	A	a	absolute value, that is positive number, e.g. ABS(–8)=8	71
AND	operator	S	s_1 AND s_2	true if both s_1 and s_2 are true	104
ASC	function	A	ASC(Q); (G)	ASCII code number for Q; G(1)	235
ATN*	function	A	a	angle (in radians)	
CHR$	function	A	n ($0 \leqslant n \leqslant 255$)	character or token for ASCII code number n	235
CLEAR	command	–	no argument	clears VDU, deletes all variables	224
CLS	command	–	no argument	clears VDU, leaves variables	224
CONT	command	–	no argument	continues program after STOP; continues program after clearing VDU	224
COS*	function	A	a (in radians)	COS a	
DATA*	statement	S	DATA G; a; b; c; v	data to be read by READ	225
DELETE	command	D	DELETE n	deletes line n	224
DIM*	statement	S	DIM G(n_1, n_2)	provides memory locations for an array with n_1 and n_2 dimensions	94
E	operator	A	a E n	gives a number in decimal standard form	
ELSE	statement	S	IF s_1 THEN s_2 ELSE s_3	an alternative statement dependent on a condition	230
END*	statement	–	no operand	terminates program	
EXP*	function	A	a	exponential raised to power a	
FOR*	statement	S	FOR Q = a TO b	sets up a loop, closed by NEXT	
GOSUB*	statement	D	GOSUB n	jumps to subroutine, line n	101
GOTO*	statement	D	GOTO n	jumps to line n; start program at line n, variables unchanged	24
IF*	statement	S	IF s_1 THEN s_2	describes a condition to be met for a branching program	35, 84
INKEY$	function	A S	no argument IF INKEY$ = v	the character representing the key pressed selects a specified variable	236
INPUT*	statement	S	INPUT v	enters a variable	24
INT*	function	A	a	a truncated integer	71
LEFT$	function	A	LEFT$ (G, n)	extracts first n characters from a string	80

word	category	syntax or argument		result	page
LEN	function	A	LEN G	gives the length of a string, i.e. the number of characters	77
LET*	statement	S	LET v = f; a	assigns a value to a variable	24
LIST	command	D	LIST (n)	lists a program on the VDU, from line n; or line Ø with no number	233
LOAD	command	D	LOAD G	loads program G from tape into computer	218
LOG*	function	A	Log a (a > Ø)	Napierian logarithm of a	
LPRINT	command	A D	LPRINT f LPRINT G	prints result of calculating f prints text from alphanumeric string	22
MID$	function	A	MID$ (G, n_1, n_2)	extracts characters n_1 to n_2 from string G	80
NEW	command	–	no argument	deletes entire program	224
NEXT*	statement	S	NEXT Q	closes loop begun with FOR	
NOT	operator	S	NOT s	reverses statement	105
ON	statement	S S	ON a, b, c GOTO n_1, n_2, n_3 ON a, b, c GOSUB n_1, n_2, n_3	executes multiple branching on value of a, b, c	229 230
OR	operator	S	s_1 OR s_2	true if either s_1 or s_2, or both, are true	105
PEEK	statement	D	PEED d	examines contents of byte d	231
PI	function	–	no argument	3.14159	34, 72
POKE	statement	D	POKE d, n	puts the value, n, into byte d	155
PRINT*	command statement	– A D S	no argument PRINT f PRINT G; v; a PRINT TAB;	blank line on screen prints result of calculating f prints a string, the value of a variable, or a number prints at a specified position	22 25
PRINT USING	statement	S	PRINT USING "##. #"	specifies number of digits and position of decimal point	227
RANDOMIZE*	statement	–	no argument	generates a new set of random numbers	
READ*	statement	S	READ G; v	reads data from DATA lines	225
REM*	statement	–	REM text	no effect on program	25
RESTORE*	statement	–	no argument	permits DATA lines to be read again	226

word	category	syntax or argument		result	page
RETURN*	statement	–	no argument	returns from subroutine to line after GOSUB	101
RIGHT$	function	A	RIGHT$ (G, n)	extracts last n characters from G	80
RND*	function	(A)	RND (n)	produces set of random numbers from Ø to 1; or from Ø to n (Ø ≤ a < 1; Ø ≤ b < n)	244
RUN	command	D	RUN (n)	deletes variables, starts program from line Ø or from line n	24
SAVE	command	D	SAVE G	records program G from computer on to tape	218
SEG$	function	A	SEG$ (G, n_1, n_2)	extracts characters n_1 to n_2 from G	99
SGN	function	A	a	–1 or Ø or +1, depending on value and sign of a	73
SIN*	function	A	a (in radians)	SIN a	
SQR*	function	A	a (a > Ø)	√a	72
STEP*	function	A	FOR Q = a TO b STEP c	specifies increment for each cycle of a loop	
STOP*	statement	D	no argument	stops execution of program, see CONT	
STRING$	function	A	STRING$ (n, ASCII code)	prints a character n times	235
STR$	function	A	STR$ v	converts numeric variable to a string	77
TAB*	function	A	TAB n; v; f	specifies print position on a line	29
TAN*	function	A	a (in radians)	TAN a	
THEN*	statement	S	IF . . . THEN S	statement depending on a condition	35
TO	function	A	a TO b; G(n_1 TO n_2)	specifies limits of loop; extracts characters n_1 to n_2 from G	80
USR	function	A	USR d	calls machine-code program starting at location d	
VAL	function	A	VAL G	evaluates string G (a numeric string)	77

Index

absolute value 71
ACC 16, 121
accumulator 16, 121
ADC 19
address 12, 143
—, absolute 163, 174
— circuit 186
— control unit 120, 137
— decoder 120
—, indexed 162
—, indirect 162
— lines, bus 186
—, method of 174
—, symbolic 166
algorithm 43
alphabetical order 88
alphanumeric arrays 96
— characters 58
ALU 16, 121
analogue 18
analogue-to-digital converter 19
AND 104
AND gate 107
architecture 119
arithmetic and logic unit 16, 121, 126
array 94
—, alphanumeric 96
—, numeric 94
—, string 96
ascenders 199
ASCII code 57
assembler 173, 174
assembly language 161
— — format 162
assign 24

Base 52
base language 179
BASIC 21, 176
baud rate 208
BCD 56
binary code 173
binary-coded decimal 56
binary complement 64
binary exponent 68
— mantissa 68
— notation 52
bit 56
block transfer 169
— transmission 211
Boolean variable 104
bootstrap loader 216
bounce 215
brackets 35
brown-out 211
buffer 125
bug 35
bus 125, 200
byte 56

Calculation 7
calculator 7
call 147
carry flag 130
cathode-ray tube 10
CCR 16
central processing unit 15, 119, 122
character code 58
— printer 212
characters 58
— per second 208
clear to send 206
COBOL 176
comma 29
command code 129
— control unit 120
— line 125
— register 209
commands 21, 150
comparator 109
compiler 60, 178
complement 63
complemented 17
compound operators 74
computer 7
— codes 57
—, mainframe 7
concatenation 80
condition-code register 16
conditional jump 37, 146
conditions 35, 228
constants 34
contact bounce 215
continuous program 157
control 15
— lines 122
— register 208
corrupt 212
counter 35
CP gate 121
CPS 208
CPU 15, 119
crash 233
CRT 10
CTS 206
cursor 24, 27

DAC 19
daisy-wheel printer 213
data 15, 24
— bus 185

— carrier detect 206
— control unit 121, 137
— set ready 206
— terminal ready 206
— transfer 185
— types 177
database 220
DCD 206
debounce 215
— status 215
debouncing circuit 215
debugging 35
decimal notation 52
decoders 135
decrement 149
definition, picture 10
descenders 199
despooling 215
device 9
dictionary 179
difference 63
digital 18
digital-to-analogue converter 19
diodes 122
directives 163
directory 216
disk 215
— sector 215
— track 215
diskette 13
displacement 144
dividend 65
divisor 65
dot-matrix printer 213
driver 200
DSR 206
DTR 206
duplex 209

Electromechanical 11
EOR gate 109
erase 27
even parity 57
execute cycle 135
— signal 138
exponent 65
exponentiation 33
expression 74

Fetch cycle 134
field 141
field label 172
file 216
fixed-point arithmetic 62
flag register 130
flip-flop 124
floating-point arithmetic 66
floppy disk 12
flowchart 42
format 141
FORTRAN 176
fraction 62
frame 211
— error 211
full duplex 209
function 223, 234

Gates 107
general purpose register 17
glitch 211
GND 206
GPR 17
graph plotter 11
ground connection 206

Half-adder 127
half-carry flag 130
half duplex 209
half-subtractor 128
handshake 207
hard disk 13
heat-sensitive paper 212
hexadecimal notation 54
high-level language 176
highway 122

Impact printer 212
increment 48, 149
index register 168
indexed instructions 122
information 7
—, processing 8
—, retrieval 8
—, storage 12
in-out request 201
in phase 203
input 9, 24, 205
input/output instructions 149
instant access 189
instruction control unit 133
instruction decoder 120
— format 162
— register 17, 120
— types 181
integer 62
integrated circuit 122
interblock gap 217
interface 15, 202
interpreter 16, 180
interval 18
inverse statement 104
IORQ line 201, 204
IR 17
iterative process 43
Joystick 14
jump 119, 147
—, conditional 146
— instruction 119
—, unconditional 146

K 186
keyboard 9, 193
keycode 195

Language 173
large-scale integration 202
last in first out 137
latch 205
least significant bit 195
LED 212
less significant byte 143
lexical analysis 178
LIFO 137
light emitting diode 212
light pen 14
line printer 11, 213
linear programming 239
location 70
logical operators 104
loop 37, 44
low-level language 173
LSB 195
LSI 202

Machine code 141
— — format 141
— — program 152, 161
machine cycle 171
— language 161
macroinstruction 171
magnetic image 212
— tape 13, 216
mantissa 65
MAR 17, 120, 137
mask 131
matrix printer 11, 213
medium 200
memory 12
— address register 19, 120
— boards 190
—, dynamic 188
— hierarchy 14, 219
—, internal 185
— map 138, 189
—, pseudostatic 189
— refresh 189
— request 201
—, static 188
—, volatile 188
menu 172, 220
—, program 220

microcomputer 7
microinstruction 16, 171
microprocessor 119
minicomputer 7
minuend 63
mnemonic 144, 161, 173
mode 24
modem 15
module 200
modulus 71
more significant byte 143
most significant bit 129
MPU 15
MREQ line 201
MSB 129
multiple conditions 46
multiplicand 64
multiplier 64

n-type silicon 122
NAND 105
negate 177
nesting loops 47
nibble 133
non-volatile 12, 189
NOR 106
NOT 105
— gate 107
— XOR 106
notation 52
number 62
— cruncher 7
numeric array 94
— character 58

Object code 161
— program 174
octal notation 53
odd parity 57
operand 121, 142
—, binary 177
—, immediate 142, 162
—, nullary 177
—, stored 142
—, unary 177
operation mnemonic code 174
— priority 177
— types 142
operators 58, 73, 223
optical character reading 10
optimisation 179
OR 105
— gate 107
origin, program 174
out of phase 203
output 10, 205

overflow register 129
overwrite 12

p-type silicon 122
paired registers 122
parallel 59
— input/output 203
— transmission 59, 203
parentheses 35
parity bit 57
—, check 57
— column 62
—, even 57
—, odd 57
parity/overflow flag 130
partial RAM 190
PASCAL 176
PC 17, 119
peek 231
peripheral device 200
— memory 13
permanent 12
phase 203
PI 72
PIO controller 203
pointers 190
poke 155
port 201
primary memory 13
print 22, 25
printing 199, 212, 227
product 64
program 24
— counter 17, 119
— modules 248
— scan 176
— status bits 130
protective ground 206
pseudo-instruction 172
pseudo-operation 172
pseudo-register 208
pulse 123
punched cards 10
— paper tape 9

Quotes 82
quotient 65
QWERTY 9

Radix 52
RAM 12, 190
random 12
— access 13
RD line 201
read/write head 13
real number 62, 65
record 215

refreshing 188
register 15, 59, 121, 143
REM 26
remainder 65
request to send 206
reserved word 21, 176
reset 124
resolution 214
RI 207
ring in 207
ROM 12, 189
rotate left 131
RTS 206
run 25

Scan 176
scientific notation 65, 67
screen 32
sector 215
semicolon 27
semiconductors 122
send signal 138
serial 59
— access 13
— transmission 59, 210
set 124
shift left 131
— register 121, 130
— right 131
signal ground 206
sign flag 130
signed number 162
significant figures 243
single-pass assembler 174
slicing strings 80
SLT 149
source language 161
— program 174
spike voltage 211
spool 214
spooling 215
SRT 149
stack 136
— pointer 120, 136
standard index form 65
start bit 210
statement 21, 223, 225
—, directive 223
—, narrative 223
static errors 212
status 15, 129, 144
status register 209
— word register 17
step 48
stop bits 210
string 74, 76
— comparison 86

—, empty 76
— names 88
—, numeric 76
— replacements 83
strobe 204
—, address 204
—, data 205
— signal 204
subroutine 49
subscripts 98
subtract flag 130
subtrahend 63
sum check 211
switches 123
SWR 17
symbolic address 162, 166
symbols 42, 173
synchronization 203
syntax 23
— analysis 178, 181
— error 23

T cycle 171
tabular information 8
tabulation 35
tape cassette 13
tape deck 13, 216
three-line interface 209
token 235
track 55, 215
transistor 122
translation 174, 178
transmission of bytes 59
— errors 211
true complement 63
truth tables 74, 108
two-dimensional array 95, 102
two-pass assembler 174

UART 202
universal asynchronous
receiver/transmitter 202
universal synchronous/
asynchronous receiver/
transmitter 203
universal synchronous
receiver/transmitter 203
universe 104
USART 203
user-transparent 189
USRT 203

Variable 24
VDU 10, 196
visual display unit 10, 196
volatile 10, 12, 188

White noise 211
word 56, 142
— length 142
— processor 8
WR line 204
write-protect notch 216

X-line interface 209
XOR 106

Zero flag 130